Southern Political Party Activists

Southern Political Party Activists

Patterns of Conflict and Change, 1991–2001

Edited by

JOHN A. CLARK
CHARLES L. PRYSBY

THE UNIVERSITY PRESS OF KENTUCKY

Publication of this volume was made possible in part by a grant
from the National Endowment for the Humanities.

This project was supported by National Science Foundation grants SES-9986501 and SES-9986523. The findings and conclusions of this study are those of the authors and do not represent the opinions of the National Science Foundation or any other government agency.

Scholarly publisher for the Commonwealth,
serving Bellarmine University, Berea College, Centre
College of Kentucky, Eastern Kentucky University,
The Filson Historical Society, Georgetown College,
Kentucky Historical Society, Kentucky State University,
Morehead State University, Murray State University,
Northern Kentucky University, Transylvania University,
University of Kentucky, University of Louisville,
and Western Kentucky University.

Editorial and Sales Offices: The University Press of Kentucky
663 South Limestone Street, Lexington, Kentucky 40508-4008
www.kentuckypress.com

04 05 06 07 08 5 4 3 2 1

Library of Congress Cataloging-in-Publication Data

Southern political party activists: patterns of conflict and change, 1991–2001 /
John A. Clark, Charles L. Prysby.
p. cm.
Includes bibliographical references and index.
ISBN 0-8131-2340-2 (alk. paper)
ISBN 0-8131-9116-5 (pbk.: alk paper)
1. Political parties—Southern States. 2. Political activists—Southern States.
3. Political culture—Southern States. 4. Southern States—Politics and
government—1951– .
I. Clark, John A. II. Prysby, Charles L.
JK2683.567 2004
324.273'0975'09049—dc22

2004010764

This book is printed on acid-free recycled paper meeting
the requirements of the American National Standard
for Permanence in Paper for Printed Library Materials.

Manufactured in the United States of America.

Member of the Association of
American University Presses

Contents

Acknowledgments

This project was very much a collaborative effort. The data collection involved a team of scholars, most of whom are also authors or coauthors of the chapters in this book. In addition to the book contributors, Frank Feigert, Michael Gant, Audrey Haynes, and Brad Lockerbie were part of the team that collected the data. We appreciate the support that was provided by National Science Foundation grants SES-9986501 and SES-9986523, without which this study could not have been undertaken. Of course, the findings and conclusions of this study are those of the authors and do not necessarily represent the views of the National Science Foundation. The University of North Carolina at Greensboro and Western Michigan University also provided support for this project.

We clearly owe an intellectual debt to the many scholars who have done previous work in this area. Most notably, the original Southern Grassroots Party Activists project, which was directed by Charles Hadley and Lewis Bowman, provided intellectual stimulation for this study. Both Hadley and Bowman encouraged us to organize a follow-up study, and we have benefitted greatly from their hard work and from the scholarship that was produced by the original study. We hope that our book is a worthy successor to the books that resulted from the first SGPA project.

Earlier versions of many of these chapters were first presented at the 2002 meeting of the Southern Political Science Association in Savannah, Georgia. We are grateful to section heads Robin Kolodny and Richard Engstrom for finding places on the program for two panels of our papers and to Kevin Hill and Peter Wielhouwer for their comments on those papers. The Symposium on Southern Politics at the Citadel provided an additional outlet for our work and a useful gathering place for project participants.

The fact that this book is appearing in such a timely fashion is due in large part to the work of the staff at the University Press of Kentucky, who have done their best to make the production process both swift and smooth. In particular, we are grateful for the support that Stephen Wrinn, the director of the press, has provided at every stage of the process. The timely appearance of the book also is due to the cooperation of our contributors, who were willing to adhere to tight deadlines and make revisions on short notice, behavior that we greatly appreciate. We are also thankful for the invaluable assistance of Michelle Anifant, a graduate student at UNCG, who labored over many details of the manuscript, and Marcella Myers, a graduate student at WMU, who presided over the preparation of the data set.

JAC
CLP

CHAPTER

1

Studying Southern Political Party Activists

John A. Clark and Charles L. Prysby

The South continues to be the most distinctive region in American politics. Its "peculiar institution" of slavery set the stage for the Civil War, which in turn led to the creation of the Democratic "Solid South." Now the South is so interesting because of the enormous political change that has occurred over the last half century. Democratic dominance has given way to the emergence of a truly competitive two-party system that leans Republican in presidential elections. In some ways, the region is increasingly like the rest of the country, yet even the degree of change and the speed with which it occurred give the South a distinctive air.

How have these changes affected the South's political parties? Political scientists widely agree that parties are essential for the operation of democracy. Scholars concerned about the vitality of American political parties in recent decades have produced considerable research on political party organizations at the national, state, and local levels. This study examines both the development of American political party organizations and the changing political character of the South, two interesting and important aspects of American politics. Our focus is on southern grassroots party activists—those who are involved in county party organizations. By studying these activists, we hope to learn about the development of party organizations in a region marked by great partisan change, an effort that we think should be of interest to both analysts of political parties and scholars of southern politics.

POLITICAL CHANGE IN THE SOUTH

For the first half of the twentieth century, the South was solidly Democratic. Republicans enjoyed very little electoral success in the region. In the latter half of the century, the pattern changed, and by the start of the twenty-first century, the old Solid South was a two-party South. Electoral change occurred first at the presidential level, emerging in midcentury. Republican presidential candidates in the first half of the twentieth century ran very poorly in the South (Bartley and Graham 1975, 7–14). The only exception to this pattern was in 1928, when Republican Herbert Hoover won five southern states, due largely to the fact that the Democrats nominated a candidate, Al Smith, who was both Catholic and anti-Prohibition (Key 1949, 318–329). Republicans became more competitive in presidential elections in the 1950s, especially in the urban Rim South. Republican Dwight D. Eisenhower carried four southern states in 1952 and five in 1956. Richard Nixon carried three southern states in 1960 and was competitive in several others. Support for Eisenhower and Nixon came disproportionately from urban areas and from the Rim South (Black and Black 1992, 176–199). The Eisenhower-Nixon voters typically were middle-class whites who favored Republicans on economic issues (Bartley and Graham 1975, 86–95).

Republican presidential voting took a new turn in 1964, when Barry Goldwater drew upon different sources of electoral support to win five southern states. Senator Goldwater, who voted against the 1964 Civil Rights Act, did his best in the Deep South, among white voters of all income levels, who largely opposed the Civil Rights Act and other attempts to integrate southern society (Black and Black 1992, 149–158). By 1972, Republican voting in the South appeared to have come full circle, as incumbent president Richard Nixon carried every state in the region by a wide margin in his reelection effort (although it should be noted that his Democratic opponent, Senator George McGovern, did poorly nationally, not just in the South). When the Democrats in 1976 nominated a more competitive candidate, former Georgia governor Jimmy Carter, they were able to win all but one of the southern states, albeit by narrow margins in several cases.

During the last two decades of the twentieth century, Republican success in presidential elections in the South became firmly established. Ronald Reagan's victories in 1980 and 1984 appear to have realigned white southerners toward the Republican Party. From 1984 on, the Republican presidential candidate has run significantly better in the South than in the North (Abramson, Aldrich, and Rohde 2002, 109). Even in 1992, when the Democrats nominated an all-southern ticket of Bill Clinton and Al Gore, they were able to win only four states in the region, and two of those were Arkansas and Tennessee, the home states of their two candidates. Perhaps the 2000 presidential election demonstrates the current Republican advantage in southern presidential voting best of all. George W. Bush carried every southern state, even though the election was extremely close nationally, in both the popular and Electoral College vote.

Republican success in other elections lagged behind the growth of presidential voting. For example, after the 1972 election, in which Richard Nixon carried the South in a landslide, Democrats still held two-thirds of the U.S. senators and representatives from the region. Democratic control of state government was equally strong. Republican success in subpresidential elections emerged first in prominent statewide contests, such as for governor or senator, then trickled down the ballot (Aistrup 1996, 211–242; Bullock and Rozell 2003b; Scher 1997, 118–159). Following the 1980 elections, five of the eleven states had a Republican governor, and ten of the twenty-two southern U.S. Senate seats were held by Republicans. Democrats did better during the remainder of the 1980s; and after the 1992 elections, only three governors and nine senators in the region were Republicans. Republicans responded with significant gains after 1992, however, and in early 2001 they had a majority of the governors and senators in the region—six governors and thirteen senators (for state-by-state summaries, see Bullock and Rozell 2003a; Clark and Prysby 2003; and Lamis 1999).

The 1990s also were the decade in which Republicans captured a majority of the southern U.S. House seats. Even as late as 1990, Democrats had a big edge in southern congressional elections, winning two-thirds of the House seats that year. In the historic 1994 midterm elections, Republicans made enormous gains in southern congressional races, winning an additional sixteen seats, giving them a majority of the region's congressional delegation. They expanded their majority in subsequent elections; and after the 2000 elections, 58 percent of the southern congressional seats were held by Republicans. The 1990s also saw Republicans make gains in state legislative elections, although Democrats continued to maintain an advantage at this level. In early 2001, Democrats still had the majority in seven state legislatures, while Republicans had control of only three (one state legislature had divided control). For Republicans, even this limited success was a substantial improvement over the situation ten years earlier, when they were in the minority—often a very small minority—in every state legislature.

At the start of the twenty-first century, the South clearly had two-party competition. While Republicans appear to have gained a clear advantage in presidential elections and at least an edge in congressional elections as well, Democrats have managed to remain competitive overall. In almost every state, both parties have a reasonable chance of winning important statewide contests, such as for governor or U.S. senator, especially when no incumbent is running for reelection. Democratic strength in southern state legislatures continues to provide the party with a farm team of potential candidates for higher office. Whether Republicans will enjoy even greater electoral success in the next decade or two is uncertain now, but at the time that the data for this study were collected, a competitive two-party system existed in the region.

The growth of a two-party South in voting patterns and election results has been accompanied by the development of party organizations in the southern states. For most of the twentieth century, the South had very weak political organizations. During the Solid South era, Republicans were too weak electorally to create a strong party organization (Key 1949, 277–297). Democrats, on the other hand, did not need to create a strong organization, as they were able to dominate without one. Moreover, Democrats were generally divided into factions, whose leaders often feared that too much organizational infrastructure would give an unfair advantage to one group or another (Key 1949, 298–311). Studies of party organization in the 1960s and 1970s conclude that southern parties were weak even after the demise of the Solid South. Mayhew's (1986) study of party organization in the late 1960s found weak party organization across the South, particularly compared to the Northeast, where traditional party organization was the strongest. Cotter, Gibson, Bibby, and Huckshorn (1984) measured the strength of state party organizations in the 1970s by examining such factors as budgets, staffing, activities, and organizational complexity. They found that both Democratic and Republican Parties in the South lagged far behind parties in the other regions in party organizational strength.

Once a foothold of two-party competition was established, party organizations became useful for recruiting candidates, providing campaign resources and assistance, and mobilizing voters. Republicans appeared to have moved first to strengthen their state organizations. The Republican Party pioneered a strategy of "top-down" organizational development by pumping money and other resources from the national party to the states (Herrnson 1994). Within the southern states, Republicans often also followed a top-down strategy, in which state party organization was emphasized over local party organization (Aistrup 1996, 65–89). Southern Democrats responded to the growing two-party competitiveness and the increased Republican organizational presence by improving their own party organizations. State headquarters for both parties became more permanent entities, engaging in activities year round. Staffing and budgets for the state parties increased dramatically. Of course, these developments varied in their extent and timing from state to state (for state summaries, see Clark and Prysby 2003; Hadley and Bowman 1995).

While southern state party organizations are much stronger than they were three decades ago, the strength of local party organizations in the South is less clear. Republicans had been more concerned with their state party organizations, but more recently they have emphasized grassroots developments (Stanley 1995). Democrats also have attempted to improve their county party organizations, which in many areas had decayed during the 1970s and 1980s. Democratic grassroots organizations have been greatly affected by the realignment of southern voters. Many conservative white Democrats who were active in earlier years ceased their activity and even became active in the Republican Party (Prysby 1998a). At the same time, blacks have become a much more important part of the southern Democratic coalition and have become more involved in the party organization (Hadley and Stanley 1998). These changes make southern grassroots party activists a very interesting group to analyze.

DEVELOPMENT OF AMERICAN POLITICAL PARTY ORGANIZATIONS

Studying southern grassroots party activists not only will enlighten us about contemporary southern politics but also will inform us about developments in American political party organizations. Some may question whether party organizations deserve more study, as elections are commonly viewed as becoming increasingly candidate-centered (Wattenberg 1991). We believe that such an endeavor is worthwhile for two important reasons. First, parties are widely considered to be essential organizations for the operation of a democratic system. Theorists like Schattschneider (1942, 1) have argued that "modern democracy is unthinkable save in terms of the parties." More empirically minded researchers have shown that parties provide structure to political conflict, among both elected officials (Aldrich 1995) and voters in elections (Schaffner, Streb, and Wright 2001). While public support for the two-party system waxes and wanes, most political scientists (even though they may be critical of the contemporary parties) share the belief that politics without parties would be worse than the system we have today (Epstein 1986, 9–39).

Second, there has been concern over the health of American political party organizations. A prevalent view in the 1970s and 1980s was that American political parties were in decline.[1] Numerous indicators seemed to point to that same conclusion. Additional limits were placed on the use of patronage in awarding government jobs, robbing party organizations in some areas of a ready-made campaign staff. The Democratic Party's McGovern-Fraser reforms led to an opening of the presidential nominating systems of both parties. At lower levels, the ability of party organizations to slate candidates for nomination was reduced. Voters seemed less aligned to the parties when casting ballots. Split-ticket voting increased, as did the number of nonaligned or independent voters. Finally, lower levels of party voting were observed in Congress. Reforms that gave more power to individual legislators appeared to weaken the already low levels of cohesion within parties (other reforms strengthening the leadership were less visible at the time). Considering all of these trends, some observers went so far as to suggest that the two major parties would soon fade into oblivion.

More recent scholarly views argue that this decline-of-party thesis is wrong. Most would agree that the parties are weaker in some ways. The number of voters who identify with the parties has not rebounded to earlier levels, for example, and party leaders have ceded control over the presidential nominations to a mix of primary voters and campaign fund-raisers. Still, the parties are stronger in other ways. The national party organizations, for example, are much larger and better financed organizations than they were thirty years ago (Herrnson 1994). Similarly, in many states, the state party organizations have improved their headquarters in recent years. The use of the "soft money" loophole provided resources for this purpose, but many state parties were effective fund-raisers in their own right (La Raja 2003; Morehouse and Jewell 2003).

Less attention has been given to local party organizations, especially outside of major metropolitan areas. The available evidence suggests that here, too, party organizations may be strengthening, at least in some places. The notoriety of Tammany Hall and other urban machines creates an image of the local party as dominant in an earlier era, yet it is not clear whether such organizations were exceptions or the norm. Perhaps more telling is the overall weakness of county parties in the South in the late 1970s (Cotter et al. 1984). The precursor to our study (Hadley and Bowman 1995) and our own state-level analyses (Clark and Prysby 2003) show markedly different levels of organizational activity in 1991 and 2001, respectively, than those uncovered by Cotter and his colleagues.

Although most local party organizations may lack the resources to provide significant services, they can and do affect electoral outcomes. Trish (1994) notes that tight networks of party and campaign officials contribute to the success of presidential candidates.[2] Strong local organizations can lead to higher vote totals for candidates farther up the ticket (Frendreis, Gibson, and Vertz 1990). Contacting voters directly, a task often handled by party workers at the grassroots, has an impact on voters' decisions (Wielhouwer and Lockerbie 1994). Overall, strong party organizations have been shown to improve citizen evaluations of and appreciation for parties (Coleman 1996).

We believe, then, that grassroots party organizations remain important. They may be less visible than state or national organizations, but that does not make them irrelevant. Candidates may no longer be dependent on them to gain access to the ballot or to mobilize voters, but that does not make them useless. Local party organizations help to recruit candidates for lower-level offices. They provide a base of possible volunteers for campaigns, especially local ones. They, along with local office holders, help to define the image that the party has at the local level. By their actions, grassroots activists can help to bring voters and activists into the party or they can drive them away. The fact that these county-level organizations are important is demonstrated by the fact that southern Republicans in many states, after first concentrating on developing the state party organization, have been working on improving their local party organizations. Democrats, to a lesser extent, have followed suit.

The substantial evolution of party competition in the South makes it a useful laboratory in which to study change in party organizations. Scholars have long posited a relationship between the competitive environment and the development of party organizations in the South and elsewhere (see, for example, Key 1949; Beck 1974; Harmel and Janda 1982). Key (1949, 386–405) noted the general weakness of local party organizations in the one-party South compared to those found in the rest of the country. The rare organization that "most closely approximates the usual concept of a party" would most likely be found in the parts of North Carolina, Virginia, or Tennessee where party competition was the greatest (Key 1949, 388). Similar conclusions for the region were reached by subsequent researchers (Crotty 1971; Beck 1974).

The corollary to this finding is that party organizations should show signs of development as electoral competition increases. As elections become more competitive, their outcomes are less certain. Likewise, the shift in voter allegiance from overwhelming Democratic support to greater balance between parties, with many nonaligned voters, gives each party the opportunity to win any given election. Under these conditions of uncertainty, every possible vote counts. As a result, candidates from the same party have greater incentive to cooperate with one another (Schlesinger 1985). Party organizations are ideally constituted for such a task. The party organization, malleable to the goals of ambitious politicians, has adapted to meet the needs of candidates for all levels of office (Aldrich 1995; Herrnson 1988; Francia et al. 2003). Of course, increased competition does not guarantee organ-izational development. Other characteristics of the political environment can encourage or discourage organizational growth. Likewise, characteristics internal to the party, notably leaders themselves, may play a role as well (Herrnson and Menefee-Libey 1990; Appleton and Ward 1994).

Aside from campaigning for candidates, the parties may have changed in other ways. Prior empirical evidence is limited, but several possible developments can be suggested. For example, the types of activists who are recruited into the party may change as the party shifts to a more competitive political environment. Activists who are attracted to a distinctly minority party may have different goals and values than those who are attracted to a party with a strong possibility of winning elections. As the level of competition increases, we might find that party activists become more concerned with winning rather than with maintaining ideological purity. Other questions also might be raised regarding changes in party activists. For example, are the policy preferences of southern party activists becoming more in line with the positions of the national parties? Is there more emphasis placed on day-to-day organizational maintenance as the level of competition increases? An environment in which change is taking place provides an opportunity to explore such questions about party organizations and the activists who work in them, questions which in many cases have not received systematic study.

THE SOUTHERN GRASSROOTS PARTY ACTIVISTS PROJECT

This study focuses on grassroots political party activists in the South, defined as the eleven states of the old Confederacy. Our approach is to consider party organizations in terms of the people who staff them. This conceptualization is consistent with Eldersveld (1964, 1):

> The political party is a social group, a system of meaningful and patterned activity within the larger society. It consists of a set of individuals populating specific roles and behaving as member-actors of a boundaried and identifiable social unit. Goals are perceived by these actors, tasks are assigned for and by them, and communication channels are maintained. The party is thus one social organism.

We believe this approach complements those who view parties in terms of candidates or officeholders, as individual citizens with partisan attachments, or at the level of the organization itself.

The data employed in this study are drawn primarily from the 2001 Southern Grassroots Party Activists Project.[3] The 2001 SGPA study is a follow-up to the original SGPA study conducted in 1991.[4] The goal of both SGPA studies was to analyze the attitudes and behavior of southern grassroots party activists, generally defined as county chairs and other members of the county executive committees.

The 2001 SGPA study surveyed over seven thousand party activists. Respondents were almost evenly divided between Democrats and Republicans. The details of the sampling plan for each state and a summary of response rates by state and party can be found in the appendix to this book. A mail questionnaire was used to collect data on the attitudes, behavior, and characteristics of party activists. In most cases, three waves of questionnaires were mailed out in an effort to maximize the response rate, which exceeded 50 percent overall. These data have been weighted as described in the appendix in order to improve the representativeness of the sample. The sample for the original SGPA study, which surveyed over ten thousand party activists, was similar to the one for the current study; a full description of that sample can be found in Hadley and Bowman (1995, 211–214).

The 2001 SGPA study asked respondents about a variety of attitudes and behavior, including their reasons for becoming and staying involved in party politics, their attitudes toward party activity, their involvement in campaign activities and in party organizational activities, their orientations on issues of public policy, and their social and demographic characteristics. Many of the questions employed in the 2001 study were also used in the 1991 study, providing an opportunity to study change in attitudes and behavior over time. Other questions asked in 2001 were not asked in 1991, so it is not possible to examine change over time for all items. A copy of the 2001 questionnaire is in the appendix to this book. A copy of the 1991 questionnaire can be found in Hadley and Bowman (1995, 219–226).

The ability to examine change over time in the attitudes and behavior of party activists rarely exists. Systematic collection of data on party activists beyond a single state is unusual. Having such data for two points in time is even more so. Moreover, the period from 1991 to 2001 is one in which much political change occurred in the South. As discussed earlier, Republicans made substantial gains in congressional and state legislative elections during this decade, making them much more competitive up and down the ballot than they were during the 1980s, when their strength was displayed primarily in presidential and statewide races. These facts suggest that this study will be of interest to many scholars interested in political parties or in southern politics.

AIMS OF THIS STUDY

The chapters in this volume examine several important research questions. One broad set of questions has to do with conflict within and between the parties. One aspect of the divisions between and within parties in the South has to do with social factors, of which race and religion are the most important. The divisions between and within the parties also can be examined in terms of the attitudes of activists. Differences in their ideological orientations, their issue positions, and their partisan attachments all are important for understanding conflict.

In addition to examining conflict between and within the parties, we are interested in the involvement of activists in their organizations. The involvement of activists can be examined from two perspectives. One has to do with the attitudes that they bring to their involvement. What motivates activists to become involved, and what kinds of orientations do the activists display toward involvement in the party organization? In particular, we are interested in determining whether the grassroots activists tend to be uncompromising ideologues who would sacrifice the prospects of electoral success for ideological purity or whether they tend to be a more pragmatic group, concerned primarily with winning elections. Another dimension of involvement is the actual activity level of the activists. Their activities can be divided into two types—involvement in election campaigns and involvement in ongoing party activities. Both are desirable for a healthy party organization.

The three chapters in Part A discuss social factors and their impact on party conflict. John Clark's chapter on religious orientations among southern political party activists (chapter 2) focuses on a key political division in the contemporary South, the split between white fundamentalist Protestants who support the Christian Right and those who oppose or at least do not support this political movement. The conflict occurs both between parties—as Democrats are unlikely to be supporters of the Christian Right—and within the Republican Party, which is divided in its enthusiasm for the Christian Right agenda.

Jay Barth's chapter (chapter 3) examines another key social division in the South—race. The Democratic Party depends on holding together a biracial coalition to achieve electoral success, but racial divisions within the party make this coalition a tenuous one. Republicans are not racially divided, as few blacks are active in the party. Race is a divisive social factor because several race-related issues, such as affirmative action, are a basis for political conflict, which occurs between the two parties as well as within the Democratic Party.

Change in the party organizations occurs not only because activists change their views but also because the activists themselves change. Some of this occurs through generational (and other) replacement. Newer activists replace older ones. The newer activists, who usually are younger, grew up in a different political environment; consequently, they often have different attitudes. Another source for newer activists is the sizable number of individuals who have moved to the South, a group that has been particularly important in the South, especially for the Republican Party. The impact of migration on the party activists is examined in chapter 4 by Laurence Moreland and Robert Steed.

In Part B we examine the political attitudes of southern political party activists, again concentrating on conflict within and between the parties. The ideological and issue orientations of activists are examined by Patrick Cotter and Sam Fisher in chapter 5. They point out how Democratic and Republican activists have become more ideologically polarized over the past decade. The deep differences between the two parties range over a wide variety of issues, but some are more divisive than others. Jonathan Knuckey's chapter on party loyalties (chapter 6) finds that the activists are also more loyal to their parties now than they were ten years ago, a development that may have much to do with the ideological polarization of the parties. Still, activists differ in their degree of attachment, and these differences are related to other differences in attitudes and behavior.

Divisions within the parties remain important, even though party differences are sharper and deeper than before. John McGlennon examines party factionalism in chapter 7. His discussion of factionalism within the

Democratic and Republican Party organizations ties together a number of points that are brought out in the preceding chapters, such as the role of race and religion. While factionalism can be based on several factors, ideology and policy issues are the key factors that underlie most divisions.

An important question regarding party activists is, how much do they resemble the broader electorate? The usual assumption is that party activists are more ideologically extreme than the electorate, meaning that Democratic activists are more liberal than Democratic voters and Republican activists are more conservative than Republican voters. Chapter 8 examines this proposition, comparing the two parties on this dimension and examining changes over time.

Another important set of research questions has to do with the strength and vitality of the party organizations. Have the local party organizations become stronger or weaker over the past decade? How do the two parties compare to each other? In Part C we attempt to assess the health of the party organization by examining several aspects of the attitudes and behavior of the grassroots activists. Chapter 9 examines the orientations that activists have toward parties and issues, distinguishing between purists and pragmatists. Purists emphasize ideological purity; pragmatists emphasize electoral success. High levels of purism among party activists may hamper the party's ability to compromise, even when necessary for electoral victory. For this reason, the differences between the parties on this dimension and the changes that have occurred over the past ten years are significant for the vitality of the party organization. A related topic, the factors that motivate individuals to become and remain active in party organizations, is covered in chapter 10. Individuals who are motivated primarily by issues are likely to differ from those who are motivated by other factors as well, such as the social benefits of involvement. The findings of this chapter complement the discussion of purism in chapter 9.

Finally, we examine the extent to which grassroots activists are actively involved in their party organizations. Robert Hogan discusses the involvement of activists in campaign activities in chapter 11, comparing the two parties and examining change in activity levels over time. John Bruce and John Clark look at another aspect of organizational involvement, communication within the organization, in chapter 12. Communication levels provide a picture of organizational involvement apart from campaign activities, involvement that is aimed more at organizational maintenance. Both of these chapters find that the grassroots party activists are more active now than they were a decade ago, suggesting that local party organizations are becoming stronger in the contemporary two-party South.

In the concluding chapter, we summarize and integrate the findings of the individual chapters. We locate the findings within two theoretical traditions important to students of parties generally, the responsible parties' perspective, and the party renewal perspective.

The focus of this book is on the South as a whole. We believe this focus is justified because there are important commonalities to party politics across the entire region, and examining these commonalities should help us to better understand politics in the South. While some of the chapters briefly examine state-by-state variations, a thorough examination of how the topics covered in this volume play out in each state is beyond the scope of this study. However, those who are interested in individual states should refer to a special double edition of the *American Review of Politics,* which contains articles that examine party activists in each of the eleven states covered by the SGPA studies (Clark and Prysby 2003).

NOTES

1. The list is lengthy and includes many (if not most) textbooks on American government. See, for example, works by Broder (1972), Crotty and Jacobson (1980), and Wattenberg (1994).
2. For an example of the opposite situation where a dysfunctional local organization *costs* candidates votes, see Blumberg, Binning, and Green (2003).
3. The 2001 Southern Grassroots Party Activists Project was funded by NSF grants SES-9986501 and -9986523. John A. Clark and Charles L. Prysby were the principal investigators. The surveys in the eleven states were administered by a set of state investigators, who also are the authors of the various articles in this study.
4. The 1991 SGPA Project was funded by NSF grant SES-9009846. Charles D. Hadley and Lewis Bowman were the principal investigators, and the surveys in the eleven states were administered by a set of state investigators, many of whom also participated in the 2001 SGPA Project.

CHAPTER

2

Religion

Culture Wars in the New South

John A. Clark

The candidate for the Republican presidential nomination in 2000 was pulling no punches in his "straight talk" assessment of his intraparty opposition. On the campaign trail in Virginia, Arizona Senator John McCain threw down the gauntlet:

> The political tactics of division and slander are not our values. They are corrupting influences on religion and politics and those who practice them in the name of religion or in the name of the Republican Party or in the name of America shame our faith, our party and our country. Neither party should be defined by pandering to the outer reaches of American politics and the agents of intolerance whether they be Louis Farrakhan or Al Sharpton on the left, or Pat Robertson or Jerry Falwell on the right.[1]

McCain's strong statement made headlines, but it failed to win adequate support from Virginia primary voters. McCain lost the state on his way to losing the nomination. Nevertheless, his words appear to echo divisions within the Republican Party in Virginia and elsewhere. Many observers have noted the split between supporters of the Christian Right and "traditional Republicans" who represent a more moderate wing of the party.[2]

The degree to which political parties have adopted the divisions associated with the "culture wars" of American society tells us much about the present—and possibly the future—of American politics. The South, as a region, has become a key battleground in the debate over religion, culture, and politics. We know that a significant realignment in the electorate has moved the South from a region characterized by Democratic domination to one in which both parties are competitive. To a large degree, this change has drawn on cultural divisions that are imbedded in the region's deeply religious electorate (Layman 2001). Supporters of Christian Right groups have been active in Republican politics for more than two decades (Wilcox 1996; Oldfield 1996b).

In this chapter, I examine the influence of religion on grassroots party activists in the South. While much scholarship has focused on the Christian Right's influence in the region, its relative importance depends on both the differences between Republicans and Democrats and possible divisions within the two parties. In addition, the role of the black church in Democratic Party politics cannot be ignored, as it may point to splits over cultural issues in that party (Clawson and Clark 2003).

In the analysis that follows, I first examine patterns of religious attachment among local party officials. Their support for Christian Right groups is of particular interest. Next, the relationship between religious attitudes and policy proposals is analyzed. To what extent does proximity to the Christian Right correspond to attitudes about policy issues? Finally, attention is given to party loyalty. Are the Christian conservative factions in each party more or less supportive of the party's goals? Do they contribute to the factional splits within the party?

RELIGIOUS TENSIONS IN THE POLITICAL PARTY SYSTEM

The party system in the United States is not directly based on religious cleavages, yet its history gives numerous examples where religion and parties intertwine (Reichley 1992). The abolitionist movement, late-nineteenth-century populism, and the civil rights movement represent episodes in which religiously based moral divisions led to realignments of the two-party system.

In more recent times, the tension between traditionalists and modernists has forced change in the coalitions of today's Democrats and Republicans (Layman 2001). The Republican Party increasingly attracts conservative Christians to its cause, while religious liberals and secularists are more likely to find a home in the Democratic Party. The New Deal alignment, based on economic divisions in society, has been altered to absorb this new cleavage.

Major changes in the party system rarely happen on their own. Instead, they result from the strategic actions of ambitious politicians whose short-term calculations often have long-term consequences (Aldrich 1995). The emergence of the Christian Right, largely grassroots in nature, was heavily influenced by activists and entrepreneurs who organized for collective action. From the Moral Majority to the Christian Coalition to a variety of lesser-known groups, organizations were formed to harness the energy of sympathizers in the mass public. They mobilized to win nominations and to control the party apparatus. Often, but not always, they were successful. In some states, and especially in the South, conservative Christians have become dominant players in the state party apparatus. An analyst in the mid-1990s estimated that the Christian Right had a dominant influence in the Republican Party organizations of eight of eleven southern states and a substantial influence in two more; only Tennessee, with a long tradition of mountain Republicanism, seemingly remained immune. In contrast, only nine of the remaining thirty-nine states faced similar levels of conservative Christian influence (Persinos 1994). By 2000, state Republican Party organizations in all eleven southern states were at least moderately influenced by the Christian Right, although the movement may have weakened somewhat across the region (Conger and Green 2002).[3]

Is the Christian Right "invasion" good or bad for the Republican Party? As with many such questions, where you stand depends on where you sit.[4] A new generation of scholarship provides some empirical evidence on which to make judgments. For example, Oldfield (1996b, 192–212) notes that many leaders of the religious right cast their lots with George Bush in 1992. This pragmatic strategy helped them gain considerable influence in the nominating process, but the divisive tone of the Republican convention in Houston set the stage for Bush's loss to Bill Clinton. Smith (2002) finds that religious right Republicans consistently support Republican candidates; members of the traditional faction are often reluctant to support candidates from the religious right.

Not all the focus has been on Christian conservatives in the Republican Party. Others have focused on the role of the African American church in mobilizing Democratic Party supporters (Harris 1999; Calhoun-Brown 1996). While religious blacks often hold conservative religious views, Republicans have made few inroads in their efforts to recruit supporters from this group. Despite shared attitudes on some moral issues, wide divisions persist on other social and economic policies (Calhoun-Brown 1997).

RELIGIOUS DIFFERENCES AMONG GRASSROOTS ACTIVISTS

Previous researchers have identified religious-based cleavages between Republicans and Democrats and within each of the two parties. The 2001 Southern Grassroots Party Activists (SGPA) survey contained several items designed to tap the religious orientations of party activists. These items included denominational preference, religiosity (church attendance), religious salience (religious guidance in one's daily life), and whether the respondent is "born again." In addition, respondents were asked how close they feel toward Christian Right groups. Where it is appropriate, data from the 2001 SGPA survey will be compared to the results of the original SGPA Project conducted in 1991.[5]

While both Republicans and Democrats are highly religious, partisan differences emerged on a number of these items (see table 2.1). Nearly all respondents held some religious affiliation, with only 4 percent of Democrats and 1 percent of Republicans indicating that they are "nonbelievers."[6] Substantial majorities of both parties ascribe to Protestant denominations (78 percent of Democrats and 84 percent of Republicans). The modal affiliation for white respondents in both parties was with mainline Protestant churches, followed by evangelical Protestants. Almost one in five Democrats was categorized as a black Protestant, although some likely belong to integrated or largely white congregations; this category contains only 1 percent of GOP activists, due in large measure to the small number of African American Republicans in the sample.[7] Slightly more than one in ten activists in both parties are Catholics.

Table 2.1 Religious Characteristics of Grassroots Party Activists, 2001 and 1991

	2001		*1991*	
	Democrats	*Republicans*	*Democrats*	*Republicans*
Religious preference				
Mainline Protestant	31	45	38	52
Evangelical Protestant	28	39	35	35
Black Protestant	19	1	12	2
Catholic	12	12	9	9
Other or none	10	3	6	3
Attend church weekly	54	62	47	52
Religion offers great deal of guidance	57	63	—	—
Born-again Christian	52	60	—	—
Closeness to Christian Right				
Very close	8	19	—	—
Close	10	29	—	—
Neutral	25	35	—	—
Far	13	9	—	—
Very far	44	8	—	—
(Minimum *N*)	(3,537)	(3,475)	(5,370)	(4,731)

Note: Entries are percentages, by column. The minimum number of respondents from each party is in parentheses.

Other measures of religion show that Republicans are only slightly more devout than Democrats, despite some portrayals of the Democratic Party nationally as being hostile to religion. With regard to church attendance, 62 percent of Republicans and 54 percent of Democrats say they attend at least weekly, and roughly the same proportions claim that their religion offers a great deal of guidance in their daily lives. Half of Democrats and 60 percent of Republicans consider themselves to be "born-again" Christians. This term has different meanings for different faith traditions (Jelen, Smidt, and Wilcox 1993), yet the overall high levels and similarity across parties are noteworthy.

Comparisons to 1991 offer mixed results in terms of the religiosity of southern party activists. On one hand, 85 percent of Democrats and 89 percent of Republicans indicated a Protestant affiliation of some sort in 1991, higher percentages than in 2001. More activists in each party belonged to mainline Protestant denominations at the earlier time point (38 percent and 52 percent, respectively), and more Democrats belonged to evangelical Protestant denominations. There were fewer Catholics in both parties and fewer black Protestants among the Democrats. Church attendance, on the other hand, was lower in the earlier sample of grassroots leaders. Only about half of the activists in each party claimed to attend church at least once a week, seven and ten percentage points lower than in 2001. Direct comparisons on the other measures are not possible.[8]

While small differences across parties exist on the previously discussed measures from the 2001 survey, the interparty differences are substantial on the last item in the battery, "How close do you feel toward Christian Right groups?" Republican activists were much more likely to respond "close" or "very close" (48 percent) than Democrats (18 percent). At the other end of the scale, 44 percent of Democratic activists felt "very far" from Christian Right groups, compared to only 8 percent of Republicans. The wording of this item was crafted to avoid reference to a specific group like the Christian Coalition. Its stimulus refers to a wide range of possible groups that are both Christian on a religious dimension and conservative on a political dimension (Hood and Smith 2002).[9] Since membership in any particular group is not required, it is possible for a respondent to feel close to a group's goals without formally joining it.

My working hypothesis in this chapter is that support for the Christian Right among Republican activists influences political attitudes and shapes internal party cleavages; in other words, support for these *religiously* based groups has *political* implications (but see Hood and Smith 2002). Before those relationships can be assessed, however, one might question the validity of the religious nature of the measurement. To test this, I divided Republican and Democratic activists into those who felt "close" or "very close" to Christian Right groups and those who did not (that is, "neutral," "far," or "very far"). These groupings were then compared to one another along the other measures of religion in the survey.

As expected, support for the Christian Right corresponds to denominational preference, church attendance, religious guidance, and born-again status. Among Republicans, 62 percent of evangelical Protestants felt close to the Christian Right, compared to 46 percent of mainline Protestants and 34 percent of Catholics. Only a quarter of the Republicans who did not fall into those categories could be classified as Christian Right supporters. Those who attend church at least weekly are more supportive than those who attend less often (60 percent to 28 percent). Sixty-one percent of Republican activists who claim that religion provides a "great deal" of guidance in their lives felt close to the Christian Right, compared to only 25 percent of those who rely less on their religious beliefs. Finally, almost two-thirds of born-again Republicans are Christian Right supporters, compared to less than one-fourth of those who do not consider themselves born again.

The pattern for Democrats clearly shows that both Christianity and conservatism are key components of the Christian Right appeal. Black Protestants form a key basis of support for the Christian Right in the Democratic Party; 37 percent of the Democrats who are both Protestant and African American feel close to the Christian Right. The percentage drops to 27 percent for evangelical Protestants and a mere 9 percent for mainline Protestants and Catholics. Less than 1 percent of the remaining Democratic activists support the Christian Right. As with Republicans, Democrats who attend church weekly were more likely to be Christian Right supporters, but the magnitudes are smaller (29 percent to 8 percent). Virtually identical differences are found for those Democrats who are (or are not) born again and for whom religion provides a great deal (or less) of guidance in their daily lives.

Although religious differences between supporters and nonsupporters of the Christian Right are meaningful and consistent, other demographics were less so. There is no gender gap in support for the Christian Right. Christian Right supporters come from the poorer and less-educated members of their parties, especially among Democrats (regardless of race).

In sum, local party officials in the South have strong religious orientations. Support for the Christian Right is especially strong among Republican activists, with nearly half feeling close to Christian Right groups. A smaller but still substantial portion of Democrats hold similar views. Not all religious party activists support the Christian Right, even among evangelicals, reflecting the complex nature of religious attachments.

ISSUE CLEAVAGES AND SUPPORT FOR THE CHRISTIAN RIGHT

Having established the presence of activists with different religious views among grassroots party activists, one might reasonably wonder whether religious differences translate into political differences. The original SGPA survey showed that Republican activists were consistently conservative and

Democrats more liberal across a range of policy issues (Steed 1998), and the same general pattern is present in 2001 (see chapter 5 in this volume). Does the consistency within parties mask religious differences? Analysis of policy issues from the 2001 SGPA survey indicates that it does; that is, activists who support the Christian Right are almost always more conservative than other activists in their party, especially on cultural (as opposed to economic) issues. A slightly different pattern emerges for African Americans in the Democratic Party, who will be examined separately.

Republicans

Respondents were asked about their overall ideology and their attitudes on fourteen specific policy issues. The responses for Republicans are displayed in table 2.2. The first two columns of numbers show the percentages taking

Table 2.2 Issue Orientations of Grassroots Party Activists, Republicans Only

Issue	*Christian Right Nonsupporters*	*Christian Right Supporters*	*Gamma*
Abortion	53	91	.695
School prayer	88	98	.477
Gay job discrimination	71	90	.466
Handgun control	80	91	.368
School vouchers	69	83	.314
Equal role for women	6	16	.271
Government services, spending	71	82	.266
Government regulation of health care	79	87	.256
Government aid for women	63	72	.225
Death penalty	80	88	.215
Hiring preferences for blacks	98	99	.210
Guaranteed job and living standard	94	93	.172
Government aid to minorities	64	72	.152
Flat tax system	79	85	.125
Overall ideology	88	98	.641
(Minimum *N*)	(1,754)	(1,588)	

Note: Entries are the percentages of respondents who "agree" or "strongly agree" with the conservative position on each issue statement. Gamma represents the amount of difference between the two groups. All gamma coefficients are statistically significant at the 0.05 level. The minimum number of respondents from each party is in parentheses.

the conservative position on the issue. The third column displays the magnitude of the difference across groups using a gamma coefficient. All differences are statistically significant at the .05 level, although the strength of the differences varies dramatically from issue to issue.[10]

The overall ideology measure indicates that both supporters and nonsupporters of the Christian Right are overwhelmingly conservative. Variation in the degree of conservatism (not shown) is quite large. Nearly three-fourths of Christian Right supporters claim to be very conservative, with another fourth claiming to be somewhat conservative. Less than 2 percent claim to be moderate or liberal. Among those who do not feel close to the Christian Right, only 36 percent identify themselves as very conservative while half identify themselves as somewhat conservative. Slightly more than one in ten adopt a middle-of-the-road stance. Almost none of the Republican activists in the survey consider themselves to be liberal, but the degree to which they are conservative reveals a potential cleavage within the party.

The specific policy issues are arrayed from the most divisive to the most consensual. Consistent with the economic/cultural divide within the Republican Party, the greatest differences are found on social issues, while the highest levels of agreement are found on economic issues. The only exception to this pattern is the support for the death penalty, which falls in the middle of the more consensual economic issues. The positive gamma coefficients indicate that supporters of the Christian Right adopt a more conservative position than nonsupporters on every issue.[11]

The most divisive issue by far is abortion. More than nine in ten Christian Right supporters disagree with the statement, "By law a woman should be able to obtain an abortion as a matter of personal choice." Two-thirds strongly disagree. In contrast, nonsupporters are almost evenly split on the issue, with less than one-fourth taking a strongly pro-life position. Remembering that these respondents are Republican Party officials, the size of the pro-choice bloc—one-fourth of the whole party in the South—is significant. On the other hand, this faction is considerably smaller than it was in 1991 when 42 percent took a pro-choice position. Moreover, only 37 percent of Republican activists strongly disagreed with the statement in the earlier study.[12]

Evidence of a religious divide in the Republican Party can be seen on the other cultural issues in the survey. They are, in descending order, school prayer, protection of gays from job discrimination, gun control, school vouchers, and the role of women in society. On this last issue, huge majorities of both groups favor an equal role for women. Support is somewhat weaker among those close to the Christian Right, though, as 16 percent oppose women's equality compared to 6 percent for the other activists.

The differences between supporters and nonsupporters of the Christian Right are smaller on economic issues: a flat tax, aid to women or minorities, government-guaranteed jobs, hiring preferences for minorities, regulation of health care, and cutting services to reduce spending. Both groups take conservative stances on these issues, especially hiring preferences and guaranteed jobs. For example, 41 percent of Christian Right supporters and 35 percent of nonsupporters strongly agree with the statement, "The federal government should adopt a flat tax system to replace the current federal income tax." Forty-three and 44 percent of the respective groups agree, 16 percent and 12 percent disagree, and 5 percent and 4 percent strongly disagree. In sum, Republican activists who feel close to the Christian Right tend to take conservative positions on almost all the issues in the survey, while those who do not feel close take somewhat less conservative positions on social or cultural issues.

Democrats

While liberal on the whole, the Democratic activists in our survey are much more ideologically heterogeneous than their Republican counterparts. Virtually all Republicans were united in their conservatism, yet substantial numbers of Democrats fail to abide by a liberal orthodoxy (see table 2.3). Among those close to the Christian Right, 42 percent are liberal, 21 percent moderate, and 37 percent conservative. For nonsupporters, 57 percent of the Democratic activists consider themselves liberal, 30 percent are moderates, and 13 percent are conservative. Supporters of the Christian Right comprise a small segment of the Democratic Party's activist base, but they move the party in a moderate-to-conservative direction.

Overall, the pattern of disagreement on specific issues between Christian Right supporters and nonsupporters among Democrats is generally similar to that of Republicans. There is greater disagreement on some of the same social issues and more consensus on some economic issues, but there are several items that do not fit this basic pattern. The flat tax, the issue on which there was the least difference in Republican supporters and nonsupporters, is quite divisive for Democrats. Two-thirds of Christian Right Democrats support a flat tax system, compared to slightly more than a third of nonsupporters. Gun control, in contrast, created less of a stir among Democratic activists than Republicans (gamma = .203).

For Republicans, the gamma coefficients were positive and statistically significant for all fourteen issues. Gammas for two issues were not significant for the Democrats, and one was significant and negative. There was much less overall consensus on questions of minority aid and hiring preferences for minorities in the party as a whole, yet there was little systematic disagreement between Christian Right supporters and nonsupporters on these issues. On the question of whether the government should guarantee a good job and standard of living, nonsupporters took a more conservative stance.

For each of these issues, the relatively large bloc of African Americans within the Democratic Party took more liberal positions than did white Democrats. Given the substantial number of African Americans who feel close to the Christian Right, these activists are analyzed separately.

Table 2.3 Issue Orientations of Grassroots Party Activists, Democrats Only

Issue	*Christian Right Nonsupporters*	*Christian Right Supporters*	*Gamma*
School prayer	57	96	.797
Abortion	13	45	.582
Gay job discrimination	24	55	.496
Flat tax system	39	67	.446
School vouchers	9	21	.411
Equal role for women	3	9	.378
Government services, spending	10	22	.306
Death penalty	46	62	.273
Handgun control	21	33	.203
Government regulation of health care	23	35	.181
Government aid for women	14	17	.099
Government aid to minorities	19	23	.007[n.s.]
Hiring preferences for blacks	73	68	−.005[n.s.]
Guaranteed job and living standard	55	46	−.120
Overall ideology	13	37	.306
(Minimum N)	(2,714)	(587)	

Note: Entries are the percentages of respondents who "agree" or "strongly agree" with the conservative position on each issue statement. Gamma represents the amount of difference between the two groups. All gamma coefficients are statistically significant at the 0.05 level unless otherwise noted[(n.s.)]. The minimum number of respondents from each party is in parentheses.

The results, displayed in table 2.4, indicate a different pattern than was found for Republicans and the Democratic Party as a whole. First, there is no meaningful difference in overall ideology between those African American Democrats who support the Christian Right and those who do not. Christian Right supporters are more conservative on six policy issues, more liberal on two, and indistinguishable on the remaining six.

Although there are significant differences on eight of the fourteen issues, there remains substantial agreement among African American Democrats. To take one example, school prayer is the issue with the highest level of disagreement (gamma = .584), yet a full 79 percent of those African Americans who do not support the Christian Right favor allowing prayer in public schools. On none of the issues is a majority of Christian Right supporters opposed by a majority of nonsupporters. Only one issue, support for a flat tax system, shows a lack of consensus among African American Democrats.

Table 2.4 Issue Orientations of African American Party Activists, Democrats Only

Issue	*Christian Right Nonsupporters*	*Christian Right Supporters*	*Gamma*
School prayer	79	97	.584
Abortion	10	28	.416
Equal role for women	3	9	.317
Gay job discrimination	17	32	.254
Government services, spending	5	9	.198
Flat tax system	52	66	.183
School vouchers	7	9	.099$^{n.s.}$
Death penalty	28	33	.046$^{n.s.}$
Government aid to minorities	3	4	.033$^{n.s.}$
Handgun control	9	7	−.029$^{n.s.}$
Government aid for women	6	4	−.040$^{n.s.}$
Government regulation of health care	23	21	−.074$^{n.s.}$
Hiring preferences for blacks	39	31	−.188
Guaranteed job and living standard	39	27	−.223
Overall ideology	12	22	.033$^{n.s.}$
(Minimum *N*)	(416)	(227)	

Note: Entries are the percentages of respondents who "agree" or "strongly agree" with the conservative position on each issue statement. Gamma represents the amount of difference between the two groups. All gamma coefficients are statistically significant at the 0.05 level unless otherwise noted $^{(n.s.)}$. The minimum number of respondents from each party is in parentheses.

The six issues on which there are no differences between groups of African Americans all deal with issues of particular interest to the black community (see chapter 3 in this volume). Each of these issues—school vouchers, the death penalty, government aid to minorities and women, gun control, and regulation of health care—has a racial dimension. On some, it is explicit (aid to minorities). On others, like the criminal justice items, the racial dimension is implicit. The important point is that, on all six issues, the differences among African American Democrats are not tied to their support for Christian Right groups.

What, then, of white Democrats? In some ways, they mirror Republicans in the effect of Christian Right support. The differences between supporters and nonsupporters reach statistical significance for each policy item (not shown). Still, Christian Right supporters in the Democratic Party are always more liberal than Christian Right supporters among Republicans, indicating the continued importance of party to these activists. The largest differences are again on social issues (school prayer, abortion, and gay job discrimination). If the Republican Party hopes to further splinter the Democratic coalition, these white Democrats appear more likely to defect than African American supporters of the Christian Right.

PERCEIVED FACTIONALISM AND SUPPORT FOR THE CHRISTIAN RIGHT

Are the differences in policy attitudes between supporters and nonsupporters of the Christian Right reflected in the politics of the activists' states? Respondents were asked about the causes of factionalism in their state parties (see chapter 7 for a more thorough discussion of this topic). For Republicans, the top causes of factionalism were differences in ideological viewpoints, between urban and rural areas of the state, by supporters of different party leaders, and over the issue of abortion. More than half of all Republican activists indicated that these divisions caused a "great deal" or "fair amount" of factionalism in their states. The only important difference across groups comes on the issue of abortion; supporters of the Christian Right were less likely to see the issue as divisive than nonsupporters. Racial and tax issues, government spending, and newcomers to the state were much less likely to be perceived as causes of factional splits.

Democrats were more likely to perceive factionalism in both their state and county parties than Republicans. Democratic activists were split on the roots of the factional divisions in their states. The most frequently mentioned cause was differences between urban and rural areas as the leading cause of factionalism, with 65 percent naming it as the cause of a "great deal" or a "fair amount" of disagreement in their party; between 50 percent and 60 percent named each of the remaining eight possible causes as causing at least a fair amount.[13] Christian Right supporters were more likely to attribute factional divisions to policy differences on spending, race, and taxes. Nonsupporters saw urban/rural and regional differences as relatively more important.[14] Combining this information with the previous evidence about the Democrats suggests that holding together an ideologically heterogeneous, multiracial coalition will continue to be a difficult task for Democratic Party leaders.

CONCLUSIONS

Evidence from the 2001 SGPA Project indicates the continuing—and perhaps even increasing—importance of religion in southern politics. Turning the religious views of its activists and potential supporters into strengths rather than weaknesses presents different challenges for each party.

For Republicans, support for the Christian Right splits the party down the middle on a regionwide basis. Two factions of almost equal size could yield no-holds-barred fights over control of the party and its nominees. As the McCain candidacy illustrated on a national level, some Republicans feel that it isn't always enough to be conservative on *most* issues if one holds the wrong positions on certain key issues, notably abortion. The same pattern can be seen in campaigns for state and local offices across the region and the country. Still, those Republican Party activists in our survey who do not feel close to the Christian Right are still a conservative group. It should be possible for some candidates to appeal to members of both factions and to unite the party in their state. Former governors Carroll Campbell in South Carolina, George Allen and Jim Gilmore in Virginia, and George W. Bush in Texas exemplify the ability to combine support from religious conservatives with the probusiness policies characteristic of New South politicians. In each case, they took the harsh edge off of the Christian Right agenda to make it more palatable for the less committed. Bush, of course, was able to translate his "compassionate conservatism" into the presidency.

For Democrats, the important challenges posed by Christian conservatives may have been faced in previous years. White southerners, many of them conservative in both politics and religion, were once an important pillar of the Democratic Party's New Deal coalition. Many of these people (or their descendants) now fall staunchly into the Republican camp (Stanley and Niemi 1999; Layman 2001). Today's Democrats find a considerable number of Christian Right supporters among their grassroots activists. The faction is more conservative on most issues than the rest of the party. Will it have success in moving the party to the right? Or will its members become alienated by the party's liberal stands? Much depends on the way Democratic candidates address issues of concern to this group.

African Americans, who comprise a substantial portion of the Democratic coalition and an even larger portion of Christian Right Democrats, are a special case. They frequently are targeted by Republican Party leaders who seek to make them welcome in the Republican Party.[15] What is the likelihood that such efforts will lead to success? Keeping in mind that our sample consists of party activists rather than the mass public, the chances appear slim. Even when statistically significant differences appear, African American Democrats generally agree with one another. Their views are largely consistent with those of white Democratic activists in the South. When they disagree with their partisan brethren—on issues like the death penalty and minority hiring preferences—they disagree even more vehemently with strongly held Republican views. On the latter issue, African American supporters of the Christian Right are even more supportive than nonsupporters of hiring preferences. Race may continue to trump cultural issues in keeping blacks at home amid the Democrats (Calhoun-Brown 1997; Clawson and Clark 2003).

NOTES

1. "The 2000 Campaign: Excerpt from McCain's Speech on Religious Conservatives," *New York Times*, February 29, 2000, A16.
2. For a thorough discussion of the Christian Right in Virginia, see Rozell and Wilcox (1996). A recent review of the literature on Republican Party factionalism can be found in Smith (2002).
3. For recent case studies of selected states, see Green, Rozell, and Wilcox (2003).
4. Similar questions have been asked about the change in Democratic Party politics since the McGovern-Frazier reforms went into effect. See, for example, the varied viewpoints presented in Ranney 1975; Kirkpatrick 1976; Polsby 1983; and Baer and Bositis 1988.
5. Many of the items in 2001 replicate questions asked in 1991. Unfortunately, longitudinal comparisons on the religion items are difficult due to a new (and arguably improved) battery of questions.
6. Only 1 percent of respondents failed to answer this question. While it is impossible to gauge the honesty of responses, almost no one avoided the question to cover a socially unacceptable response.
7. Rather than separate out traditionally African American denominations (like the National Baptist Convention or African Methodist Episcopalian church), this category contains all African Americans who affiliate with Protestant churches. The decision rule avoids the difficulty in characterizing denominations as either "mainline" or "evangelical," as the distinctions are often blurred in predominantly black congregations (Lincoln and Mamiya 1990; Calhoun-Brown 1997, 120–121).
8. A different question was used in 1991 to see if respondents thought of themselves as born again. Less than a third responded in the affirmative. It is impossible to tell how much of this difference is due to changes in attitudes and how much results from changes in question wording. The questions on religious salience and the Christian Right were not asked in 1991. For a discussion of religion in the original SGPA study, see Baker, Steed, and Moreland (1998).
9. While most respondents seemed to understand our meaning, a few took exception to our word choice. A few comments written into the margins of the survey instrument asked if we were comparing the Christian Right to the "humanist left" or "non-Christian wrong." That so few such comments appeared in more than 7,000 completed surveys leads me to believe that our wording was both understandable and appropriate.
10. For overall ideology, respondents were asked to place themselves on a five-point scale ranging from very liberal to very conservative. For the issue items, they were given single-stimulus statements about various policies and asked whether they strongly agreed, agreed, disagreed, or strongly disagreed with each statement. The percentages in table 2.2 represent the sum of both conservative categories. The gamma coefficients measure the strength of disagreement across the two groups of activists. The larger the coefficient, the greater the difference between groups. Positive scores indicate that Christian Right supporters are more conservative.
11. On one issue, whether "the government in Washington should see to it that every person has a job and a good standard of living," it appears that nonsupporters of the Christian Right are slightly more conservative than supporters. When the full four-point scale is taken into account, the opposite conclusion is reached. Sixty percent of

Christian Right supporters *strongly* disagree with the statement compared to only half of nonsupporters. Overall, very few Republican activists agree with the statement.

12. There is some evidence of polarization among Democrats, too. In 1991, 73 percent took a pro-choice position. The figure rose to 81 percent a decade later.

13. These included different ideological viewpoints; different party leaders; longtime residents and newcomers; different regions of the state; and issues of taxes, abortion, race, and government spending.

14. In some states, urban and rural divisions would overlap completely with regions of the state. In others, urban areas might be found in more than one part of the state.

15. The most recent attempts involve President Bush's faith-based initiative program (see, for example, Edsall and Cooperman 2002).

CHAPTER

3

The Continuing Role of Race in Southern Party Organizations

Jay Barth

As emphasized by the previous chapter, the social forces that shape party politics in the South have become increasingly complex in the contemporary era. It is now much too simplistic to say, in V. O. Key's oft-quoted phrase from his 1949 text, "In its grand outlines the politics of the South revolves around the position of the Negro" (Key 1949, 5). That said, race has only moved from its place as *the* defining characteristic of the region's politics to *a* defining characteristic of party politics in the South. As the considerable amount of previous research on southern party organizations noted in chapter 1 makes clear, a void would exist in any analysis that failed to examine the cleavages created by race in the region. Still, as this chapter shows, an essential stability to the racial dynamics of party politics at the grassroots level has arrived in the South. Table 3.1 shows the race and ethnicity of the two parties' local activists in 2001. There is much similarity between these data and those collected from activists in 1991, which are also in table 3.1.

While the percentage of Democratic activists who are African American has grown to just over 20 percent from slightly under 15 percent a decade before (and the white percentages have declined a bit), the party's local party organizations remain decidedly biracial as has been the case since African Americans entered electoral politics in large numbers throughout the region after the passage of the Voting Rights Act (VRA) of 1965. The first two decades after the passage of the initial VRA showed, of course, not just the entrance of African Americans into the ranks of the voters and activists into the political party that, at the national level, had led the fight for the VRA (and

Table 3.1 Southern Grassroots Party Activists, by Race and Party, 2001 and 1991

	2001		*1991*	
Race/Ethnicity	*Democrats*	*Republicans*	*Democrats*	*Republicans*
White	76	96	83	96
African American	21	1	14	2
Latino/Latina	2	1	2	1
Other	1	1	1	1
	100%	100%	100%	100%
(*N*)	(3,568)	(3,493)	(5,390)	(4,769)

Note: Entries are percentages, by column. Percentages may not total to 100 percent because of rounding.

accompanying civil rights legislation) but also the departure of whites from what was the only consequential political party in the South during the first six decades of the twentieth century. This white "departure" included both literal party switching by white Democrats who became Republicans and the absence of Democratic allegiance by new white voters and activists coming of age. So, while local Democratic Party organizations have continued to show openness to the entrance of the traditional "out" group in southern politics, as shown by Clawson and Clark (1998) in their analysis of the 1991 SGPA data, white activists, as a group, have not continued to flee the party in large numbers.

The examination of racial and ethnic demographic data for Republicans shows the picture that has been consistent since the civil rights era as conservative whites fled to the empty shells that were Republican Party organizations in southern states. Reiterating the findings from a decade earlier, the Republican Party has shown no ability to diversify its activist ranks in terms of race and ethnicity, with only a relative handful of Republican loyalists identifying themselves as anything other than white.

Just as interesting as these now familiar racial patterns is the general absence of Latino and Latina grassroots activists in either party in 2001. Many southern communities throughout the region have been transformed by the arrival of Latinos and Latinas in the past decade; and observers, following upon 2000 census findings, have analyzed the more generalized impact of the enlarged Latino/Latina population in several southern states and in the region as a whole.[1] While Spanish-language campaign appeals have become increasingly common in a number of southern states, the 2001 SGPA survey data indicate that neither party has brought Latino and Latina community leaders into their local organizations. As a result, the survey responses present no enhanced clarity about the partisan path that the first generation of new immigrants will take in the coming election cycles. While future analysis of grassroots political activists in the South will likely need to be enhanced to reflect ethnic diversity, for the purposes of this analysis the three categories of political actors—white Republicans, white Democrats, and African American Democrats—who have shaped modern southern dynamics remain the focus. The bulk of this chapter therefore focuses on differences and commonalities across those three groups, with two important—and, as will be emphasized, interrelated—questions in mind: What diagnosis is the result of this checkup on the oft-troubled Democratic biracial coalition? What distinctive contributions to the work of their party do activist African Americans, the traditional outsiders in southern politics, provide to their contemporary political home?

THE HEALTH OF THE DEMOCRATIC BIRACIAL COALITION

As numerous scholars of the modern South have noted, Democratic success in the region is dependent upon the enlivening of a biracial coalition. Black and Black (1987, 138–144) were most clear in presenting the mathematical realities present for the Democratic candidates in the region; they must pull together biracial coalitions of sufficient size and cohesiveness to win elections in the region. Most of the threats to the coalition had come from the departure of whites from the party. And, it was the shocks to the coalition that had arisen from white flight that were the appropriate focuses of analysis of the region's politics from the time of the Voting Rights Act until the Clinton era.

Despite these jolts to the party's fragile coalition, in their analysis of the 1991 Southern Grassroots Party Activists data, Hadley and Stanley (1998, 22) concluded that "while the biracial Democratic coalition in the South was far from rock solid, neither was that coalition on the verge of collapse." The 2001 data indicate that fissures remain in the coalition at the activist level, but that white and African American party activists increasingly share much demographically and see the political world in similar ways; thus, the Democratic coalition no longer seems in dire threat of self-destruction at the activist level.

Some of the deepest demographic and ideological divides within the Democratic coalition are religious in their roots, as noted in the previous chapter, and serve as a potential source of angst for African Americans, who may see persons who understand their religiosity better in the other party. Yet it is these activists who are decidedly most loyal attitudinally and behaviorally to the Democratic Party. This African American fealty, combined with the perceived hostility of the modern Republican Party to their interests, therefore serves as an effective block against large-scale African American abandonment of the Democrats, at least at this level of southern party politics.

Most of the divisiveness in the post-VRA Democratic Party revolved around issues related to race. The data analyzed below show that divisions indeed persist in the Democratic Party on issues related to African American civil rights. But, more than the flight of white activists from the party that served as the key threat to the biracial Democratic coalition in the past, it is now the potential *deactivation* of African American activists—a set of activists who play a distinctive role in the workings of the party in the electoral arena—that is the direst threat to the continuing health of the coalition.

Intraparty divides generally arise from either of two fundamental points: who the activists are and what the activists believe. Thus, it is crucial to examine the demographic attributes and attitudinal orientations of activists. As noted earlier, the overwhelming majority of grassroots party activists in the South fall into three distinct groups that include racial and party differentiators: white Republicans, white Democrats, and African American Democrats. Therefore, the most straightforward analysis of the interaction of race and party in the region at the beginning of the new century involves the comparison of these three groups into which almost all party activists can be categorized. As the questions posed at the start of this chapter suggest, the focus of this analysis of the three groups will be on evaluating whether party or race is, on the whole, more potent as a differentiator of the attributes, attitudes, and political work of grassroots activists in the South.

THE DEMOGRAPHIC ATTRIBUTES OF WHITE AND AFRICAN AMERICAN ACTIVISTS

As shown in table 3.2, women activists near parity with men among white and African American Democrats. In both groups, the percentage of female activists has grown since 1991, but change is most striking among white Democrats. In 1991, only 35 percent of white Democratic activists were female, the smallest percentage in any of the three groups. In the 2001 survey results, the percentage of women among white Democratic activists has grown to 43 percent.

Findings regarding women in the ranks of African American activists reflect a similar percentage change over the decade; in 1991, 43 percent of African American Democratic activists were female; as of 2001, just under half were. Nearly one in four (23 percent) female Democratic activists in the South are now African American, showing the importance of this doubly deprived group in the party's base. The factors that potentially promote disproportionate races of activism in this group include their work in other social organizations (especially churches), the enhanced political consciousness that comes with double deprivation, and the influence of black female elected officials (who compose a disproportionate percentage of all female elected officials in the region).[2] All told, the survey data show that the

Table 3.2 Demographic Characteristics of Party Activists, 2001

Characteristic	*White Democrats*	*African American Democrats*	*White Republicans*
Age			
Mean (Years)	58	58	57
18–40	12	10	15
65 and up	32	31	30
Native southerner	79	93	76
Female	43	50	32
Education			
Less than college	15	15	9
Some college	28	30	30
College graduate	21	21	33
Post-college	35	35	29
Family income			
Under $25,000	9	18	5
$25,000–$49,999	28	36	30
$50,000–$74,999	25	25	26
$75,000–$99,999	18	13	18
$100,000–$149,999	13	6	15
Above $150,000	6	2	10
(Minimum *N*)	(2,602)	(703)	(3,139)

Note: Entries are percentages, by column.

openness to traditional outsiders in the Democratic Party has moved beyond race to include gender. In stark contrast, the Republican Party organizations of the region have, if anything, become less welcoming of women at the grassroots level over the same period. In 1991, 36 percent of white Republican activists were women; by 2001, the percentage had shrunk to 32 percent. The face of the Republican Party in local communities in the South is, therefore, overwhelmingly male, perhaps serving as another factor in pushing rank-and-file women voters away from the party. At the most superficial level, it is the Democratic Party that looks most like the southern communities in which it operates.

Another important demographic force—geographical migration—will be examined in detail in the chapter that follows. While a full analysis can be found there, it is relevant to note that one of the most clear racial divides across the demographic profiles can be seen in one of the two areas: where activists came of age. In 1991, the largest gap on southern nativity was partisan: white Democrats and African American Democrats—86 percent and 93 percent southern-bred, respectively—were both decidedly more likely to be native southerners than were Republicans (with one in four nonnative). According to the 2001 survey, while the high levels of nativity among African

Americans remain constant and while little change can be seen on this measure among white Republicans, white Democrats have become markedly less native. In 2001, over one in five came of age outside the region, only a slightly smaller percentage than among their Republican counterparts.

Race and party are both important in dividing activists on family income. Over half (54 percent) of African American Democratic activists have family incomes below $50,000, followed by 38 percent of white Democrats and 31 percent of white Republicans. At the other end of the income spectrum, 26 percent of the Republicans surveyed have incomes above $100,000, followed by 19 percent of white Democrats and only 8 percent of African American Democrats.

On the other most potent determinant of socioeconomic status, educational attainment, white and black Democrats are essentially indistinguishable: over one in three activists from each group have some educational training following their college graduation. The relatively small difference among activist groupings that shows itself on this demographic attribute is a partisan one with white Republicans more likely both to have attended some college and to be college graduates than their Democratic counterparts but less likely to have advanced educational experiences. All told, while differences between white and African American Democrats show themselves on the demographic characteristics presented in table 3.2, they are certainly not of a nature to create deep intraparty divisions and they are generally less striking than the differences between Republican and Democratic activists, white and black.

RELIGION: THE VITAL EXCEPTION

In a variety of ways, however, the three groups differ significantly on religious attributes. And, in contrast to the pattern shown with the previous demographic characteristics, white Democrats do not fall between their African American partisans and white Republicans; the middle ground on these gauges of religiosity and an acceptance of a linkage between religion and politics among the three groups is filled by white Republicans. Thus, the potential for damaging intraparty tensions within the Democratic Party activist base is clearly present here.

As shown in table 3.3, white southern Democratic activists are, as a group, anything but secularists. All but a small percentage of this group identify with a religious denomination, including 36 percent who term themselves evangelical Protestants. And, nearly half of white Democrats attend church at least once per week, and a similar percentage note the significant role that their religion provides in guiding their life decisions on a daily basis.

Still, the importance of religion in their personal lives is strikingly greater for the other two groups, especially for the white Democrats' partisan comrades. With the exception that a larger percentage of Democrats identify themselves as Jewish or as atheist or agnostic, white Republicans appear quite similar to white

Table 3.3 Religious Characteristics of Party Activists, 2001

	White Democrats	*African American Democrats*	*White Republicans*
Religion			
Mainline Protestant	40	—	46
Evangelical Protestant	36	—	39
Black Protestant	0	92	—
Jewish	4	—	1
Roman Catholic	12	7	12
Atheist/Agnostic	5	0	1
Other	4	1	1
Attend church weekly or more	48	75	62
Religion provides "great deal" of guidance in day-to-day life	50	84	63
(Minimum *N*)	(2,669)	(717)	(3,282)

Note: Entries are percentages, by column.

Democrats in terms of the the religious affiliations with which they identify. But, white Republican activists attend church more regularly (62 percent at least weekly) and are more cognizant of the role that their religion provides for their daily lives (63 percent say a "great deal"). It is for African American Democrats, most all of whom are Protestant, that religion is an even more significant part of their lives. Three in four of the members of this group say that they attend church weekly or more often. And, an incredible 84 percent state that religion provides a great deal of guidance for their daily lives.

Most importantly, and similar to the worldview of many white Republicans, this is a group for whom the lines between the secular and the spiritual are not sharply drawn. As such, the influence of black Democrats' religious beliefs on their political views are noticeable, as the next section clearly points out. But, while the hints of common ground between religious African American Democratic activists and white Republican activists are present on certain social issues, these are more than overwhelmed by the liberalism on many other issues that divides the parties, which results from African Americans' unique religious perspective.

THE ATTITUDES AND ACTIVITIES OF AFRICAN AMERICAN ACTIVISTS

As shown in table 3.4, African American activists are indeed more conservative than white Democratic activists on the civil liberties issues of prayer in schools and abortion rights. On prayer in schools, only 6 percent of African American activists take the most liberal position, that is, strong opposition to

Table 3.4 Position on Issues for Democratic and Republican Party Activists, 2001

Issue	*White Democrats*	*African American Democrats*	*White Republicans*
Sexual equality issues			
1. Gay job discrimination	22	25	2
2. Equal role for women	58	61	38
3. Government aid for women	32	50	5
Civil liberty issues			
1. School prayer*	21	6	2
2. Abortion	51	47	9
Social safety net issues			
1. Government services/spending*	36	48	2
2. Government regulation of health care	29	32	3
3. Guaranteed job and living standard	11	30	1
Criminal justice issues			
1. Handgun control	42	65	5
2. Death penalty*	16	19	2
Civil rights issues			
1. Government aid to minorities	26	73	4
2. Hiring preferences for blacks	3	28	0
(Minimun *N*)	(2,537)	(652)	(3,184)

Note: Entries are the percentage claiming "strong" agreement with more liberal stance. For the wording of each issue item, see the copy of the questionnaire in the appendix.

*Indicates that liberal position is indicated by "strongly disagree" response.

school prayer. On this issue, and reflecting the trend shown in 1991 data, they look much more like Republican activists (2 percent oppose school prayer) than white Democrats (over one in five oppose school prayer). In addition, African American activists are less likely than white Democrats to see the legal protections of a woman's right to choose abortion as appropriate. Here, however, the difference between the two groups of Democrats is tiny compared to the partisan divide that exists on the issue of abortion rights.

In addition, religious beliefs likely do mute African Americans' support for the promotion of women's equality in business and politics and for the expansion of civil rights protections to gay men and lesbians. The patriarchal

Table 3.5 Ideological Self-Identification of Party Activists, 2001

Political Beliefs	*White Democrats*	*African American Democrats*	*White Republicans*
Very liberal	9	23	0
Somewhat liberal	29	36	1
Moderate	25	25	7
Somewhat conservative	18	12	39
Very conservative	13	4	54
(Minimum *N*)	(2,630)	(674)	(3,272)

Note: Entries are percentages, by column.

nature of the black church (and, by extension, key components of the civil rights movement grounded in that church) has been noted by numerous scholars.[3] Still, this religious-based conservatism only results in lessening the liberalism of African Americans on these issues; they remain slightly more supportive than white Democrats of promoting women's equality in the public sphere and of civil rights expansions to gay men and lesbians in the job arena.

The larger impact of African American religious tenets on political predispositions actually comes in the form of enhancing their liberalism on a wide range of issues, thus more than outweighing any shared ideological space with Republican Party activists on social issues. While it is important not to overgeneralize, a key tenet of the teachings of most African American churches emphasizes the importance of creating social change that enhances justice, that is, the social gospel. As the key civil rights movement leader (and present congressman) John Lewis (1988, 87) puts it in his autobiography: "[Martin Luther King's notion of] the Beloved Community was nothing less than the kingdom of God on earth."[4]

Despite the elements of conservatism present in the religious beliefs so fundamentally important to the vast majority of African American activists, these more progressive tenets of that same religious tradition are more important in shaping their ideologies. As shown in table 3.5, nearly six in ten African American activists describe themselves as "very" or "somewhat" liberal. And, despite the fact that on most issues there are not huge differences in the stances of white and black Democratic activists, "liberals" only outnumber "conservatives" among those activists by a small margin (38 percent to 31 percent). Even on this measure of ideology, it is party rather than race that matters more in dividing activists, as white Republicans are emphatically conservative ideologically.

Combined with the relative economic disadvantage of African American families, this ideology leads naturally to the stances expressed by African American activists on a variety of social safety net issues shown in table 3.4. Generally reiterating the findings reported by Hadley and Stanley using the 1991 data, African Americans have more faith than other activists in the capacity of government to be a force for protecting and promoting the interests of the less powerful in society. Still, while African Americans are more emphatic about the importance of a strong government in regulating businesses (such as HMOs) and the maintenance of government activity in funding domestic programs, the differences between white and African American Democrats pale in comparison with differences across party lines. Similarly, while African Americans are more liberal on issues related to the use of force, it is differences between Democrats and Republicans on gun control and the death penalty that are more decisive.

While the numbers vary from issue to issue (on those questions that are replicated exactly in the two surveys), on these issues white Democratic activists of 2001 have liberalized slightly from 1991. It is this movement on these non-African American civil rights, civil liberties, social safety net, and use of force issues that is responsible for most of the closing of the gap between white and African American activists on issue stances that has occurred. The more intense change—leading to the growing gap between white activists from the two parties—is the increasingly rigid and consistent conservatism of white Republican activists in the region.

CIVIL-RIGHTS-BASED TENSIONS AND THE DEMOCRATIC BASE

So, the religious differences between white and African American Democratic activists, important as they are in creating cultural differences between whites and blacks in the South, are not serious enough to create threats to the biracial coalition. The threats to the coalition, not surprisingly considering the region's history, are grounded in race. But, it is increasingly African American frustrations with fellow Democrats rather than the white Democrats' sense that their party has left them behind on issues related to race that appear to present the true threat to the ongoing vitality of the Democratic coalition.

Undeniably, some of the issues analyzed previously have implicit racial components. For instance, both gun violence and the death penalty have important racial components, especially in the South. African Americans are more likely to be victims of gun violence and, even more disproportionately, they are more likely to be recipients of death sentences. But, as shown in table 3.4, it is as political issues move into explicit racial turf that the divisions between activists move from the partisan to racial. The most explicitly racial political issues about which activists were asked their views are the especial role of the government in bettering the economic position of African Americans and the appropriateness of hiring policies that would preference racial minorities. On both of these issues, white Democrats are more in sync with white Republicans than with their fellow partisans.

Moreover, on these issues, the chasm between African American activists and white activists from both parties is larger than in the 1991 survey with both white groups moving in the conservative direction.

The white Democratic activists are not particularly cognizant of the sharp attitudinal divisions that show themselves on African American civil rights issues in the party. According to the survey, only 16 percent of white Democrats note a "great deal" of disagreement on racial issues within their state parties. More than twice as many African American Democrats (35 percent) are conscious of these divisions; indeed, over two-thirds of black activists (67 percent) note a "great deal" or a "fair amount" of disagreement with state parties on the issues. So, African American activists, as a minority of Democratic activists, are aware they are on the short end within their party on issues that are deeply important to them as activists.

Despite these divisions about which African Americans are concerned, there is absolutely no worry that these activists will bail out on their party. They are decidedly loyal in their partisan allegiance and in their support for the party's candidates. As shown in table 3.6, African Americans are as cohesive in their party affiliation and support for their party's presidential candidates as are the deeply committed white Republican activists. Indeed, in state politics, African American activists are the most committed group. And, as is the case with all three groups (especially with white Democrats and their views of their national party), the strength of partisanship has grown in activists as compared to 1991.

Thus, the racial divisions noted and noticed by African American activists do not threaten their core allegiance. But, just as troublesome for Democrats is the potential muting of support of African Americans that could imperil the important work that they do in reaching out to rank-and-file African American

Table 3.6 Strength of Partisanship and Presidential Voting Behavior of Party Activists, 2001

	White Democrats	*African American Democrats*	*White Republicans*
Identify as "strong" partisan in national politics	81	89	92
Identify as "strong" partisan in state politics	86	92	89
Voted for party's candidate in 2000 presidential election	87	98	98
(Minimum *N*)	(2,658)	(695)	(3,284)

Note: Entries are percentages, by column.

voters at election time. As African American turnout is just as important a variable in the mathematics of modern biracial southern politics described by Black and Black as is the voting group's cohesiveness, such prospects of lessening of the activists' energy for party work are a real threat to the vitality of the coalition.

THE ESSENTIAL WORK OF AFRICAN AMERICANS

Table 3.7 shows the activities in which county activists in the South engage on behalf of their parties. The pertinent differences among the groups are race based rather than partisan. Not surprising considering the income differences noted earlier, white activists of both parties are more likely to contribute money themselves and to engage in other activities where raising or spending money is the focus of the work. Money obviously matters in driving turnout, but African American activists report engaging in a series of

Table 3.7 Campaign Activities in Which Party Activists Report Having Participated, 2001

Activity	*White Democrats*	*African American Democrats*	*White Republicans*
Organized door-to-door canvassing	27	50	30
Organized events	42	37	44
Arranged fund-raising activities	34	26	40
Sent mailings to voters	43	34	50
Distributed literature	68	73	74
Organized telephoning	32	43	36
Purchased billboard space	6	4	6
Distributed posters or signs	70	69	79
Contributed money	72	54	80
Conducted voter registration drives	26	51	26
Utilized public opinion surveys	10	11	11
Dealt with media	26	20	30
Helped maintain or create Web site	4	3	6
(Minimum *N*)	(2,728)	(731)	(3,344)

Note: Entries are the percentage of respondents indicating performance of the specific campaign activity.

activities that are much more directly related to actually "getting out the vote" on election day and in the days leading up to that event. African Americans are decidedly more likely to work in voter registration efforts, to go door to door on behalf of candidates, to distribute campaign literature, and to make get-out-the-vote phone calls. This is the time-intensive work at which volunteers are particularly effective. And, as has been shown in analyses of the relationship between contact and turnout that controls for other important variables explaining African American turnout, this work makes a significant difference in enlivening the African American component of the biracial coalition (Wielhouwer 2000).[5]

Because of the investment of time necessary for these activities to be done effectively, a threat to the biracial coalition does arise if African American activists no longer feel that their work is worthy of the personal cost. Moreover, working to get out the vote in the African American community may become even more difficult if less committed rank-and-file African Americans also come to believe that their traditional political party is no longer working on behalf of them and their community or if significant numbers of African Americans begin to be drawn to elements of the social conservative platform of the Republican Party. The potential threat to the work of African American activists is highlighted when the survey data that examine the incentives that drive grassroots activists to become and stay involved in their party are examined, a topic examined in considerably more detail in chapter 10.

Following upon the work of Clark and Wilson (1961) that provides the foundation for the analysis in chapter 10, incentives for activism can be clumped into three major categories: purposive incentives (i.e., the desire to promote public policy change), solidary incentives (i.e., the desire to interact with others on a task), and material incentives (i.e., the desire for self-interested benefits). Fortunately, the survey instrument in use in the 2001 SGPA Project tapped each of these incentives with multiple questions, the results of which for the three groups are shown in table 3.8.

Like all party activists, African American Democratic activists are decidedly purposive. For this reason, the threats that arise from doubts about the commitment of their party to their interests and ideology are potentially serious ones. As the data indicate, the two "minority" groups reflected here—African Americans and the traditional "out" party in the South, Republicans—are both more purposive than white Democrats. Interesting patterns also show themselves in two other categories. First, Democrats are decidedly more driven by solidary incentives than are Republicans. When the ideologies of the two parties are considered, it is not surprising that the antigovernment Republicans would be less inspired by working with others in activities related to the acquisition and maintenance of governmental power. Activists from all three groups are least likely to identify self-interest-oriented incentives as reasons for their involvement in party politics. But, African American Democrats are the group most likely to note

Table 3.8 Incentives for Party Activists, 2001

Incentive	*White Democrats*	*African American Democrats*	*White Republicans*
Purposive			
Concern with public issues	67	74	74
Belief in particular candidates	73	73	75
Solidary			
Political work is part of a way of life	42	41	33
Excitement of campaign	32	30	25
Friendship/social contact	33	37	25
Personal advantage			
Obtaining community recognition	11	20	7
Making business contacts	5	13	3
Building personal position in politics	10	14	8
(Minimum *N*)	(2,487)	(639)	(2,602)

Note: Entries are the percentage claiming the incentive is "very important."

their desire for personal and economic gain in party work. Considering that the other primary social outlet for African Americans, the church, is a segregated institution, it makes sense that African Americans would see this one biracial social institution in which they are involved as a venue that would give them access to the economic and social power that, in most southern communities, remains in the hands of whites.

This finding that African Americans are more driven by material incentives than other activists leads to an additional potentially problematic area for the Democratic coalition. While compared to the findings reported by Clawson and Clark (1998) that African Americans are enlarging their leadership roles in the party, they still lag significantly behind white Democratic activists in positions of power in local parties despite two generations of African American commitment to the Democratic coalition. In 1991, just over 6 percent of Democratic local party chairs were African American; in 2001, the percentage of African American leaders had grown to just over 10 percent indicating some movement up the party hierarchy by the traditional "out" group. But, the continuing disproportionate lack of power held by African Americans in local Democratic Party organizations is made more clear from a different cut of the 2001 data: just over 8 percent of African American activists hold chair positions as compared to 18 percent of white activists.

CONCLUSIONS

The 2001 Southern Grassroots Party Activists Project data, much like the survey data from 1991 analyzed by Hadley and Stanley, show a Democratic biracial coalition that is generally stable. Indeed, white Democrats' comfort with their party seems enhanced over that of their predecessors. For most of the contemporary era, analysts of electoral politics in the South have focused on the angst about the direction of their party expressed, attitudinally and behaviorally, by white Democrats. But, if anything, the divisions that now are shown in the coalition at the grassroots level are putting more pressure on African American activists, the continued minority group in the biracial coalition that recognizes that whites see public policy issues where race is a factor in a decidedly different way than they do. These data certainly do not indicate that a bailout of the party by African American activists is on the horizon. Indeed, this is a decidedly loyal and committed group of activists. But, some warning signs appear here that, if African Americans come to feel taken for granted and/or ignored in the operations of their parties at a state and local level, then the Democratic Party and its candidates could feel the effects of African Americans' no longer feeling that the hard work in which they engage on behalf of their party is sufficiently benefiting them. This tension—along with the enhanced diversification of one or both parties at the grassroots that will come with the entrance of Latinos and Latinas that will likely produce new ethnic and racial tensions—and the other intraparty tensions discussed elsewhere in this text indicate that the dynamics of party politics in the South in the coming decade will be increasingly complex and consequential.

NOTES

1. On this issue, see, for example: Dorie Turner, "The Changing South," *Chatanooga Times Free Press,* August 17, 2003; Suzi Parker, "Hispanics Reshape Culture of the South," *Christian Science Monitor,* June 10, 1999; Gary Martin, "Candidates Targeting Hispanic Leaders, Voters," *San Antonio Express-News,* June 4, 2003; Mark Niesse, "Census Numbers Show South Seeing Boom in Hispanic Population," *The Associated Press,* September 17, 2003.

2. The initial examination of African American women active in the church and their political involvement by Clawson and Clark (2003), using the 1991 data, indicates the potency of this impetus. On this issue, also see Frederick (2003).

3. See, for instance, Dyson (2000, 197–222) and Frederick (2003). As Martin Luther King Jr. himself said in indirectly promoting the notion of separate spheres for men and women, "The primary obligation of the woman is that of motherhood" (quoted in Garrow 1986, 99). D'Emilio (2003) also writes extensively on the impact of the homosexuality of 1963 March on Washington organizer Bayard Rustin in limiting his visible role in the movement.

4. A number of authors have argued that the roots of these tenets are found in the distinctive African American religion that grew up during the era of slavery. As Genovese (1976, 252) has written, "Black eschatology emerges more clearly from the slaves' treatment of Moses and Jesus. The slaves did not draw a sharp line between them but merged them into a single deliverer, at one this-worldly and otherworldly."

5. Interestingly, many of these activities that focus on one-on-one communication are also disproportionately engaged in by women—another traditional "out" group in the region's public life—according to the survey data (Barth 2002).

CHAPTER

4

Population Movement and Southern Party Activists

Laurence W. Moreland and Robert P. Steed

Scholars in a wide range of fields have long identified population movement as an important variable. Demographers and economists, for example, have analyzed the effects of population movement on such matters as patterns of industrialization, income change, generational change, and race relations (see, e.g., Long 1975; Shin 1978; Biggar and Biasiolli 1978; and Biggar 1984). Political scientists also have long seen population movement as important. Early research by Lubell (1952) and Harris (1954) focused on some of the key political consequences of movement of people from central cities to suburbs. Campbell, Converse, Miller, and Stokes (1960), in their groundbreaking analysis of political behavior in the 1950s, noted the political importance of interregional population movement, a line of inquiry later extended by others such as Feigert (1973) and Brown (1988). Scammon and Wattenberg (1970) pointed to population shifts as a factor contributing to the modification of the American party system; and Dye (1966), Sharkansky (1969), and Katzman (1978) examined the consequences of population mobility for state and local policy.

Similarly, and more relevant to the central focus of this chapter, examinations of political parties in the post–World War II South have frequently pointed to population movement into the region as one important factor in the dramatic transformation of the South's party system from a one-party Democratic stronghold to one of Republican strength.

In this regard, despite some research findings to the contrary (e.g., Nie, Verba, and Petrocik 1976, 221; Petrocik 1987; Beck 1977), the impact of (especially white) in-migration has been generally identified as an important variable in the development of Republican Party strength in the southern electorate as nonsoutherners moving into the region brought their party identifications and voting habits with them. For example, a broad examination of Republican Party growth in the South between the 1940s and the mid-1960s by Topping, Lazarek, and Linder (1966) concluded that in-migration made a significant contribution to the development of southern Republicanism. Other research in Tennessee found that, in comparison with native southerners, nonsouthern in-migrants in that state tended to be more affluent, more Republican, and more inclined to support changes in existing morality legislation and in existing state political structures (Lyons and Durant 1980). Similarly, Campbell (1977b), in examining survey data for the 1952–1972 period, reported that in-migration explains roughly 25 percent of the change in southern partisanship during those two decades. He speculated, moreover, that the influence of in-migration might well be greater than these figures suggest inasmuch as "[t]he arrival of northern Republicans . . . may well have served to catalyze a movement into the Republican Party among large numbers of formerly Democratic southerners" (Campbell 1977b, 755). Additional research by Converse (1972, 314), Wolfinger and Arseneau (1978, 185), Welch and Brown (1979), Wolfinger and Hagen (1985, 10), Black and Black (1987), and Van Wingen and Valentine (1988, 131–134) further support the argument that population movement contributed significantly to southern partisan change in the electorate (for a good summary, see Stanley and Castle 1988).

While much of the research on in-migration has focused on its impact on partisanship and voting patterns in the South, there is some evidence that it has affected the region's politics in other ways as well. For example, Black and Black (2002) cited a recent public opinion survey that reveals a number of attitudinal and ideological differences between native southerners and in-migrants. Focusing especially on the data for white men, they noted that by 1999 native white men tended to be more Republican than white men who had moved into the region and that they tended to be more conservative on a number of social, racial, and religious issues than in-migrants (see Black and Black 2002, 425, n. 11).

There is also a body of research that examines the impact of population movement into the South on the party organizations in the region. For example, Bowman, Hulbary, and Kelley (1990) found that in-migrants had become heavily involved in Florida's party organizations inasmuch as almost two-thirds of precinct officials in both parties had moved into the state from outside the South; in turn, they found that these in-migrants had contributed significantly to the ideological realignment of the state's parties. Similarly, analyses of data on state convention delegates and on precinct officials in South Carolina demonstrated that in-migration has had a clear impact on party organizations and activities in the state, particularly by pulling the Democratic Party ideologically to the left (see, e.g., Steed,

Moreland, and Baker 1981; Moreland, Steed, and Baker 1986; Steed, Moreland, and Baker 1990; Moreland 1990b; Steed, Moreland, and Baker 1991; Steed, Moreland, and Baker 1995; Moreland and Steed 1998a; Moreland and Steed 1998b; Moreland and Steed 2001).

DATA

The Southern Grassroots Party Activists Project survey invites a regionwide examination of in-migration's impact on local party organizations. Here, we analyze data from the 2001 Southern Grassroots Party Activists Project to assess the current impact of in-migration on the South's local party organizations (and to update the earlier findings of the 1991 Southern Grassroots Party Activists Project; see Feigert and Todd 1998). For our analysis here, we divide Democratic and Republican respondents into two groups each: natives (those who grew up in one of the eleven southern states) and nonnatives (those who grew up outside the South). For both parties, over a quarter of the respondents—26 percent of the Democrats (n = 929) and 29 percent of the Republicans (n = 1,020)—reported having grown up outside the South. Most of the nonnatives immigrated to the South from either the eastern or midwestern regions of the United States (see table 4.1).

FINDINGS

Penetration of In-Migrants into Local Party Organizations

As already noted, in-migrants constitute over a quarter of local party activists in each party. Table 4.2, which reports data by state, suggests two observations: generally, Rim South states show greater penetration than Deep South states, and local Republican Party organizations show greater penetration than Democratic organizations. Among Deep South states, South Carolina and Georgia show the most penetration, with Louisiana showing, by far, the least. Between the two parties, not surprisingly, in-migrants were more heavily involved in the local Republican Party organizations in almost every state in the region, although the overall pattern of greater penetration in the Rim South than in the Deep South still held. This latter pattern tends to confirm the important role in-migration has played in the development of Republican strength in the South during the past half century. When we compare the current data with data from the 1991 Southern Grassroots Party Activists Project, several differences are apparent. First, in-migrants still constitute larger percentages of local party officials in the Republican Party than in the Democratic Party, although the gap has narrowed considerably in

Table 4.1 Region of Childhood of Respondents in Southern States' Local Party Organizations, by Party

Region of Childhood	*Democrats*	*Republicans*
South	*74*	*71*
Current state	66	55
Another southern state	8	16
Non-South	*26*	*29*
Eastern U.S.	14	11
Midwestern U.S.	8	13
Western U.S.	2	4
Outside U.S./more than one place	2	2

Note: Entries are percentages, by column. In this table as well as the following tables in this chapter, columns may not total to 100 because of rounding error.

Table 4.2 Penetration of In-Migrants into Southern States' Local Party Organizations, by Party and State

State	*Democrats*	*Republicans*
Deep South		
Alabama	9	10
Georgia	15	31
Louisiana	3	2
Mississippi	9	12
South Carolina	22	33
Average	13.2	18.8
Rim South		
Arkansas	9	26
Florida	56	46
North Carolina	14	26
Tennessee	13	22
Texas	25	28
Virginia	34	33
Average	25.0	30.8

Note: Entries are percentages nonnative to the state.

almost every state. Second, in-migrants are somewhat more prominently involved in the southern Democratic Party in 2001 than in 1991 (with South Carolina having the most notable change as the proportion of in-migrant local party activists has jumped from 9 percent in 1991 to 22 percent ten years later). Just the reverse has happened in the Republican Party where the proportion of in-migrants has tended, on the whole, to decline. Finally, the gap between the Deep South and Rim South remains—more in-migrants

Table 4.3 Socioeconomic Backgrounds of Local Party Officials in the South, by Childhood Region and Party

	Democrats		*Republicans*	
Background Characteristic	*Natives*	*In-Migrants*	*Natives*	*In-Migrants*
Gender				
Male	58	52	66	64
Female	43	48	34	36
Age				
Under 30	3	1	4	3
30–40	10	5	13	9
40–50	17	18	20	20
50–60	28	23	21	29
Over 60	44	53	43	39
Race				
White	75	90	94	95
African American	20	6	2	1
Hispanic American	4	2	2	2
Other	1	1	1	2
Education				
High school or less	13	7	10	4
Some college	29	25	31	25
College degree	23	23	33	38
Graduate or professional degree	34	45	27	34
Income				
Under $25,000	11	8	6	4
$25,000–$49,999	31	27	26	21
$50,000–$74,999	24	26	27	25
$75,000–$99,999	18	14	17	22
$100,000–$150,000	11	16	15	17
Over $150,000	5	9	10	11

Note: Entries are percentages, by column.

are active in local party organizations in both parties in the Rim South than in the Deep South—but it has narrowed slightly in each party.

Demographic, Socioeconomic, and Religious Backgrounds

In most respects, in-migrants in both parties vary only marginally from natives, although women are better represented among in-migrants, and in-migrants tend to be somewhat better educated, tend to earn higher incomes, and tend to be somewhat older than natives. Among Democrats, in-migrants are also less likely to be African American as compared with natives (see table 4.3).

Table 4.4 Religious Backgrounds of Local Party Officials in the South, by Childhood Region and Party

	Democrats		*Republicans*	
Background Characteristic	*Natives*	*In-Migrants*	*Natives*	*In-Migrants*
Religious preference				
Protestant	79	45	86	68
Catholic	13	22	12	23
Jewish	1	15	*	3
Other	3	5	1	3
Nonbeliever	3	13	1	3
Religious attendance				
More than once a week	24	11	28	22
Once a week	29	20	33	29
Almost every week	13	9	13	10
Once or twice a month	10	10	9	14
Few times a year	18	27	14	19
Never	7	23	3	6
Religious guidance in daily life				
Great deal	55	31	62	49
Fair amount	23	19	24	25
Some	13	20	10	18
Very little	5	14	3	6
No guidance	4	15	1	3
Born-again Christian?				
Yes	51	17	62	36
No	49	84	38	64
Closeness to Christian Right				
Very close or close	16	4	48	37
Neutral	25	12	35	35
Far or very far	59	84	17	28

Note: Entries are percentages, by column.

*Indicates less than 0.5 percent.

The religious variables, however, show greater differences (see table 4.4; also see chapter 2 of this volume for a detailed examination of the importance of religious attitudes and behavior). On the whole, in-migrants tend to be substantially less Protestant and less religious, regardless of party. Among Democrats, natives tend to be significantly more Protestant than in-migrants (79 percent to 45 percent), less Catholic (13 percent to 22 percent), and less Jewish (1 percent to 15 percent). Native Democrats are also less likely to say they are nonbelievers (3 percent to 13 percent). Among Republicans, there is a similar pattern in that natives tend to be more Protestant (86 percent to 68 percent) and less Catholic (12 percent to 23 percent).

Similarly, and not surprisingly, native southerners tend to exhibit greater religiosity on other dimensions than in-migrants: they attend church more often and more regularly. Among Democrats over half (53 percent) of the natives attend church once a week or more, compared with less than a third (31 percent) of the in-migrants. Among Republicans, the pattern is not quite so striking, but natives remain more likely to attend religious services at least weekly (61 percent to 51 percent).

On other religious dimensions as well, natives differ from in-migrants. Among Democrats, natives are more likely to indicate a great deal or a fair amount of religious guidance in daily life (78 percent to 50 percent) and are much more likely (51 percent to 17 percent) to indicate a "born-again" experience. Among Republicans, the pattern is similar, although the differences are not as great. These patterns on religious attendance and on born-again status are generally consistent with those found in the 1991 data and suggest that in-migrants continue to constitute a significant secularizing influence on the southern Democratic Party.

Finally, on a political-religious dimension—a measure of closeness to the Christian Right—in-migrant Democrats are the least supportive among the four groups (84 percent indicate that they are very far or far from the Christian Right, compared with 59 percent of native Democrats). Among Republicans, while support for the Christian Right is much stronger, still less than half (48 percent) of natives and less than two-fifths (37 percent) of in-migrants indicate closeness to that movement.

These patterns suggest that in-migrants constitute a diversifying influence as well as a secularizing influence on both parties, although the pattern is stronger among Democrats. Conversely, population movement into the South has had less of a diversifying effect on the Republican Party's local organizations than on the Democratic Party's.

Political Backgrounds

In-migrants differ from natives in mixed patterns with respect to their political backgrounds (see table 4.5). In both parties, natives tend to have longer histories of political activity and evince more political experience overall than in-migrants, but the differences are small and do not extend to every variable listed (e.g., holding a previous party office).

The most noteworthy political background differences occur on party switching and family political activity (see table 4.5). Among Democratic officials, slightly larger percentages of in-migrants are party switchers (15 percent to 8 percent) while the reverse is true among the Republican officials (26 percent of natives have switched parties compared to 21 percent of the in-migrants). Natives in both parties tend to come from politically active families more than in-migrants, and natives are more likely to come from families where one or both parents were Democrats. This latter point is

Table 4.5 Political Backgrounds of Local Party Officials in the South, by Childhood Region and Party

	Democrats		*Republicans*	
Background Characteristic	*Natives*	*In-Migrants*	*Natives*	*In-Migrants*
Years politically active				
10 years or less	22	27	29	31
11–20 years	21	24	23	27
21–30 years	24	20	22	21
Over 30 years	33	29	27	22
Political experience				
Held previous party position	32	33	43	44
Held previous appointed office	20	17	22	18
Held elective public office	25	18	22	17
Ran unsuccessfully for elected office	24	14	27	20
Family political patterns				
Parents or other relatives politically active	55	48	46	45
Father's party affiliation				
Democrat	79	58	48	26
Republican	10	24	37	57
Independent	4	9	8	9
Other or don't know	7	9	7	7
Mother's party affiliation				
Democrat	80	62	47	30
Republican	8	23	35	52
Independent	4	9	10	10
Other or don't know	7	7	9	8

Note: Entries are percentages, by column.

a continuing reflection of the persistent impact of the Democratic dominance of the southern political system well into the 1970s and 1980s. Consequently, it is not surprising that in-migrants in both parties are more likely to have had Republican parents than natives. The most interesting groups, perhaps, are the most "deviant" ones, that is, in-migrant Democrats (nearly a quarter of Democratic in-migrants) who had Republican parents and in-migrant Republicans (over a quarter of Republican in-migrants) who had Democratic parents. While the data do not allow us to confirm this, we might speculate that some of those in-migrants who had Republican parents and who moved to the South might have found the very socially conservative southern Republican Party to be sufficiently different from the party systems from which they came that they found the southern Democratic Party to be a more congenial home. On the other hand, those in-migrants who had Democratic parents and who subsequently became active in the southern Republican Party might have found that party—a strikingly ascendant party, particularly among white suburbanites—to be a more natural resting place.

Party Attachment and Campaign Activity

Within parties, respondents' state and national party identifications and feelings toward the parties at the national and state levels vary only marginally, and their voting patterns in the 2000 presidential election are nearly identical (see table 4.6). The main exception to this is found in examining the data for the Democrats on feelings toward the national party. Natives are somewhat less likely to say they feel close to the national party than in-migrants (71 percent to 77 percent). Moreover, while the percentages of both natives and in-migrants saying they feel close to the national party are lower than the corresponding percentages saying they feel close to the state party, the gap is larger for the natives. This suggests that some vestiges of the disaffection southern Democrats felt toward the national Democratic Party, and which haunted the party during the 1980s and 1990s, remain (see chapter 6 of this volume for a more detailed analysis of the data on party loyalty and party attachment).

When asked about their activity at different electoral levels, in both parties larger percentages of natives than of in-migrants said they are "very active" in local and state elections. However, the pattern is reversed in both parties in national elections. Moreover, the differences in each case tend to be small enough so as to be essentially inconsequential. The picture that emerges for both groups of officials in both parties is that they are quite active at all electoral levels. Even so, there is one other point worth noting in these data. Consistent with the data on feelings toward the national party versus feelings toward the state party, native Democratic officials are considerably less active in national elections than in state and, especially, local elections. Looking at those saying they are "very active," there is a drop among natives from 63 percent (local) to 50 percent (state) to 43 percent (national). Of the four groups in the analysis, only native Democrats demonstrate this pattern. It appears, then, that one of the ways in which in-migration is impacting the southern Democratic Party is by helping to reduce the support gap between southern Democratic Party officials and the national Democratic Party, a gap that has been a nagging problem for the Democratic Party since at least the late 1960s.

IDEOLOGY AND ISSUE ORIENTATIONS

The 1991 data on local party officials showed a sharp ideological (and issue position) division between Democratic and Republican activists (Steed 1998; McGlennon 1998b). This picture of party sorting among party officials is consistent with a wide range of research on southern party activists at various

Table 4.6 Party Attachment and Levels of Campaign Activity of Local Party Officials in the South, by Childhood Region and Party

	Democrats		*Republicans*	
Orientation Characteristic	*Natives*	*In-Migrants*	*Natives*	*In-Migrants*
Switched parties?				
Yes	8	15	26	21
No	92	85	74	80
National party identification				
Strong	83	88	91	87
Weak	8	4	4	4
Independent, leaning toward own party	5	5	3	6
Independent	2	1	1	2
State party identification				
Strong	87	88	89	89
Weak	6	6	6	5
Independent, leaning toward own party	5	4	4	6
Independent	1	1	1	1
Feelings toward the national party				
Close	71	77	85	82
Neutral	17	13	9	12
Distant	12	10	6	6
Feelings toward the state party				
Close	79	81	91	89
Neutral	13	12	5	7
Distant	8	7	5	4
2000 presidential vote				
Gore	91	93	1	1
Bush	8	5	97	98
Other, didn't vote	2	3	1	1
Level of campaign activity				
Local elections, very active	63	54	58	54
State elections, very active	50	48	54	50
National elections, very active	43	55	55	56

Note: Entries are percentages, by column.

organizational levels (see, e.g., Bowman, Hulbary, and Kelley 1990; Steed, Moreland, and Baker 1995; Moreland 1990a). In general the consistent pattern over the past two decades has been for Republican activists to be heavily conservative and for Democratic activists to be comparatively more moderate to liberal but also to be more widely spread across the ideological spectrum.

Table 4.7 Ideology of Local Party Officials in the South, by Childhood Region and Party

	Democrats		*Republicans*	
Ideological Characteristic	*Natives*	*In-Migrants*	*Natives*	*In-Migrants*
Very liberal	18	31	*	*
Somewhat liberal	34	42	1	2
Moderate	31	19	6	10
Somewhat conservative	13	7	39	42
Very conservative	4	1	53	47

Note: Entries are percentages, by column.

*Indicates less than 0.5 percent.

This pattern holds for local party officials in the South in 2001 as well, both in terms of general ideology and in terms of stands on specific issues (see chapter 5 and chapter 8 of this volume for more detailed examinations of the role of ideology). Both native and in-migrant Republicans overwhelmingly tend to classify themselves as some type of conservative with natives only slightly more likely than in-migrants to call themselves very conservative (see table 4.7). Democrats, on the other hand, are more heterogeneous ideologically than the Republicans. However, unlike in the Republican Party, there are some ideological differences between the natives and the in-migrants. Most clearly, in-migrants tend to be more liberal than natives when comparing only those who label themselves "very liberal" (31 percent to 18 percent) and when comparing those in the two liberal categories combined (73 percent to 52 percent). Conversely, natives tend to be more moderate (31 percent to 19 percent) and more conservative (17 percent to 8 percent) than the in-migrants.

These same patterns are found in table 4.8, which presents data on these officials' positions on a series of twenty social, economic, and political issues, roughly grouped into three broad categories (social/lifestyle issues, governmental program issues, and spending/tax issues). First, on every issue listed the Democrats are more liberal than the Republicans, and these differences are quite large in a majority of the cases. Still, in spite of this differentiation, Democrats are not uniformly liberal. For example, on two issues—federal welfare spending and preferential hiring of blacks—a majority of Democrats, both natives and in-migrants, are conservative (just less conservative than Republicans), and on an additional three issues—school prayer, the death penalty, and government provision of jobs—a majority of native Democrats are conservative. Second, among Democratic activists, natives tend to be less liberal than in-migrants on eighteen of the twenty issues; on a number of these issues—school prayer, the death penalty, environmental spending—these differences are substantial, and on eight issues the differences equal or exceed ten percentage points. The consistency of the pattern

Table 4.8 Issue Orientations of Local Party Officials in the South, by Childhood Region and Party

Issue	*Democrats* Natives	*Democrats* In-Migrants	*Republicans* Natives	*Republicans* In-Migrants
Social/lifestyle issues				
Gay job discrimination	70	88	20	24
Handgun control	76	87	15	17
School prayer	34	73	7	11
Death penalty	50	67	16	23
Abortion	83	90	28	36
Hiring preferences for blacks	29	36	2	2
Equal role for women	96	97	90	93
Governmental program issues				
Government aid for women	85	90	33	28
Government aid to minorities	81	88	33	30
Guaranteed job and living standard	49	55	8	4
Government regulation of health care	76	85	17	18
School vouchers	89	85	24	22
Spending and tax issues				
Government services/spending	88	94	25	19
Social Security spending increase	67	61	23	20
Public education spending increase	82	85	29	22
Defense spending increase	69	80	19	21
Health care spending increase	82	87	20	19
Environmental spending increase	60	79	12	12
Welfare spending increase	22	32	1	1
Flat tax approval	55	71	18	16

Note: Entries are percentages reported liberal, by column. For the wording of each issue item, see the copy of the questionnaire in the appendix.

more than the size of the differences underscores the ideological variations between native and in-migrant Democrats. Third, with the lone exception of supporting an equal role for women, the traditional conservative homogeneity of the Republicans shows up on these issues. Moreover, unlike the Democrats, there is relatively small variation between the natives and in-migrants (on no issue do the differences reach 10 percent and on sixteen of the twenty issues they are 5 percent or less), and the variations that do exist do not run consistently in one direction (natives are more conservative on nine of the issues, in-migrants are more conservative on eight issues, and the percentages are identical on three issues). To tease as much as possible out of these data, though, it is worth noting that on the seven social/lifestyle issues, in-migrant Republicans are somewhat more likely to take a liberal position on six of them, although the likelihood is modest. On governmental program issues and spending/tax issues, Republican in-migrants are somewhat less likely to be liberal than natives.

Consistent with the 1991 data, the data in the 2001 Southern Grassroots Party Activists Project show that in-migrants tend to pull the ideological center of gravity of the Democrats in a more liberal direction while, for Republicans, in-migrants tend to reinforce the already strongly conservative orientations of native Republicans. This also suggests that there is greater potential for intraparty divisions to develop along ideological lines between natives and in-migrants within the Democratic Party than within the Republican Party. Somewhat paradoxically, however, the broader potential for intraparty ideological divisions among Democrats is probably lessened somewhat by the presence of in-migrants who serve to pull the party more fully toward the liberal end of the scale, thus contributing to greater homogeneity than would otherwise exist.

CONCLUSIONS

Population movement into the South following World War II affected the region's party system in a number of ways. Its major early impact was to boost the initial growth of the Republican Party as Republicans moving into the South brought their voting habits and organizational skills with them. Vestiges of this early pattern remain in the early twenty-first century in that in-migrants still generally constitute larger percentages of local party officials in the Republican Party in the South than in the Democratic Party (though the gap has narrowed in recent years).

Research on party activists at different organizational levels in the 1980s and the 1990s revealed that a second key effect of in-migration was to diversify the ranks of party officials in both parties, and especially in the Democratic Party. Our data show that this is still the case in the contemporary southern party system. Local party officials native to the South are different from those who have moved into the region from other parts of the country on a number of background variables, particularly on those related to religion. Even in the Republican Party, with its greater homogeneity, in-migrants differ on these religious variables rather consistently and thus serve to diversify the party. In the 1980s and early 1990s in-migrants and native party activists also tended to differ rather sharply in terms of their political backgrounds (see, e.g., Steed, Moreland, and Baker 1981), but in this regard diversification has lessened by the turn of the century.

A third major area of impact for in-migration historically concerned its role in helping to differentiate the parties in terms of their ideological and issue positions. The past pattern has been for in-migrants to pull the

Democratic Party toward the liberal end of the ideological scale both on subjective self-identification of personal ideology and on more specific positions on a range of policy issues; at the same time on these points, in-migrants differed little from natives in the Republican Party and, thus, they served more to reinforce the long-standing conservativism of the party's activists. Our data show these patterns to be applicable still in both parties in 2001. Clearly, in-migration has worked to further the process of party sorting that has taken place in the South over the past two decades and that has pretty much resulted in the region's party system coming to mirror the national party system.

This process in the Democratic Party represents the most dramatic picture. The party that was once the standard bearer of southern traditionalism as it related to such matters as race relations, economic conservatism, states' rights, defense of the status quo, and individualism has undergone a significant transformation that has brought it ever closer to the national party. A number of factors have had an impact—older, more conservative Democratic Party leaders have left the political arena through death or retirement, or they have switched parties in an effort to resolve the dissonance resulting from the party's liberal makeover, and blacks have become more heavily involved in party organizational work, to mention two of the more important factors. Our data, coupled with earlier research demonstrating the same pattern, demonstrate that in-migration should be given a great deal of credits as well. The Southern Republican Party has become the party more closely aligned with the values and symbols of the traditional, conservative South, and, in this, in-migrants have served as reinforcing agents. Indeed, there is some irony in the conclusion that over the long term the Southern Democratic Party has been changed qualitatively more by in-migration than the Southern Republic Party.

One final observation in this vein is relevant to the discussion. Much of the earlier research on the effects of in-migration generally concluded that the impact of population movement on the South's parties was limited by the relatively small numbers of party activists who were nonnative. Feigert and Todd (1998, 143) noted in their analysis of the 1991 data that this no longer held true inasmuch as in-migrants were present in sufficient numbers to make substantial contributions to the alteration of southern politics in recent years. The 2001 SGPA data confirm this observation and point to in-migration as a key factor in understanding the contemporary southern parties.

CHAPTER

5

A Growing Divide

Issue Opinions of Southern Party Activists

Patrick R. Cotter and Samuel H. Fisher III

Politics often involves conflict. Thus, important for understanding southern politics is knowledge of the region's political conflict. Similarly, understanding how southern politics have changed requires knowing how the nature of the South's political conflict has shifted. Among the most frequent forms of political conflict are disputes over public policies. In this chapter, we use the results of the Southern Grassroots Party Activists surveys to examine three aspects of policy-based conflict in the South—interparty policy conflict, intraparty policy conflict, and change in policy conflict over time.

First, we compare the policy opinions of the region's Democratic and Republican Party activists. The results of this examination will show which policy areas most or least divide the region's parties from one another. Second, political conflict does not, of course, only occur between parties. It can also take place within a party. Thus, this chapter also examines the level of policy agreement within each group of party activists across a number of specific issues. This examination of intraparty divisions shows which policy areas are potential "wedge" issues that a party may use to generate dissension and splits within its opposition. Finally, we compare the results of the issue-related items contained in both the 1991 and 2001 SGPA studies. The results of this examination show how the size and character of the region's political conflict have changed.

By most accounts, the policy preference of political activists would have provided little insight into the region's politics during the days of the Solid South. Then, according to V. O. Key (1949, 37, 142, 186), political conflict within the region centered around splits along "irrelevant" lines, on matters upon which everyone already "agrees ought to be done," or on an "appeal to support the home-town boy." While variations existed among southern states, issue-based debates and divisions generally played an exceptionally small role in the region's partisan politics. "Issues?" Key (1949, 94) quotes a Florida county judge as declaring, "Why, son, they don't have a damn thing to do with it."

However, as discussed in chapter 1, during the last half century the Solid Democratic South has disappeared and a new, more competitive, politics has developed within the region. Investigations of the region's political transformation, as well as discussion of partisan change generally, suggest that policy questions played an important role in the demise of the South's one-party political system.[1] Studies examining the issue-related measures contained in the 1991 SGPA survey also show the importance of policy questions in the recent politics of the region (Brodsky and Cotter 1998; McGlennon 1998b). Thus, unlike previously, an examination of partisan issue differences is likely to shed considerable light on the nature of contemporary political conflict in the South.

Further, it is appropriate to investigate the character of the region's political conflict by examining the issue opinions of party activists. These individuals, through their work in political campaigns, attendance at party conventions and caucuses, and performance of the organization's mundane but necessary administrative tasks, have an important influence on the issue stances taken by the parties. These issue positions, in turn, affect who wins the parties' nominations for office, the focus and substance of election campaigns, the types of voters the parties attract, and the actions of officeholders in government.[2] Recent research exploring the influence of "elites" on citizens' policy preferences suggests that the policy views of party activists may also have an important impact on public opinion and, thus, the nature of political conflict generally (see, for example, Zaller 1992).

DATA

The 2001 SGPA survey contains several measures of the policy or issue views of the region's party activists. First, respondents' general policy views were measured by an item asking the activists to describe their "political beliefs" as (1) very liberal, (2) somewhat liberal, (3) middle of the road/moderate, (4) somewhat conservative, or (5) very conservative. Second, the questionnaire contains a set of items in which respondents were asked their opinions about fourteen different domestic issues. In order to make the results of the analysis of the different types of policy measures more comparable, the issue items were recoded so that the most conservative response was given a score of 5, while the most liberal response received a score of 1. Finally, the 2001 study includes seven items asking respondents if "federal spending should be increased, decreased, or kept the same" in seven policy areas. Again for purposes of comparability, responses to these spending items were recoded so that scores ranged from 1 (decrease spending) to 5 (increase spending).[3]

We begin the analysis by considering regionwide patterns. However, because the sampling methods employed in the SGPA surveys vary across state and party (and year), care and caution are required in aggregating the individual state results into findings for the region as a whole. The analysis conducted here addresses this issue by first calculating unweighted individual state scores. Then, using the states as the unit of analysis, overall regional measures are calculated by averaging the state scores. The measure used to investigate the policy views of Democratic and Republican Party activists is the state mean scores for each available issue item. The analysis of intraparty differences employs the average state standard deviation scores for the different policy items included in the SGPA survey. The larger a standard deviation, the greater the level of division within the party.

RESULTS

Self-described Ideology

Figure 5.1 shows that there is a wide division, and relatively little overlap, in the self-described political ideology of southern Democratic and Republican Party activists. In 2001, most Democrats described their political beliefs as "very liberal" (18 percent) or "somewhat liberal" (35 percent). However,

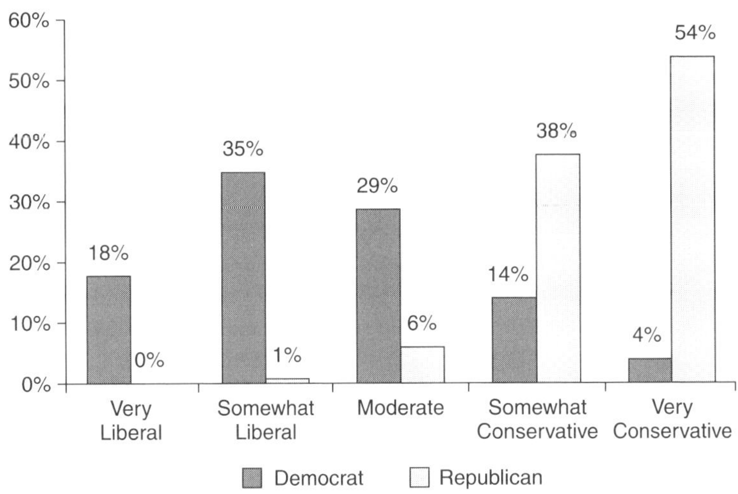

Figure 5.1 Party Activist Ideology—2001.

a substantial number—about one in five—of the Democratic activists identified themselves as either somewhat (14 percent) or very (4 percent) conservative.

In contrast, Republican Party activists in 2001 overwhelmingly and thoroughly described themselves as conservatives. Indeed, a majority (54 percent) of southern Republican activists said that they are very conservative. An additional 38 percent described themselves as somewhat conservative. An extremely small proportion of Republican activists identified themselves as moderates (6 percent) or liberals (1 percent).

The results presented in table 5.1 also show that important changes have occurred in the self-described ideology of Democratic and Republican activists. In his analysis of the 1991 study, McGlennon (1998b, 87) reported that Democratic activists were found "completely across the ideological spectrum but tend to cluster in the middle, from 'somewhat liberal' to 'moderate' to 'somewhat conservative.' " The 2001 study, however, shows that Democratic activists have generally become more liberal. In particular, the number of self-described liberals among Democrats increased from about 36 percent in 1991 to about 53 percent in 2001. While Democratic activists have shifted in the liberal direction, the standard deviation scores show that they remain about as ideologically heterogeneous as they were previously.

Table 5.1 Self-described Political Ideology among Party Activists, 2001 and 1991

	Democrats	*Republicans*
2001		
Very liberal	18	0
Somewhat liberal	35	1
Middle of road/moderate	29	6
Somewhat conservative	14	38
Very conservative	4	54
State mean score	2.51	4.45
Mean standard deviation	1.04	0.66
1991		
Very liberal	10	0
Somewhat liberal	26	2
Middle of road/moderate	35	13
Somewhat conservative	22	48
Very conservative	6	37
State mean score	2.86	4.19
Mean standard deviation	1.04	0.75

Note: Entries are percentages, unless otherwise indicated.

At the same time Republican activists have become more conservative. However, this change is not the consequence of a decrease in the number of moderates or liberals within the party. In both 1991 and 2001 almost no Republican activists identified themselves as anything other than conservatives. What has changed is the distribution among conservatives. McGlennon (1998b, 87) found in the 1991 survey that there was a relatively even balance among Republican activists between those who said that they were "somewhat" conservative and those describing themselves as "very" conservative. Now, however, a majority of Republican activists say that they are "very" conservative. As a result of this change, Republican activists, while already more ideologically homogeneous than Democrats, have become even more so in 2001, as indicated by the standard deviation measure.

Issue Opinions

Democratic and Republican Party activists are expected to differ when it comes to political issues, and the results presented here support that belief. In particular, on each of the issues examined in the 2001 SGPA survey, Democrats are, on average, more liberal (or less conservative) than their Republican counterparts (table 5.2). Specifically, the typical Democrat is more likely than the typical Republican activist to favor public provision of social services, including health care and employment; women having an equal role with men in society; women's right to an abortion; stricter gun control laws; the government working to improve the social and economic

Table 5.2 Average State Mean Scores on Issues by Party, 2001

Issue	*Democrats*	*Republicans*	*Difference*
School vouchers	1.70	3.78	2.08
Handgun control	2.08	4.17	1.99
Government services/spending	1.90	3.85	1.95
Abortion	1.97	3.78	1.81
Health care regulation	2.26	4.03	1.77
Gay job protections	2.49	4.02	1.53
Government aid for women	1.96	3.47	1.51
Government aid for minorities	2.06	3.50	1.44
Government job guarantee	3.03	4.42	1.39
Flat tax system	2.82	4.00	1.18
Death penalty	2.98	4.01	1.03
Hiring preferences for blacks	3.62	4.61	0.99
School prayer	3.48	4.41	0.93
Equal role for women	1.52	1.82	0.30

Note: Entries are mean scores on a five-point scale, where 1 represents the most liberal position. For the wording of each issue item, see the copy of the questionnaire in the appendix.

positions of women, blacks, and other minorities; laws protecting gays from job discrimination; and giving preferences to blacks in hiring and promotion decisions. Similarly, Democratic activists are more opposed than the typical Republican Party activists to school prayer, the death penalty, a flat tax, and school vouchers.

Further, the conservatism of the Republican activists extends beyond their being relatively more conservative than Democrats. Republican activists are also "absolutely" conservative in their opinions. Specifically, a conservative position (as indicated by a mean score greater than the scale's midpoint of 3.0) is taken by Republican activists on all but one of the policy issues examined. This single exception involves the issue of whether "women should have an equal role with men in running business, industry, and government." The issues that generate the highest level of conservatism among Republican activists involve preferential hiring and promotions for blacks, government responsibility to provide jobs and a good standard of living, and allowing prayer in public schools.

While consistently less conservative than their Republican counterparts, southern Democratic grassroots party activists are, on average, not uniformly liberal in their policy beliefs. On some issues, such as equality for women in society, school vouchers, the provision of social services, government efforts to "improve the social and economic situation for women," and abortion, Democratic activists are generally liberal (i.e., have an average mean score of less than 3.0). However, on issues such as preferences for blacks in hiring and promotion decisions, school prayer, and a government of a good standard of living, Democratic activists express a more even mix of liberal and conservative views.

Table 5.2 also shows that several traditional "New Deal" social-welfare-type policy questions generate the largest difference in average issue opinions between Democratic and Republican activists. This reflects differences in partisan attitudes toward Depression era programs at that time, ranging from bank and stock market regulations to government work projects to provide employment. At the time, Democrats pushed for greater assistance by the federal government, while Republicans opposed such an expanded role and pushed for greater reliance on the free market. This divide still exists. Specifically, large gaps in opinions are found between the two groups of activists regarding issues such as school vouchers and the provision of social services and health care.

In recent decades new social issues involving lifestyle concerns such as gay rights, abortion, school prayer, and gun control have become the province of political disputes. There is, however, no consistent pattern regarding differences between the party activists on these issues. For two of the cultural issues—gun control and abortion—there are large differences in preferences between Democratic and Republican activists. Yet partisan differences are relatively small on issues such as whether women should have an equal role with men in society;

school prayer; and, somewhat surprisingly, given the region's political history, preferences for blacks in employment decisions (see chapter 3 for a more detailed discussion of the role of race). In the instance of equality of women and men, both groups fall on the liberal end of the scale; however, the issues of school prayer and employment preferences for blacks elicit more conservative responses from both Democrats and Republicans.

In terms of intraparty divisions, the results show that Democrats are most in agreement on the issues of women having an equal role with men in society, the provision of government services, school vouchers, and government working to improve the social and economic situation for women (table 5.3). Conversely, the level of agreement among Democrats is lowest on the flat tax and school prayer issues. Among Republicans, consensus is highest on the issues of black preferences in hiring and promotion decisions, a government guarantee of jobs, and school prayer. Abortion is the issue that most divides Republicans.

The results also show that on some issues Republican activists are more unified than Democrats. Republicans are especially united on the issues of a government guarantee of jobs and a good standard of living, school prayer, and whether preferences should be given to blacks. On each of these three concerns the Republican Party enjoys a considerable advantage in party unity.

Table 5.3 Average State Standard Deviations on Issue Items by Party, 2001

Issue	*Democrats*	*Republicans*	*Difference**
School vouchers	1.01	1.21	−0.20
Handgun control	1.29	1.09	0.20
Government services/spending	1.00	1.13	−0.13
Abortion	1.24	1.38	−0.14
Health care regulation	1.21	1.09	0.12
Gay job protections	1.28	1.15	0.13
Government aid for women	1.01	1.18	−0.17
Government aid for minorities	1.14	1.18	−0.04
Government job guarantee	1.30	0.83	0.47
Flat tax system	1.48	1.12	0.36
Death penalty	1.36	1.05	0.31
Hiring preferences for blacks	1.22	0.59	0.61
School prayer	1.47	0.86	0.61
Equal role for women	0.75	1.13	−0.38

Note: Entries are the mean standard deviations for the issue items. For the wording of each issue item, see the copy of the questionnaire in the appendix.

*Negative score indicates Democrats are more unified than Republicans. Positive score indicates Republicans are more unified than Democrats.

On other issues, however, Democrats enjoy the greater level of internal consensus. Specifically, Democrats are more unified (sometimes slightly) on four issues generally involving the role and size of government: school vouchers, provision of social services, assistance to women, and assistance to blacks. Democrats are also more internally united than Republicans on the issues of abortion and women having an equal role in society.

Eight of the specific issue items were asked in both the 1991 and 2001 SGPA surveys. Comparisons of the two surveys show overall that the two parties generally retained their relative issue positions, but the interparty gaps have grown while intraparty divisions have declined. Specifically, the opinions of Democratic activists have generally become more liberal (table 5.4). In particular, the level of support among Democrats has increased for government services, government efforts to improve the social and economic position of minorities, preferences for blacks in employment decisions, and women having an equal role with men in society. Similarly, Democrats have become more opposed to (though they still generally favor) school prayer. The typical Democrat, however, has not shifted position regarding the issues of a government guarantee of jobs or government efforts to improve the social and economic conditions of women.

Conversely, Republican activists have generally become more conservative in their issue positions. The one exception to this pattern of increased conservatism involves the issue of women having an equal role with men in society, where Republicans have shifted to a more liberal position in 2001 compared to 1991. Further examination of the standard deviations shows that the level of internal unity among Democrats has increased on some (government services, government assistance to blacks and other minorities, and abortion) but not all the issues examined. However, among Republican activists the level of internal consensus increased (though marginally on the government assistance to blacks and other minorities question) on each issue.

Overall, then, the results from the two surveys show that during the last decade Democratic activists have generally become more liberal while their Republican counterparts have become more strongly, and uniformly, conservative. The net result of these changes is that the two parties have become more polarized in terms of the policy preferences of their activists.[4] In particular, on each of the issues examined, the differences between the two groups of party activists are larger in 2001 than they were in 1991. It might be expected that differences should be sharpest on economic issues and less on social issues, but there is no clear differentiation. While the economic issue divisions arising out of the New Deal continue to be a factor, newer social issues also provide a line of division. However, there is no consistent pattern. On some issues, such as equal role for women, the gap between the parties increased by only a small amount. On other issues, such as abortion and government services, the polarization between the parties increased by a substantial amount.

Table 5.4 Means and Standard Deviations on Issue Positions among Party Activists by Party, 1991 and 2001

	1991 Dem.	*2001 Dem.*	*1991 Rep.*	*2001 Rep.*	*1991 Diff. D-R**	*2001 Diff. D-R*
Means						
Government services/ spending	2.34	1.90	3.73	3.85	−1.39	−1.95
Abortion	2.24	1.97	3.28	3.78	−1.04	−1.81
Government aid for women	1.93	1.93	2.96	3.47	−1.03	−1.51
Government aid to minorities	2.46	2.06	3.52	3.50	−1.06	−1.44
Guaranteed job/ living standard	3.01	3.03	4.07	4.42	−1.06	−1.39
Hiring preferences for blacks	3.77	3.62	4.53	4.61	−0.76	−0.99
School prayer	3.72	3.48	4.29	4.41	−0.57	−0.93
Equal role for women	1.88	1.52	2.17	1.82	−0.29	−0.30
Standard deviations						
Government services/ spending	1.27	1.00	1.21	1.13	0.06	−0.13
Abortion	1.37	1.24	1.61	1.38	−0.24	−0.14
Government aid for women	0.98	1.01	1.26	1.18	−0.28	−0.17
Government aid to minorities	1.26	1.14	1.19	1.18	0.07	−0.04
Guaranteed job/ living standard	1.31	1.30	0.99	0.83	0.32	0.47
Hiring preferences for blacks	1.19	1.22	0.73	0.59	0.46	0.62
School prayer	1.41	1.47	1.00	0.86	0.41	0.61
Equal role for women	0.92	0.75	1.07	1.13	−0.15	−0.38

Note: Entries are mean scores or standard deviations, as indicated. For the wording of each issue item, see the copy of the questionnaire in the appendix.

*Negative score indicates Democrats are more unified than Republicans. Positive score indicates Republicans are more unified than Democrats.

Spending Preferences

Partisan differences are also found when Democratic and Republican activists are asked about federal spending (table 5.5). Democratic Party activists are more likely than Republicans to favor increased federal spending on health care, public school, social security, environmental protection, crime, and

Table 5.5 Average State Mean Scores and Standard Deviations on Spending Issues by Party

	Democrats	*Republicans*	*Difference**
Means			
Health care	4.60	2.89	1.71
Public schools	4.57	2.91	1.66
Environment	4.10	2.58	1.52
Welfare programs	2.91	1.49	1.42
Social security	4.30	3.15	1.15
Crime	3.95	3.59	0.36
National defense	3.37	4.63	−1.26
Standard deviations			
Health care	0.83	1.33	−0.50
Public schools	0.90	1.48	−0.58
Environment	1.11	1.23	−0.12
Welfare programs	1.36	0.89	0.47
Social security	0.99	1.20	−0.21
Crime	1.14	1.25	−0.11
National defense	1.28	0.84	0.44

Note: Entries are mean scores on the spending items, which run from 1 to 5 (1 = more spending, 3 = same spending, and 5 = less spending). For the wording of each issue item, see the copy of the questionnaire in the appendix.

*Negative score indicates Democrats are more unified than Republicans. Positive score indicates Republicans are more unified than Democrats.

welfare. Republicans are more in favor of increased spending for national defense than are Democrats.

Among Democrats, the highest level of support for increased spending is found in the areas of health care and education. Neither group of activists supports increased spending for welfare programs. Besides lowering federal financial support for welfare, Republican activists are most likely to favor lower federal spending for environment protection and health care. Further, the largest partisan gaps in spending preferences are found in the areas of health care, education, and protecting the environment. In these policy arenas, most Democrats favor higher spending while most Republican activists lean toward reduced spending. The smallest partisan difference in spending preferences was found when respondents were asked about the crime issue. Here, both Democratic and Republican activists express mixed feelings about whether federal spending should be increased or decreased.

The standard deviations show that, when asked about federal government spending, Democrats are generally more unified in their opinions than are Republicans. This is particularly the case with regard to spending in traditional "New Deal" policy areas such as education, health care, and social security. The level of consensus among Republican activists is higher than is the case among Democrats regarding federal spending for national defense and welfare programs.

STATE-LEVEL CONFLICT

Many of the most important elections within the South—for president, U.S. senators, and governor—occur at the state rather than the regional level. Further, while similarities among southern states are to be expected, there is no reason to assume that each state's party system is a carbon copy of the others. Thus, understanding political conflict within the region requires, in addition to a regionwide analysis, separate investigations of the policy views of party activists within each of the eleven former Confederate states. Conducting a detailed state-based analysis is, unfortunately, beyond the scope of both this chapter and volume as a whole. Still, a limited analysis of the self-described political ideologies of each southern state's party activists provides some information about this important topic (see Clark and Prysby 2003 for more extended discussions of individual states).

The results shown in table 5.6 show that between 1991 and 2001 Democratic activists in each southern state became more liberal. In seven of the states (Alabama, Florida, Mississippi, North Carolina, South Carolina, Texas, and Virginia) a majority of the 2001 Democratic activists label themselves as very or somewhat liberal (results not shown). In three of the remaining states (Arkansas, Louisiana, and Tennessee), liberals constitute more than 40 percent of the Democratic activists. Only in Georgia are less than 40 percent of Democratic activists self-described liberals.[5] Conversely, the number of conservatives among Democratic activists declined between 1991 and 2001 in each state examined. Finally, the results show that in 2001 the most "liberal" Democratic Party organizations in the South are found in Virginia and Florida, while the least liberal party organizations exist in Mississippi, Louisiana, Arkansas, and Georgia.

Within each of the region's states, Republican activists have moved in the opposite ideological direction. In every southern state except Florida, a majority of the 2001 Republican activists say that they are "very" conservative. In three of the states—Arkansas (67 percent), Georgia (63 percent) and South Carolina (60 percent)—at least six in ten Republican activists describe themselves this way. Even in Florida, the number of self-described conservatives among Republican activists increased between 1991 and 2001.

The net result of these changes is that in each southern state, the two parties have become more polarized in terms of the self-described ideologies of their activists. The two parties are most polarized in Florida, North Carolina, Texas, South Carolina, and Virginia. The smallest partisan ideological difference among activists is found in Louisiana.

Table 5.6 Mean and Standard Deviation for Self-described Political Ideology among Party Activists by State, 1991 and 2001

	1991 Dem.	*2001 Dem.*	*1991 Rep.*	*2001 Rep.*	*1991 Diff. D-R*	*2001 Diff. D-R*
Means						
Alabama	3.07	2.55	4.21	4.44	−1.14	−1.89
Arkansas	3.04	2.74	4.21	4.64	−1.17	−1.90
Florida	2.58	2.18	4.08	4.18	−1.50	−2.00
Georgia	2.98	2.80	4.22	4.56	−1.24	−1.76
Louisiana	3.03	2.74	4.27	4.38	−1.24	−1.64
Mississippi	2.91	2.69	4.19	4.45	−1.28	−1.76
North Carolina	2.75	2.41	4.25	4.44	−1.50	−2.03
South Carolina	2.84	2.41	4.30	4.54	−1.46	−2.13
Tennessee	2.94	2.54	4.14	4.43	−1.20	−1.89
Texas	2.79	2.38	4.23	4.42	−1.44	−2.04
Virginia	2.57	2.13	4.01	4.52	−1.44	−2.39
Standard deviations						
Alabama	1.10	1.09	0.76	0.70	0.34	0.39
Arkansas	1.06	1.08	0.78	0.55	0.28	0.53
Florida	1.04	0.97	0.79	0.69	0.25	0.28
Georgia	1.06	0.97	0.73	0.63	0.33	0.34
Louisiana	1.04	1.09	0.72	0.72	0.32	0.37
Mississippi	1.11	1.16	0.77	0.70	0.34	0.46
North Carolina	0.98	0.99	0.77	0.70	0.22	0.29
South Carolina	1.04	1.13	0.70	0.60	0.34	0.53
Tennessee	0.98	0.96	0.73	0.65	0.25	0.31
Texas	1.07	1.05	0.76	0.72	0.31	0.33
Virginia	0.93	1.00	0.77	0.63	0.16	0.37

Note: Entries are mean scores or standard deviations, as indicated. For the wording of each issue item, see the copy of the questionnaire in the appendix.

The reason states vary in the ideological polarization of party activists is not altogether clear. It could be that repeatedly experiencing highly competitive, and sometimes acrimonious, political campaigns results in the increasing polarization of Democratic and Republican activists. Alternatively, states may vary in the degree to which activists have completed the process of sorting themselves ideologically into the "proper" party.

CONCLUSIONS

The location and magnitude of the policy differences existing between and among Democratic and Republican Party activists are important aspects of the political conflict occurring in the South. Overall, the results of the SGPA surveys show that there are many areas of partisan policy differences, and these gaps between Democrats and Republicans are often wide. Specifically, the results show that the two sets of activists are quite different in their self-described ideology. Democratic activists generally identify themselves as somewhat or very liberal, while a majority of southern Republican activists label themselves as very conservative. The results further show that, in terms of self-described ideology, the two parties have become more polarized.

The results of the SGPA surveys also show that Democratic and Republican activists hold distinct opinions on a variety of important political issues. Specifically, southern Democratic activists are consistently more liberal in their views than are their Republican counterparts. Additionally, Democratic and Republican activists often hold widely different opinions concerning government spending—especially in traditional "New Deal" policy areas such as health care, education, and social security. Moreover, neither party has a consistent advantage in intraparty unity. There are suggestions, however, that both groups, especially Republicans, are becoming more internally unified. Further, comparing the results of the 1991 and 2001 SGPA studies shows that, overall, southern Democratic and Republican Party activists have become increasingly distinct in their issue positions. Southern Democrats have become more liberal while southern Republicans have become more conservative. Finally, the analysis shows that this pattern of increased policy polarization has occurred within each of the southern states. Variations, however, are found across states in the degree to which the parties have grown apart. The reasons for these state level differences remain an important question for future examination.

Altogether, the ideological and issue divisions currently existing between southern Democratic and Republican activists suggest that future election campaigns within the region will typically involve candidates offering voters starkly different ideas and choices regarding a variety of social, economic, and political policy concerns. As a result, the voters attracted to a party are also likely to hold distinctive policy views. Further, Democratic and Republican Party members are likely to follow distinctly separate issue agendas when elected to public office. Greater polarization may also lead to much more bitter struggles over the direction of government policy. Finally, the substantial—and growing—policy and ideological differences found between the two groups of southern party activists confirm the belief that a lack of issues no longer characterizes the region's politics. Rather, issues now have quite a bit "to do with it."

NOTES

1. For discussions of partisan changes in the South, see for example, Aistrup 1996; Beck 1977; Black and Black 1987, 1992; Campbell 1977a, 1977b; Glaser 1996; and Lamis 1988. For research examining the general topic of party system change, see, for example, Carmines and Stimson 1989; Key 1967; MacDonald and Rabinowitz

1987; Marchant-Shapiro and Patterson 1995; Miller and Schofield 2003; and Schattschneider 1960.

2. For earlier studies of activists' policy opinions see McClosky, Hoffman, and O'Hara 1960; Nie, Verba, and Petrocik 1976; Montjoy, Shaffer, and Weber 1980; Jackson, Brown, and Bositis 1982; Kirkpatrick 1976; Miller and Jennings 1986; Moreland 1990a; Brodsky and Cotter 1998.

3. See the discussion in chapter 8 concerning why the spending items are not easily placed on a liberal-conservative continuum.

4. These results demonstrate that the region's parties have participated in the national trend toward increasingly polarized parties. For recent studies showing this increased polarization, see Abramowitz and Saunders 1998; Hetherington 2001; and Layman and Carsey 2002.

5. See the methodological appendix to this volume for a discussion of the Georgia sample.

CHAPTER

6

Partisan Attachments of Southern Party Activists

Jonathan Knuckey

The American South has long made for a fascinating case study for the examinations of the causes and consequences of changes in the underlying distribution of partisan attachments. Once a region where the overwhelming majority held Democratic Party identifications (Key 1949), the South at the beginning of the twenty-first century is now divided between Democratic and Republican identifiers. Indeed, when the focus shifts just to southern whites, a majority now hold Republican Party identifications (Black and Black 2002). This partisan transformation occurred gradually, resembling what Key (1959) referred to as a secular realignment.

One major explanation for the slow pace of changes in partisan identifications emphasizes the notion of split- or dual-party identification—that is, holding identification with different parties at the state and national level. The notion of different partisan identifications at multiple levels was introduced by Jennings and Niemi (1966) and applied to the South by Converse (1966), although the latter found little evidence to suggest that southern whites held split-party identifications. However, as scholars began to question the dimensionality of the traditional measure of partisanship (Petrocik 1987; Katz 1979; Valentine and Van Wingen 1980; Weisberg 1980) and as the notion of multiple levels of partisanship appeared applicable in other federal political systems, most notably Canada (LeDuc, Clarke, Jenson, and Pammett 1984), there was renewed interest, both in the South and at the national level, in the concept of dual or multiple partisanship (Hadley 1985; Niemi, Wright, and Powell 1987; Wekkin 1991; Barth 1992). The concept appeared especially appropriate to the study of southern partisanship, given the high incidence of split-ticket voting in the region (Hadley and Howell 1980). Applying the notion of split partisanship to party activists in the South, Clark and Lockerbie (1998) found that identification with different parties at different levels (or differing strength of partisanship at different levels) was most evident among Democratic activists, who increasingly eschewed national Democratic identification due to the perceived liberal drift of the party, but who continued to find the party acceptable at the state and local levels. However, among Republicans there was also evidence to suggest greater attachments to the national party than to the state party. This may reflect the weak Republican Party organization at the grassroots level as well as the emphasis placed by southern Republicans on a "top-down" strategy (Aistrup 1996).

A focus on party attachments utilizing data from the 2001 SGPA is important for two reasons. First, the 1990s produced a culmination of the realignment among southern whites that had been developing for decades (Black and Black 2002; Lamis 1999). A Republican advantage at the presidential level along with continuing Democratic success at the state and local level had characterized party competition in the post–Voting Rights South (Black and Black 1987, 1992; Petrocik 1987; Swansbrough and Brodsky 1988; Stanley 1988; Lamis 1990; Glaser 1996). However, in the 1990s, southern whites increasingly brought their subpresidential voting behavior and party identifications into line with their presidential vote choice (Black and Black 2002). Indeed, the South is now witnessing some of its most partisan voting patterns in elections below the presidency (Knuckey 2000; Prysby 2000; Shaffer, Pierce, and Kohnke 2000; Bullock, Gaddie, and Hoffman 2002). Second, a focus on the party attachments of activists is important as it is likely to provide some insights into future party competition in the region. Carmines and Stimson (1989) argue that realignment is first evident at the elite level before moving downward to the mass level. At the same time, party activists provide a cadre of potential candidates for elected office. Thus, an examination of party attachments of activists ought to provide a reflection of the partisan upheavals of the 1990s, as well as providing some indicators about the potential for further realignment, the nature of party competition, and the coalitional bases of party support in the region.

MEASURING STRENGTH OF PARTY ATTACHMENTS

Scholars have examined party attachments in different ways. One approach has been to focus on split or dual partisanship by examining the partisan identifications at the national and state levels (Hadley 1985; Clark and Lockerbie 1998). On the other hand, Steed and Bowman (1998) refined this concept to focus on the *strength of party attachment* based on responses to both the national and state party identification as well as items measuring affective feelings toward the national and state parties. As the overwhelming majority of party activists held consistent party identifications based on the first measure (85 percent of Democrats and 90 percent of Republicans),[1] the more inclusive measure of strength of party attachment is used here.

Following Steed and Bowman (1998), activists in each party were placed into three groups based on their strength of party attachments: consistently strong, mixed, and consistently weak. The consistently strong are those who held strong identifications with both their national and state parties,[2] *and* said they felt very close to both national and state parties. Very close was defined as positions "1" and "2" on a seven-point scale (1 being "extremely close" and 7 "extremely distant"). The consistently weak are those who did not hold strong identifications with both their national and state parties *and* did not feel very close to both their national and state parties (positions 3 through 7 on the seven-point scale). The mixed category includes any other combinations of responses on the four partisan variables, that is, one, two, or three inconsistent responses to these items.

The distributions of these categories for each set of party activists are presented in table 6.1, which also disaggregates by party position (county committee chair or member). Among both sets of party activists, fewer than 10 percent hold consistently weak party attachments, a reflection of the more partisan environment in southern politics since the 1990s. Compared to the percentages reported by Steed and Bowman (1998, 186) using the original SGPA data, the number of Democratic activists holding weak attachments almost halved (15 percent in 1991), while the number of Republicans with weak attachments also declined, although in 1991 there were already few Republicans with weak attachments (7 percent). As in 1991, a majority of Republican activists held consistently strong attachments. While the proportion of Democrats with strong attachments has increased over the past decade, a plurality hold mixed attachments, as in 1991. Thus, it is the

Table 6.1 Strength of Party Attachment among Local Party Activists

	Democrats			*Republicans*		
	All Activists	*County Chairs*	*Committee Members*	*All Activists*	*County Chairs*	*Committee Members*
Consistently strong	41.9	47.3	40.8	56.3	66.5	53.8
Mixed	49.3	46.4	49.8	39.3	31.8	41.1
Consistently weak	8.8	6.3	9.3	4.4	1.8	5.1
(*N*)	(2,929)	(474)	(2,455)	(3,142)	(626)	(2,516)

Note: Entries are percentages, by column. *N*s are in parentheses.

Republicans who appear to possess the most committed base of activist support. Disaggregating by party position reveals, as one would expect, that chairs in both parties are more likely to possess consistently strong attachments than members, with Republican chairs exhibiting the strongest attachments and Democratic committee members the weakest attachments. These patterns broadly held across each state, although some variation did exist. Among Democrats, Tennessee and Texas had the highest incidence of consistently strong attachments (47 percent in each case), while Louisiana and Mississippi had the lowest incidence of consistently strong attachments (33 percent in each case). There was more variation among Republicans, the consistently strong being most numerous in Arkansas (74 percent) and least numerous in Florida (46 percent).[3]

Having identified variation across each category of strength of party attachment, the chapter pursues three broad questions. First, are personal and political background characteristics of party activists systematically related to strength of party attachment? In addressing this question it is hoped that one might identify the cleavages that contribute to variations in party attachments. Second, to what extent do different degrees of party attachment affect the political behavior and nature and degree of participation by party activists? Third, how does the strength of party attachments affect orientations of activists toward the party organizational norms? The specific focus here is on purist-pragmatic orientations, patterns of communication with the party hierarchy, and the perceptions and sources of internal party factionalism. In addressing each of these questions, consideration will be given to the extent to which differences appear among Democratic and Republican activists by degrees of party attachment.

CORRELATES OF PARTY ATTACHMENT

Personal Characteristics

In examining personal characteristics that correlate with strength of party attachment, the assumption made is that members of groups most closely tied to the party electorally will exhibit somewhat stronger party attachments. Additionally, the analysis will allow one to discern the extent to which social group cleavages are evident, both between and within the parties at the elite level. Table 6.2 shows that there appears to be little variation in levels of party attachments caused by socioeconomic characteristics such as income and education for either set of party activists. At the same time, strength of party attachment seems to vary little based on whether a respondent is a native southerner or an in-migrant. Racial divisions have existed as a potential source of division within the Democratic Party, as discussed in more detail in chapter 3. Although white Democratic activists are slightly

Table 6.2 Selected Personal Background Characteristics of Local Party Activists by Strength of Party Attachment

	Democrats			*Republicans*		
	Strong	*Mixed*	*Weak*	*Strong*	*Mixed*	*Weak*
Race						
White	80	79	85	96	93	90
Black	15	17	10	1	2	6
(*N*)	(1,208)	(1,414)	(254)	(1,738)	(1,211)	(138)
Gender						
Male	53	57	71	66	66	70
Female	47	43	29	34	34	30
(*N*)	(1,266)	(1,443)	(259)	(1,758)	(1,229)	(139)
Education						
High school or less	10	8	7	8	7	5
Some college	24	26	39	28	27	33
College degree	24	26	26	34	38	22
Graduate/ prof. degree	42	39	28	30	28	40
(*N*)	(1,215)	(1,432)	(257)	(1,760)	(1,227)	(138)
Income						
Under $25,000	11	7	8	4	5	4
$25,000 to $49,999	31	27	21	23	23	22
$50,000 to $74,999	25	25	33	27	25	34
$75,000 to $99,999	14	21	19	20	18	18
$100,000 to $150,000	12	14	15	15	19	12
Over $150,000	7	6	3	11	10	10
(*N*)	(1,174)	(1,393)	(248)	(1,668)	(1,147)	(135)
Age						
Under 40	11	14	11	15	18	30
40–49	16	21	23	18	24	21
50–59	28	28	28	24	23	17
60–69	25	22	25	27	22	24
70+	19	15	13	17	14	8
(*N*)	(1,217)	(1,435)	(257)	(1,751)	(1,218)	(139)
Region where grew up						
South	72	73	76	75	65	68
Non-South	28	27	24	25	35	32

Note: Entries are percentages, by column. *N*s are in parentheses.

less prone to possess strong party attachments, racial differences across each category of party attachments appear less salient than a decade ago, again possibly because those whites with the weakest attachments are either no longer active in the party organization or have realigned and become Republicans. Among Republicans, blacks were slightly more likely to hold consistently weak attachments, but black Republican activists are so few in number that the difference in percentages is too small to be meaningful.

The gender gap has been especially visible in the South, primarily as a result of white southern men becoming more Republican in their party identifications at a more rapid rate than white southern women (Miller and Shanks 1996, 143; Norrander 1999; Black and Black 2002, 251–254). It appears that there is something of a gender gap at the elite level, too, with male Democratic activists being more numerous among those with consistently weak party attachments. In contrast, men and women are more evenly divided in the other two categories, especially among those with consistently strong attachments.

Surprisingly, age does not appear to be systematically related to strength of party attachment. According to the sociopsychological model (Campbell et al. 1960; Miller and Shanks 1996), party attachments should increase in intensity over the lifecycle. However, this pattern is only mildly evident among Republican activists, with the consistently weak tending to be younger than the other two categories, although even then only 30 percent of those with consistently weak attachments are under the age of forty.

Table 6.3 presents several items concerning religion and religiosity. The items that appear to affect strength of party attachment among both sets of activists are religiosity and orientations toward the Christian Right. The rise of the "Christian Right" in southern state and local Republican Party organizations has been widely discussed, with many arguing that religiosity has emerged as an important interparty as well as intraparty cleavage (Green et al. 2002; Green, Rozell, and Wilcox 2003; Wilcox 2000; Baker, Steed, and Moreland 1998; Schneider 1998; Smith 1997; Oldfield 1996a). Moreover, this has increasingly been evident at the elite level, as discussed in chapter 2. It should be stressed that *denominational* differences do not appear to be important correlates of party attachment, with similar distributions across each major denomination in each category of party attachment. However, when examining frequency of church attendance, a pattern does appear. Among Democratic activists, the consistently weak tend to be more likely to be frequent church attenders than those in the consistently strong or the mixed categories; indeed, a majority of the weakly attached (55 percent) report attending church frequently, that is, once a week or more often. In contrast, among Republican activists, frequent church attenders tend to be more numerous among the consistently strong than among the mixed category and especially the consistently weak. Indeed, a minority of Republicans with consistently weak attachments (37 percent) are frequent church attenders.

Table 6.3 Religion and Religiosity of Local Party Activists by Strength of Party Attachment

	Democrats			*Republicans*		
	Strong	*Mixed*	*Weak*	*Strong*	*Mixed*	*Weak*
Religion						
Mainline Protestant	33	32	35	44	43	44
Evangelical Protestant	20	19	27	38	32	22
Black Protestant	13	15	9	1	1	6
Catholic	17	15	20	15	17	17
Jewish	6	5	4	1	2	6
(*N*)	(1,200)	(1,410)	(253)	(1,730)	(1,215)	(136)
Church attendance						
Frequently	45	41	55	63	53	37
Occasionally	23	23	19	21	25	32
Seldom/never	32	35	26	16	22	31
(*N*)	(1,218)	(1,432)	(258)	(1,759)	(1,231)	(138)
Born-again Christian?						
Yes	38	38	50	59	49	40
No	62	62	50	41	51	60
(*N*)	(1,205)	(1,419)	(247)	(1,735)	(1,216)	(137)
Closeness to Christian Right						
Very close/close	9	11	25	53	37	15
Neutral	16	20	33	34	35	32
Very far/far	74	69	42	13	27	53
(*N*)	(1,217)	(1,435)	(257)	(1,750)	(1,223)	(137)

Note: Entries are percentages, by columns. *N*s are in parentheses.

A similar pattern appears when considering whether a respondent considered himself or herself to be a "born-again" Christian, as well as when considering general feelings toward the Christian Right. For example, among Democratic activists, only 38 percent of both the consistently strong and mixed categories consider themselves "born-again" Christians, whereas half of those with consistently weak attachments do so. Among Republicans the percentage that consider themselves "born-again" Christians increases with strength of party attachment—59 percent among the consistently strong, 49 percent among the mixed, and just 40 percent among the consistently weak. Thus, consistently weak Democrats were *more likely* to consider themselves "born again" than consistently weak Republicans. In terms of feelings toward the Christian Right among Democrats, the overwhelming majority of the consistently strong and mixed categories placed themselves as being either far or very far from the Christian Right. However, only 42 percent of Democrats with consistently weak attachments did so. Among Republican activists, feelings toward the Christian Right among the consistently strong and consistently weak are almost the mirror image of each other. While a majority of the consistently strong felt close or very close to the Christian Right, only 15 percent of the consistently weak did so. Indeed, a majority of those Republicans with weak attachments felt far or very far from the Christian Right. Again, it is interesting to note that consistently weak Democratic activists felt *closer* to the Christian Right than consistently weak Republican activists. It should also be noted that among Republicans in the mixed category, only 37 percent felt close or very close to the Christian Right, and just over a quarter placed themselves far or very far from the Christian Right. While tensions between social and economic conservatives may have abated somewhat in state and local Republican Party organizations, these findings, nonetheless, continue to illustrate the potential that the Christian Right possesses as a source of internal divisions within the Republican Party.

Ideology and Issue Preferences

Scholars have emphasized a process of "ideological sorting" of the party coalitions in the South at the mass and elite levels (Black and Black 2002; McGlennon 1998b; Steed 1998; Knuckey 2001; Carmines and Stanley 1990). Given the effect of group orientations on political attitudes (see, for example, Singer 1981), a plausible hypothesis is that just as the ideological polarization of the two parties accelerated in the 1990s—a phenomenon evident outside the South as well (Abramowitz and Saunders 1998)—those activists with weaker party attachments are likely to hold ideological and issue preferences that are at odds with the mainstream views of their respective parties. Specifically, weaker party attachments should produce a moderating effect on each party (Bruce and Clark 1998). Table 6.4 presents the ideological orientations and preferences on specific issues for each set of activists by strength of party attachment.

Table 6.4 confirms that ideology is related to strength of party attachments, with 69 percent of Democratic activists considering themselves liberal and an overwhelming 96 percent of Republicans considering themselves conservatives. This underscores the process of ideological realignment in the South at the elite level culminating in the 1990s as discussed in detail in chapter 5. Indeed, only 5 percent of consistently strong Democrats considered themselves conservatives while no consistently strong Republicans considered themselves liberal. This general pattern also held for those in the mixed categories for each party, especially among Republicans, with 89 percent considering themselves conservative, while 58 percent of Democrats considered themselves liberal. It is only among Democrats with consistently weak attachments that one finds a majority considering themselves conservative. The ideological composition of the consistently weak is in marked contrast to the consistently strong and mixed categories, as only 12 percent considered themselves liberal. The ideological distance between Republicans with consistently weak attachments and the other categories is not quite as dramatic, as a plurality (44 percent) still consider them-

Table 6.4 Ideological and Issue Preferences of Local Party Activists by Strength of Party Attachment

	Democrats			*Republicans*		
	Strong	*Mixed*	*Weak*	*Strong*	*Mixed*	*Weak*
Ideology						
Liberal	69	58	12	—	1	24
Moderate	26	28	37	4	10	31
Conservative	5	14	51	96	89	44
(N)	(1,190)	(1,403)	(256)	(1,738)	(1,234)	(139)
Issues						
Gov't services/spending	4	11	37	81	76	36
Equal role for women	2	4	10	8	10	8
Abortion	9	16	42	76	65	33
School prayer	47	55	74	95	91	64
Gov't aid to minorities	8	20	53	69	70	50
Death penalty	40	43	67	85	81	53
Gov't regulation of health care	15	22	43	87	81	60
Gov't aid for women	7	16	42	70	72	52
Handgun control	13	23	56	90	83	54
School vouchers	4	9	37	82	75	46
Hiring preferences for blacks	66	68	93	99	97	90
Flat tax system	33	40	70	84	83	74
Gay job discrimination	17	24	57	83	79	42
Guaranteed job and living standard	46	51	69	94	94	84
(Minimum *N*)	(1,194)	(1,399)	(245)	(1,715)	(1,197)	(135)

Note: Entries are percentages, by column. For the issue items, entries are the percentages giving the conservative response ("agree/strongly agree" or "disagree/strongly disagree") to each issue preference. *N*s are in parentheses. For the wording of each issue item, see the copy of the questionnaire in the appendix.

selves conservatives, while around a quarter consider themselves liberal. Overall, these findings suggest that the relationship between ideology and strength of party attachment, already strong in 1991, has become even stronger, and this is even more evident among Democrats than it is among the already ideologically homogenous Republicans.[4]

Ideological differences between each category of party attachment were also evident in regard to the specific issue preferences presented in table 6.3. Among Democrats, the stronger the party attachment, the less conservative the preference on every issue. Large differences existed between the consistently strong and the consistently weak, with, on average, the consistently strong being thirty-one percentage points less conservative (more liberal) than the consistently weak. The distance on each issue between the consistently strong and the mixed categories was not as great, the consistently strong being, on average, just seven percentage points less conservative than the mixed category. Among Republicans, a similar pattern exists, with the consistently strong being more conservative than the mixed, who were more conservative than the consistently weak. The largest distances were between the consistently strong and the consistently weak, the former being, on average, twenty-six percentage points more conservative across the fourteen issues. The differences between the consistently strong and the mixed category were much more modest, the former being, on average, just four percentage points more conservative than the latter across the fourteen issues; and only on the abortion issues did the difference reach double digits.

Overall, ideology and issue preferences appear to provide the best explanation for variations in strength of party attachment. Those with consistently strong attachments in both parties are also the most ideologically polarized, and this seems to support the notion of the culmination of an ideological sorting at the elite level. While the consistently weak hold dissonant ideological and issue preferences from their respective party mainstreams, the scope for ideological and issue-based divisions seems less than it was a decade ago as a result of the very small number of activists in both parties who hold consistently weak attachments.

CONSEQUENCES OF PARTY ATTACHMENTS

Political Behavior and Activity

Strength of party attachment has long been regarded as an important predictor of a variety of modes of political behavior and participation among individuals (Lazarsfeld, Berelson, and Gaudet 1944; Campbell et al. 1960; Miller and Shanks 1996). Thus, party activists with weak party attachments should exhibit patterns of partisan behavior and activity that are less strong and widespread than those with strong party attachments. While activists should represent the core electoral base of the support in the party, differences in strength of party attachments do produce variation in the voting behavior of activists in both parties. Among Democrats, both the consistently strong and the mixed were almost unanimous in their support of both Bill Clinton in 1996 (99 percent and 94 percent, respectively) and Al Gore in 2000 (98 percent and 93 percent, respectively). However, among the consistently weak, a majority *failed* to support both Clinton in 1996 (48 percent) and Gore in 2000 (45 percent). Indeed, in 2000 a majority (51 percent) of Democratic activists with consistently weak attachments actually voted for George W. Bush. These defections, based on the findings presented here, appear to be attributable to the conservative ideology and issue preferences of the consistently weak. Fortunately, from the perspective of the Democratic Party, these defections are yielding fewer votes for Republican candidates given the decline in the size of activists holding consistently weak party attachments. Among Republican activists, there was also near unanimous support for Bob Dole in 1996 and for Bush in 2000 among both the consistently strong and the mixed categories. Some defections are evident among the consistently weak, 31 percent voting for Clinton in 1996 and 20 percent for Gore in 2000, although overall consistently weak Republicans tended to be more loyal to their party's candidates than consistently weak Democrats were to their candidates.[5]

Strength of party attachment also appears to be related to patterns of political behavior beyond the simple act of voting, specifically with respect to levels of campaign activity. Among Democrats, 66 percent of those with consistently strong attachments reported being "very active" in local elections, and this dropped only slightly to 59 percent in both state and national elections. This pattern is also evident among Republicans, with virtually no variation across level of election—60 percent reporting that they were very active in local and state elections and 62 percent saying that they were very active in national elections. The degree of activity in elections among the mixed and consistently weak categories in both parties shows less commitment to campaign activity. While a majority in the mixed category for both Democrats and Republicans reported that they were very active in local elections (58 percent and 52 percent, respectively), only a minority reported being very active in state elections (42 percent and 41 percent, respectively), as was also the case in national elections (37 percent and 46 percent, respectively). As one might expect, among those with consistently weak attachments, less than half of the activists in both parties reported being very active at *any* level. Election activity among the consistently weak is most evident at the local level, with 46 percent of Democrats and 47 percent of Republicans reporting that they were very active. This drops off dramatically at the state level, with 26 percent of Democrats and 29 percent of Republicans being very active, and especially at the national level for Democrats, with only 18 percent reporting that they were very active, while 28 percent of Republicans did so.

The effects of strength of party attachment are also evident when considering specific activities performed in recent election campaigns. The first part of table 6.5 shows the percentage of activists claiming to have performed each of thirteen campaign activities. Those with consistently strong attachments in both parties report the greatest levels of activities, which generally decline as party attachments weaken. Again though, the largest differences appear between the consistently strong and the consistently weak, with the average difference across the thirteen activities being sixteen percentage points among Democrats and ten percentage points among Republicans. Differences between the consistently strong and the mixed categories were fairly slight, on average about five percentage points among Democrats and four percentage points among Republicans.

Table 6.5 Activities Performed in Recent Campaigns by Local Party Activists by Strength of Party Attachment

	Democrats			*Republicans*		
	Strong	*Mixed*	*Weak*	*Strong*	*Mixed*	*Weak*
Campaign activities[a]						
Org. door-to-door canvassing	40	32	25	36	32	31
Organized events	48	40	22	50	42	30
Arranged fund-raising activities	36	35	16	43	35	30
Sent mailings to voters	55	46	35	55	54	55
Distributed literature	78	71	49	80	72	57
Organized telephoning	39	33	18	40	36	23
Purchased billboard space	4	4	3	5	4	4
Distributed posters or signs	78	73	55	83	74	58
Contributed money	76	71	48	83	76	61
Conducted voter registration drives	39	31	17	30	29	23
Utilized public opinion surveys	11	11	8	12	13	14
Dealt with media	28	22	17	33	27	25
Helped maintain or create Web site	6	6	3	7	7	4
(Minimum *N*)	(1,226)	(1,443)	(259)	(1,770)	(1,234)	(139)
Communication with other party members[b]						
County chair	72	62	39	77	70	56
County committee members	72	64	42	80	72	54
State chair	17	10	5	20	11	3
State committee members	28	20	7	34	21	9
National committee members	11	7	4	14	6	2
(Minimum *N*)	(1,166)	(1,391)	(245)	(1,691)	(1,184)	(134)

[a]Entries are the percentages of those performing each activity in recent campaigns.

[b]Entries are the percentages responding "very often" or "often."

These findings about voting behavior and campaign activity indicate the robust health of southern parties at the grassroots level. Specifically, the problems once faced by southern Democrats in mobilizing their base in national elections seem to have been resolved by the decline in those with consistently weak attachments. Again, while this pattern is still evident among Democrats with weak attachments, it is less consequential given the size of this group. At the same time, when one compares the consistently strong and mixed categories of both sets of party activists, there is little evidence now of large interparty differences. Among the consistently strong, for example, Republicans were only three percentage points more likely than Democrats to be very active in national elections.

Party Norms and Orientations toward the Party Organization

Strength of party attachment should be related to a variety of measures that assess the extent to which party activists are integrated into the party organization at the grassroots level. Differences over party norms are related to some degree to strength of party attachment, although there are some important interparty differences. Mean scores on the purism index, as discussed in chapter 9, show that among both sets of party activists, the weaker the party attachment the higher the purism score. For example, among Democrats the mean scores for the strong, mixed, and weak categories were, respectively, 2.40, 2.55, and 2.87. These scores are on a four-point scale, with 4.0 being the most purist score. Among Republicans, a similar pattern was evident; the mean scores for the strong, mixed, and weak categories were, respectively, 2.63, 2.69, and 2.83. This is interesting, as chapter 9 suggests that purism is correlated with ideological extremism, and, as discussed earlier in this chapter, so too is strength of party attachment. Arguably, those activists with stronger attachments may have nonetheless adopted more pragmatic orientations as a consequence of the competitive elections in the South for all political offices.

The extent to which party activists communicated with other party officials also demonstrates a general level of integration into the party organization at the grassroots level. The second part of table 6.5 shows patterns of communication across each party attachment category. Those activists in both parties with consistently strong attachments were much more integrated into the communication network of their respective party organizations than those with mixed attachments and especially than those with consistently weak attachments. While the overall level of communication declines dramatically the farther one goes up the party hierarchy, this general pattern persists. One other point to note is that Republicans in each category of party attachment tended to report communicating "often" or "very often" more than Democrats. For example, even though consistently weak Republicans reported least communication with the party hierarchy at the county level, a majority still reported communicating very often or often with other county committee members (56 percent) and county chairs (54 percent). In contrast, Democrats with consistently weak attachments were much less likely to report communicating often or very often with county party members and chairs.

Perceptions and Sources of Factionalism

As discussed in chapter 7, internal party factionalism—or at least the perception of factionalism—remains evident in both parties. As strength of party attachment is related to ideological and issue preferences, and the latter contribute most toward perceived factionalism (see chapter 7), it is hypothesized that activists with weaker attachments will be more likely to perceive factionalism in the state and local party organizations. The differences discussed earlier about a religiosity cleavage may also produce perceptions of factionalism, especially among Republican activists.

The first part of table 6.6 shows that among Democrats, those with consistently weak attachments do tend to perceive greater internal party factionalism, with a majority saying that factionalism was either "very high" or "moderately high" in both the state and county party organizations (58 percent and 50 percent, respectively). This pattern also holds among Republicans with consistently weak attachments, with 53 percent and 54 percent, respectively, perceiving very high or moderately high levels of factionalism in the state and local party organizations. Among both sets of activists, perceptions of factionalism decline as party attachments strengthen. Indeed, among Democrats and Republicans in both the mixed and consistently strong categories, less than 10 percent perceived a very high level of factionalism.

The second part of table 6.6 shows the sources of the perceived factionalism in the state party organizations. The general pattern for activists in both parties was for the consistently weak to see each source as contributing "a great deal" or "a fair amount" to party factionalism more than the consistently strong or the mixed categories. Among Democrats, the largest difference in perception of the sources of factionalism does appear to be issue based. For example, the consistently weak were twenty-one percentage points more likely to perceive racial issues as contributing a great deal or a fair amount to state party factionalism than the consistently strong, and nineteen percentage points more likely to perceive differences on abortion and government spending to be the sources of factionalism. Among Republicans, the biggest differences on perceived sources of factionalism between the consistently strong and the consistently weak were differences between new and old residents (twenty-one percentage points), region (twenty-one percentage points), and urban-rural differences (twenty percentage points). However, Republicans in each category of party attachment seemed to be united in acknowledging that the abortion issue was an important source of factionalism. This was the only item, other than general ideological differences, cited by a majority in *each* category of party attachment as contributing either a great deal or a fair amount to state party factionalism. Overall, it is interesting to note that activists with weaker

Table 6.6 Perceived Levels of Party Factionalism and Sources of Factionalism by Local Party Activists by Strength of Party Attachment

	Democrats			*Republicans*		
	Strong	*Mixed*	*Weak*	*Strong*	*Mixed*	*Weak*
State party factionalism						
Very high	4	8	14	4	7	15
Moderately high	36	43	44	29	38	38
Moderately low	52	44	37	54	47	39
Very low	8	4	5	13	8	7
(*N*)	(1,157)	(1,322)	(234)	(1,704)	(1,169)	(130)
County party factionalism						
Very high	8	8	10	5	9	17
Moderately high	26	30	40	17	22	37
Moderately low	41	41	35	43	39	30
Very low	25	21	15	35	30	15
(*N*)	(1,163)	(1,328)	(232)	(1,693)	(1,174)	(131)
Sources of state party factionalism[a]						
Ideological viewpoints	52	60	63	51	54	64
Party leaders	50	56	54	48	52	49
New vs. old residents	44	48	55	30	37	51
Region	60	64	66	44	52	65
Urban-rural	67	69	68	49	58	69
Taxes	49	50	63	28	30	42
Abortion	47	54	66	50	57	69
Racial issues	39	49	60	23	27	34
Government spending	47	52	66	30	31	46
(Minimum *N*)	(1,156)	(1,335)	(230)	(1,710)	(1,178)	(130)

[a]Entries are percentages of those saying that each source contributed "a great deal" or "a fair amount" to state party factionalism.

attachments—especially Republicans—tended to view as important *each* source contributing to state party factionalism. This suggests that it is not just the ideological dissonance of those with weak attachments that produces the perceptions of factionalism. Of course, this raises an important question of cause and effect. Do perceptions of greater levels of party factionalism contribute to weaker party attachments, or do weaker party attachments produce a greater perception of factionalism? Resolving this question is beyond the scope of this chapter, but it does suggest an interesting area for further research.

CONCLUSIONS

Party organizations in the South today consist of a cadre of activists who exhibit increasingly strong attachments to their respective parties. Compared to a decade ago the proportion of those with consistently weak attachments has fallen, and this has been especially evident on the Democratic side. It appears that the "weakest links" on the Democratic side are either no longer active or have realigned to fill the ranks of Republican Party activists. Among Republicans, those with consistently weak attachments, already small in number a decade ago, now account for less than 5 percent of all Republican Party activists. It should be noted, though, that a plurality of Democratic activists and a sizable minority of Republican activists continue to hold inconsistent attachments on at least one of four partisan variables.

In terms of explanations for different levels of party attachment, ideological and issue orientations seem to be most important. Among Democrats, the consistently strong were the most liberal; and among Republicans they were the most conservative. Differences based on religiosity and orientations toward the Christian Right also appear to be important determinants of party attachments. As a "values" or "secular-religiosity" cleavage appears to be coming more important in American politics more generally (White 2002), so it also appears that party elites in the South are polarizing around this cleavage. Those on the "wrong" side of this cleavage, that is, religiously committed Democrats and "secular" Republicans, evidently acknowledge this dissonance by exhibiting weak attachments.

The effect on the parties of activists with different levels of party attachment is not without consequence. Those with stronger party attachments exhibit much greater loyalty to party candidates and, more generally, are more involved and more committed to the party organization. As differences between the two categories of party attachment in which over 90 percent of activists in both parties are placed—the consistently strong and the mixed—were not very large, this suggests that southern party organizations now consist of intensely partisan and intensely committed individuals. This will certainly have ramifications on southern partisan and electoral politics in the years ahead. Candidates for political office will need to respond to the wishes of the base of their party, suggesting that elections in the South increasingly will present contests between a liberal Democrat and a conservative Republican. Such choices will, in turn, further widen the ideological and issue gap between the parties. Overall, the existence of strongly attached, committed, and ideologically distinct activists in both parties suggests that at the elite level there has been a culmination of partisan realignment. Southern party politics in the early twenty-first century can genuinely be characterized as possessing a rational and mature two-party system.

NOTES

1. These percentages are based on those who held either strong national and strong state Democratic (Republican) Party identifications, or weak national and weak state Democratic Party identifications. Only 2 percent of both Democratic and Republican activists held split partisanship.

2. The party identification item differed slightly from that used by the American National Election Studies. Rather than the branching question format used by the NES, respondents were asked to locate themselves on a seven-point scale ranging from strongly Democratic to strongly Republican. The seven-point scale is identical to the NES party identification scale, however.

3. A detailed examination of state-by-state variations in strength of party attachments is beyond the scope of this analysis, but more information on state patterns is in Clark and Prysby (2003).

4. For example, in 1991, 53 percent of Democrats with strong attachments identified as liberals while 40 percent of Democrats in the mixed category did so (Steed and Bowman 1998, 195).

5. Interestingly, the defection rate in 2000 among Democratic activists is *less* than that found in 1988 when 67 percent of those with consistently weak attachments defected and voted for George H. W. Bush rather than Michael Dukakis. Also the Republican defection rate in 2000 was *greater* than that in 1988 when 13 percent voted for Dukakis rather than Bush. These data are taken from the analysis of the 1991 SGPA data by Steed and Bowman (1998).

CHAPTER

7

Factional Transformation in the Two-Party South

It's Getting Harder to Pick a Fight

John J. McGlennon

The study of factionalism and its effects on southern politics has evolved with the development of two-party competition in the region. In an era when the South's politics were distinguished by the absence of Republican organization, voters, and even candidates, factionalism provided a basis for explaining particular patterns of competition for political power and public office.

During the first half of the twentieth century, the eleven states of the Confederacy routinely cast their lot in national politics with the Democrats and maintained a nearly universal attachment to the Democratic Party. "No Southerner," wrote John Crowe Ransom, "ever dreams of heaven, or pictures his Utopia on earth, without providing room for the Democratic Party" (Ransom 1930, 26). With all southerners assembled under the same party label, ambition and cleavage worked their ways in less formal vehicles of competition, party factions.

Often the "Solid South," as it was described by historians and political scientists, was seen as a unified region without electoral division. The nearly unanimous Democratic label on public officials of the region overshadowed any consideration of contests for public office and policy outcomes. Challenging the notion of a monolithic Democratic South was one of the most significant contributions of V. O. Key's *Southern Politics* (1949). Key recognized that this collection of eleven states may have been bound together by their common heritage of secession and Reconstruction, but their individual polities contained vast differences. Key's identification of variations in factional competition in the southern states set the agenda for research on political competition in the region for decades. His classifications of states as having multifactional competition, bifactionalism, or a dominant faction within the dominant party led Key to suggest ongoing patterns in southern voting behavior. These patterns fell along regional or sociodemographic lines in some cases and around support for or opposition to personalities in others. He went on to hypothesize that the type of factionalism would affect the policy orientation of state government, with states exhibiting the characteristics closest to two-party competition also opting for policies geared to assisting the "have nots" of society (Key 1949, 307).

FACTIONALISM AND PARTY SYSTEMS

Key's theories of factionalism were the basis for more research. Some focused on the public policy implications of his research, testing the hypothesis that party competition would lead to policies more attentive to the poor. Others focused more on the electoral mechanics of factionalism and how it would structure the choices for voters in one-party states. Black (1983) and Canon (1978) in separate studies tested the impact on factionalism of factors such as the primary system at use in each state (single versus runoff primary), the presence of an incumbent governor on the primary ballot, and the existence of a durable electoral faction. These studies were useful in testing the ways in which party nominations were contested even as the importance of the Democratic nomination was declining. They did not focus on the role that factionalism might play in the then-emerging two-party South. But as the South shed its one-party legacy and began to experience competition between Republicans and Democrats, factionalism took on a different importance.

Studies of competitive party systems have looked at the impact of factionalism on party organization and electoral success. Geer and Shere (1992) examine the effect of party primary contests on organizational strength and conclude that intraparty competition is important in aiding party responsiveness to voter wishes. Stone, Atkeson, and Rapoport (1992) find that candidate-centered factionalism may not be damaging to a party as even supporters of losing candidates are recruited to party activity, and Stone (1982) further finds that even delegates motivated by ideology put great stock in candidate electability.

Factionalism is often seen as having as much potential for growing support for a party organizationally and electorally as for being a serious source of party division. Studies of both U.S. political parties and parties in other nations show that factionalism can be a benefit for the party (Belloni and Beller 1976; McAllister 1991; Reiter 1981). While conventional wisdom often assumes that contests for party nominations are disruptive to electoral objectives, the contests often reflect a party that is expanding and broadening.

So most studies of factionalism have considered the phenomenon as an alternative to interparty competition in the one-party South or to test its implications for harm or good in two-party systems. Few efforts have attempted to look at the impact of factionalism specifically in the southern states as they have become two-party systems. One exception is an examination of Florida by Echols and Ranney (1976), which analyzed the impact of growing competition in Florida on the state's Democratic factionalism.

FACTIONALISM AND PARTY TRANSITIONS

The emergence of competition in the South over the past half century was accompanied by factionalism within both parties. For the newly enlarging Republican Party, growth carried with it tensions between loyal, longtime activists and newcomers or party switchers. Factional disputes often were identified by dominant personalities but reflected more persistent regional and ideological bases. The cleavages represented by U.S. Senator Jesse Helms and Governor James Holshouser in North Carolina, Governor Linwood Holton and party chairman Richard Obenshain in Virginia, and Senators Bill Brock and Howard Baker in Tennessee all neatly packaged regional and issue orientations in personally identified factions.

The formerly dominant Democratic Party found itself confronting a difficult transition. The winners of intraparty tests were rewarded with public office in the Solid South. The two-party South's Democratic candidates won a nomination that did not guarantee victory and, in fact, had often served to drive the losing faction toward competitive and eagerly awaiting Republicans. John Tower became the first southern Republican elected to statewide office in 1961 because liberal Democrats believed that they were better off supporting a one-term Republican than backing the conservative Democrat who won the party's nomination. Over the course of three decades, Republican successes in most southern states often resulted from ideological cleavages in Democratic primaries, as the party gradually moved toward the profile of northern Democrats.

The decade between 1991 and 2001 brought the culmination of party realignment to the South. Despite the national success of southern Democrats Bill Clinton and Al Gore in both 1992 and 1996, and Gore's popular vote victory in 2000, regional Democrats completed the twentieth century with their worst share of elected offices since the establishment of the post-Reconstruction Solid South.

President Clinton's first two years in office proved especially unpopular among southern white voters, who opposed his policy of toleration for homosexuals in the military and saw his health care proposals as an expansion of "Big Government." In combination with congressional scandals and redistricting, which matched a number of new "majority-minority" congressional districts with an even larger number of newly configured Republican-friendly suburban districts, Republicans won a majority of southern U.S. House seats in 1994. They also regained a majority of the twenty-two Senate seats from the South, and in both cases, their southern margins provided the majorities that gave them unified control of Congress for the first time in forty years.

Despite their losses, Democrats demonstrated a continuing ability to compete. After the 1994 debacle, they managed to elect new Democratic senators and/or governors in all of the states except Tennessee and Texas (and have since won the Tennessee governorship).

Organizationally, both parties generally recognized the need to strengthen their recruitment of candidates and activists, improve their technology, and raise money. There was no doubt that the parties had to adapt to changed circumstances. Factionalism was bound to be part of the new party structure in the South.

CHANGES IN PARTY FACTIONALISM

This chapter examines the evolving nature of factionalism in the southern parties as seen by the precinct activists of those parties. Utilizing the Southern Grassroots Party Activist surveys conducted in 2001, we examine their perceptions of factional divisions and compare these results to the study conducted a decade earlier. We also consider whether the perception of factional division is related to the characteristics of the party membership and whether it appears to influence their views of the party's organizational and campaign effectiveness. The first SGPA Project provided the opportunity to measure the level of factionalism among precinct-level party organization members in the eleven states of the Confederacy (McGlennon 1998a). It also allowed examination of the relationship between perceptions of party factionalism and party organizational strength.

The current project allows for a further examination of the factionalism confronting the parties. As the parties have continued to evolve, we can observe whether they have become more internally consistent or diverse. It should be evident whether party factionalism is currently seen as more or less of a party problem and whether it bears any relationship to perceptions of party effectiveness.

Factional divisions within the parties were inevitable outgrowths of the changes in party competitiveness and party composition. As discussed elsewhere, realignment of the southern electorate increasingly meant that conservative activists would find their homes in the Republican Party and moderates and liberals would be found in the Democratic Party. The preponderance of black voters in the Democratic Party is reflected by an even more racially polarized set of party activists than in 1991.

Table 7.1 Level and Sources of Perceived Factionalism among Activists, by Party, 1991

	Democrats	*Republicans*
Level of factionalism		
Fairly high	19.9	16.8
Moderate	54.3	47.2
Low	15.4	27.4
None	10.4	8.6
Source of factionalism		
Personal followings	77.3	73.6
Ideology	61.5	59.4
Issues	57.7	63.7
Geography	57.1	36.4
Old vs. new residents	49.0	40.1

Source: Reproduced from McGlennon 1998a, 153.
Note: Entries are percentages, by column.

In many ways, the parties became more internally consistent over the decade between the two SGPA studies, and the activists' perceptions of party cleavage reflect this in an apparent lessening of tension. Table 7.1 shows how activists viewed the presence of party factionalism in 1991. Almost two-thirds of Republicans and nearly three-quarters of Democrats viewed factionalism as being "fairly high" or "moderately high."

In this earlier survey, activists were also asked to indicate which of five sources of factionalism existed within the party. Democrats saw division almost everywhere, with a majority saying four of the five sources were present in their party. The fifth was identified by 49 percent. Personal followings were most commonly mentioned, with 77 percent of Democrats saying they had seen evidence of such schisms. Ideological tension ranked second.

Republicans found fewer causes of factionalism present, but again personal followings ranked first, with slightly less than three-quarters noting its presence. Issues were next, followed by ideology, while fewer than half found tensions caused by geographical division or rivalries between new and old residents of their states.

By 2001, factionalism seemed to be a less significant problem in both parties, though differences in question wording make direct comparison problematic. Still, when asked to describe the level of factionalism in their state and county party organizations, solid majorities of both Democrats and Republicans described it as "very low" or "moderately low" at the state and county levels.

Though the levels of factionalism might be low, the party activists still found it to be present and based on numerous sources, as shown in table 7.2. Activists in 2001 were presented with nine potential sources of

Table 7.2 Level and Sources of Perceived Factionalism among Activists, by Party, 2001

	Democrats	*Republicans*
Level		
Very high	7	6
Moderately high	41	33
Moderately low	46	50
Very low	6	11
Source of factionalism		
Ideology	57	54
Party leaders	55	50
New vs. old residents	47	35
Region	62	48
Urban/rural	67	53
Taxes	52	30
Abortion	54	54
Racial issues	47	26
Government spending	53	32

Note: Entries are percentages, by column.

factionalism, and majorities of Democrats claimed high levels of factionalism in seven of the cases (with 47 percent adding the last two). In contrast, Republican activists perceived high factionalism in only four of the nine causes.

Democrats most commonly cited urban/rural and regional division, with ideology next. Party leaders were fourth on the list of sources of factional division. Republican activists were most likely to name ideology and abortion as causes of division, with urban/rural conflict and support for contending party leaders ranking close behind.

The overall decline in perception of factionalism is consistent with the ongoing realignment of the parties. Even so, the continuing identification of ideology by activists in both parties, as well as issue differences on abortion for Republicans, suggests the continuation of friction under a unified surface. Not surprisingly, table 7.3 shows that the identification of factionalism over ideology tracks with an activist's own ideological positioning. The more conservative the Democratic activist, the more likely he or she is to see factionalism over ideology. Among Republicans, who primarily distinguish themselves in shades of conservatism, the less conservative the activists, the more likely they are to see factionalism. In these cases, it appears that the perception of factionalism may be enhanced by holding a less common view within the party. The increasing polarization of the parties means that there are fewer conservative Democrats or moderate Republicans to feel engaged in a factional dispute within the organization.

Table 7.3 Perception of Factionalism among Party Activists by Ideology and Abortion Attitude

Percentage Perceiving High Factionalism (Very or Moderately High)	*Democrats*	*Republicans*
Ideology		
All activists	48	39
Very liberal	36	43*
Somewhat liberal	46	67
Moderate	51	53
Somewhat conservative	55	41
Very conservative	59	34
Abortion attitude		
Strongly favor legal abortions	47	57
Favor legal abortions	46	43
Oppose legal abortions	57	41
Strongly oppose legal abortions	58	31

Note: Entries are percentages, by column.
*$N = 3$.

Similarly, the identification of abortion policy as a source of factionalism appears closely related to a respondent's position on legalized abortion. The closer to the dominant party position an activist is, the less likely he or she is to see this as a highly factional issue in the party.

How does the perception of factionalism match actual disagreements or varying perceptions among party members? And how do changes in party composition serve to explain declining levels of factionalism?

It must first be recognized that the parties have become less ideologically diverse than they were ten years earlier. On the five-point scale of party identification, a majority of Republicans in 2001 identified themselves as "very conservative," up 13 percent from the earlier study. Liberals and moderates dropped from 15 percent to 9 percent of Republican Party members. Democrats experienced a similar if more modest trend toward ideological unity. Liberals constituted 57 percent of Democratic activists, an increase of 20 percent over 1991. Moderates and conservatives dropped to 43 percent among Democrats. In both cases, the level of factional diversity in the party has declined, but the perception of ideology as a divisive force remains.

Abortion was seen by a majority of both parties as an important explanation for factionalism, despite the fact that both parties saw increasing consensus among their activists. Republican support for legal abortion fell from more than 40 percent to just 30 percent. Democratic support jumped from just below 75 percent to 85 percent. Those on the minority side in each party were even more likely to see abortion as a cause of factionalism, suggesting that they were increasingly aware of their divergence from their party's majority opinion on the issue. The sensitivity may come as party leaders and candidates increasingly reflect a consensus position that these activists do not share. It also suggests the possibility that these activists may be the remnants of a larger group who have already exited each party over issue differences.

Those among the activists who have switched parties give us some indication of the impact that issue factionalism may have. Among the activists who reported that they had been members of another party previously (about 5 percent of Democrats and more than 10 percent of Republicans), the overwhelming reason reported for the party change was that the new party of the activists had a better stand on issues. Two-thirds of those who switched to the Democrats and 84 percent of Republican converts selected issue stands as the most important reason for the change. For both sets of partisans, their positions on the issue of abortion were consistent with their new party's dominant stance and at variance with their former party. Issue factionalism both explains the movement of party switchers and suggests a continuing impact on those who increasingly feel themselves at odds with their own party.

NEW SOURCES OF CLEAVAGE

The emergence of regional and urban/rural factionalism reflects a different dynamic at work in the southern party systems. Regionalism is not new in southern politics, of course. Key devoted considerable attention to the concept of "friends and neighbors" voting and to identifying ongoing geographic or regional bases for candidates and even parties. But the return of regional factionalism does suggest more stable patterns of intraparty competition.

While ideological and issue differences were disappearing among local party activists, they seemed to be increasingly cognizant of differences among party members based on where they lived. The distinction did not seem to be between newcomers and longtime residents or natives, but rather among sections of states and metropolitan versus rural areas. With the South as a whole still more rural than the rest of the country, but large sections of it rapidly urbanizing, a clash of values is predictable. It also presages a more permanent source of controversy as urban areas require higher levels of service, exhibit more diversity and tolerance, and are oriented toward economic and social expansion.

Examples of urban/rural divisions in southern state politics abound, whether it is the split between congested South Florida and the Panhandle, the Atlanta metropolitan gargantuan and the peanut farms of Plains, or Northern Virginia's constant battle over state resources with Southside. Regional rivalries have been well documented in Tennessee's Grand Divisions, the Delta versus the Hills, and the Low Country of South Carolina against the Upcountry. But as party competition has come to the South, other factors have often weakened regional tendencies from early eras.

With the emergence of factionalism based on region and urbanism in both parties, it suggests a more fundamental change in the organization of politics. Different perspectives on the need for and extent of state services are likely to be seen in both parties and to result in conflicts at all levels: elections, state and local governments, and party organizations. As metropolitan areas grow, it becomes more difficult for either party to hold together a coalition that includes varied regional and locational interests.

These results suggest that the overall decline in factionalism experienced by the parties over the decade is largely the result of increasingly unified opinions among party activists. It also suggests that as party competition has become more regularized, party positions and bases of support become more stable. If this is true, it should be evident in differences among state party systems.

STATE PARTY VARIANCES

In the 1991 survey of activists, three results stood out in the analysis of activists in the individual state parties. First, the perception of factionalism was high across the board, with a majority of the party activists in both parties in every state so indicating. While Mississippi Republicans barely hit the majority, in most cases well over 60 percent of activists of other state parties cited high factionalism as present in their organization. Second, Democrats perceived higher levels than Republicans in nine of eleven states, tying with Republican activists in Florida and Georgia. Third, the range among each party by state was relatively small, clustering close to the average score in all but a handful of cases.

The 2001 results show greater variance, as shown in table 7.4. In fourteen of the state parties (ten Republican and four Democratic), perceptions of high factionalism had declined to minority levels. In two states, reported factionalism by Republicans actually exceeded the Democrats' reports. Finally, the range of percentages was much higher, especially for the Democrats.

Consistent with the reports that regional and urban/rural divisions are among the leading sources of factionalism, party activists report much less disagreement within their county organizations (table 7.5). Reports of divisions between urban and rural activists and among activists from different regions are in some contrast to the harmony reported at the local level. With some important sources of factionalism not relevant (local committees will be comprised of activists from one region and most often from counties that are either urban, rural, or suburban), factionalism overall should be much lower.

Of course, factionalism's impact will be felt differently in the varied states of the region. The 1991 SGPA survey found that while majorities in

Table 7.4 Perception of Factionalism in State Parties, 1991 and 2001

	Democrats			*Republicans*		
State	*1991*	*2001*	*Change*	*1991*	*2001*	*Change*
Alabama	79	56	−23	61	35	−26
Arkansas	72	51	−21	64	41	−23
Florida	76	39	−37	76	35	−41
Georgia	71	51	−20	71	41	−30
Louisiana	84	65	−19	73	67	−6
Mississippi	75	72	−3	50	33	−17
North Carolina	79	44	−35	69	38	−31
South Carolina	74	51	−23	61	32	−29
Tennessee	74	55	−19	57	43	−14
Texas	73	40	−33	67	34	−33
Virginia	67	39	−28	62	45	−17

Note: Entries are the percent indicating existence of "very high" or "moderately high" levels of factionalism.

Table 7.5 Perceptions of Factionalism in County Party Organizations, 2001

State	*Democrats*	*Republicans*
Alabama	42	33
Arkansas	44	23
Florida	37	23
Georgia	27	22
Louisiana	57	32
Mississippi	51	21
North Carolina	44	36
South Carolina	40	30
Tennessee	39	33
Texas	35	31
Virginia	24	21

Note: Entries are the percent indicating existence of "very high" or "moderately high" levels of factionalism.

both parties in all states found factionalism to be high, the level of recognition ranged from a low of 50 percent to a high of 84 percent. Among Republicans, there was a spread of 26 percent between the high and low states, while the Democratic range was only 17 percent, including the state with the highest level of reported factionalism. While much more detailed discussion of factionalism in individual states can be found in Clark and Prysby (2003), some state variations are worth commenting on here.

The significantly lower levels of factionalism reported in 2001 were largely consistent across both parties and most states. While activists in a couple of state parties still found factionalism to be high, it was reported by fewer than half among Republicans in ten states and Democrats in four. Each party experienced a 24 percent overall decline in reported high factionalism. South Carolina, Mississippi, Texas, and Florida had the lowest levels among Republican activists, while Florida, Virginia, Texas, and North Carolina had the Democratic Party organizations with the lowest rates. Louisiana stood out in both parties as highly factional, with only Mississippi Democrats reporting a higher level.

IMPLICATIONS OF STATE VARIANCES IN FACTIONALISM

The explanations for low and high levels of factionalism are not immediately evident from this data, but their experiences in party development are suggestive. For the Republicans, the least factional states are ones in which they have experienced enormous success and have established their power in state and national elections. The Democratic states with low factionalism are generally those that faced strong Republican opposition early and have had the most time to adapt to a changing political environment. Their members may represent a more coherent body of activists who recognize that they no longer have the luxury of internal division.

The three high factionalism state parties represent a different set of circumstances. Both Louisiana parties operate in an electoral system that works against party unity and discipline, at least in its early stage. The "free-for-all" primary makes each candidate, regardless of party, put together a personal coalition of support with the goal of winning a spot in a runoff against another candidate who may even be of the same party. That electoral mechanism is tailormade to encourage factionalism. The Mississippi Democrats presumably face the difficulty of holding together a party consisting of traditional white Democrats, who continue to hold local and state legislative positions, and African Americans, who are the electoral backbone of the Mississippi Democrats. With African Americans comprising 47 percent of Mississippi's Democratic activists, the state presented a unique racial profile. No other state party came close to the nearly equal division of Mississippi, with South Carolina's African Americans constituting less than a third of the total activists.

Another source for trying to understand the interstate variations is the identification of specific sources of factionalism by the party activists. The results lend support for the contention that Louisiana's high rate of reported factionalism is due to candidate-centered politics, as 71 percent of Democrats and 61 percent of Republicans from the Pelican State cited factionalism based on party leaders. Georgia Republicans, who have had a series of close statewide nomination contests in recent years, also reported a high level of personal factionalism.

Georgia and North Carolina Democrats and Tennessee Republicans identified the split between new and old residents as a source of unusually high factionalism, consistent with the relatively high growth rates these states have experienced. However, this finding did not appear in other fast-growing states. Regional divisions were noted most frequently by both Democrats and Republicans in Virginia, and by Tennessee Republicans. Members of both parties in Georgia, Louisiana, and Virginia pointed to urban/rural division, as did North Carolina Democrats and Tennessee Republicans.

Though Republicans across the South found little to disagree on over tax policy, in Tennessee it was a source of deep division. Compared to only 30 percent of Republicans overall naming tax policy as a source of factionalism, 68 percent of Tennessee's Republicans found tax policy a source of division. With the Volunteer State in the midst of a bitter fight over adoption of an income tax proposed by Republican Governor Don Sundquist, the issue was a top source of Democratic friction as well. Louisiana Democrats also cited this issue as a source of factionalism.

IMPACTS OF FACTIONAL DIVISION

Although factionalism may have declined, we have seen that it remains a concern among significant numbers of southern party activists. The sources may be different than a decade earlier, but the implications of a divided party can be serious. In order to investigate the impact of factionalism, we focus on those who reported their perception of party factionalism to be very high. These activists, as we have seen, are likely to be disproportionally in the minority in their own party on those dimensions that lead to factionalism. If there are consequences to their sense of division, they are likely to be among this group.

In order to examine the implications, we first consider how strongly these activists identify with their party and its candidates at the state and national levels. We then turn to the level of activity that these precinct party members report and finally look to their views on the appropriate roles for party members to play when confronted with sources of division.

Do party members who report high levels of factionalism in their state organizations retain strong attachments to their parties? Not surprisingly, precinct organization members view themselves as strong partisans. If they lose attachment to their party, why would they continue to hold even lower level positions in the organization? That question must frequently come to the minds of activists who see themselves in a divided organization, as they do report lower levels of strong affiliation.

As it turns out, large majorities of precinct activists do see themselves as "strong" partisans, but among both parties, the activists who find high factionalism (hereafter referred to as "factionals") are much less likely to profess this strong attachment (table 7.6). Concern over factionalism is also evident in levels of support for the presidential candidacies of both parties in both 1996 and 2000. While large majorities of activists supported their party's nominee each time, factionals were consistently (though only modestly) less supportive. In addition, when describing their attachment to their state and national parties, factionals were much less likely to identify themselves as close to either their state or local party.

This loosening of attachment to the party by some factionals manifests itself in the perception of the party's strength and effectiveness as well. Republicans overwhelmingly view their party organizations as having gotten stronger over the past decade, and Democrats are more restrained in their evaluation, but factionals consistently have a more pessimistic view of the party change in organizational and campaign effectiveness and in effectiveness with voters.

So factionals have weaker attachment to their party and its candidates and are less likely to believe that it has strengthened itself in recent years. Does this affect the way in which these activists function within the party? To answer this question, we examined the reported activity levels of factionals compared to other party activists and how they resolve the tension between electability and ideological purity.

Table 7.6 Perception of Factionalism and Attachment to Party

	Democrats		*Republicans*	
	Factionals	*Nonfactionals*	*Factionals*	*Nonfactionals*
Strong national partisan	73	89	80	93
Strong state partisan	79	91	77	94
Presidential vote for party 1996	88	92	86	94
Presidential vote for party 2000	85	91	92	98
Feel close to national party	62	75	71	88
Feel close to state party	67	89	83	92
Perceptions of increased party strength				
County organization weaker	43	28	8	2
Campaign effectiveness weaker	44	27	8	3
Effectiveness with voters weaker	42	31	10	2

Note: Entries for the first six rows are the percent indicating existence of "very high" or "moderately high" levels of factionalism. Entries for the final three rows are the percent who perceived that the party was weaker on the specified dimension.

Democratic factionals show a predictable pattern of activity: they are most active in local elections and least active in national campaigns. While those Democrats who reported little factionalism maintained consistent levels of activity in local, state, and national campaigns, factionals put in their strongest effort for the local candidates who were more likely to match their own ideological and issue preferences.

Republican factionals worked at the same level as other Republicans in local and national campaigns but were less active at the state level. Since factionalism generally was reported to be at higher levels in state parties than local ones, it is not surprising that activists were more likely to sit out a state election. For Republican factionals who took less conservative positions on issues, moderate southern Democrats running for state office might provide less motivation for involvement than more liberal national Democrats. A fuller discussion of questions relating to the pragmatism and purism of party activists can be found in chapter 9.

CONCLUSIONS

The second Southern Grassroots Party Activists survey paints a picture of political parties in a newly competitive system with declining and changing causes of factionalism. As ideological and issue variations within each party have narrowed, both the Democrats and Republicans report lower levels of factional division within their respective organizations. Ideological polarization continues, and, as it does, the parties may continue to experience factionalism, but it is declining.

As the traditional source of factionalism is easing, however, a new and important source of potential division is being recognized: conflict based on regional and urban/rural distinctiveness. This source of factionalism reflects both a more stable and predictable cause of cleavage within the parties and a potentially significant wedge within party organizations.

Metropolitan growth is transforming the South and challenging dominant political views in ways that carry the possibility of pitting party members against each other. Rural communities with strong attachments to traditional values will more frequently confront policy initiatives coming from urbanizing areas, both in state parties and state government. The challenges confronted by politicians of both parties in keeping together disparate coalitions in the face of issues and controversies such as the design of state flags, abortion, homosexual rights, religion, and government services are seen increasingly.

Georgia's Democratic Governor Roy Barnes lost his reelection bid unexpectedly in 2002 despite increased support in metropolitan areas because of the wholesale abandonment of his candidacy by rural voters, partly over the state flag issue. Republican Sonny Perdue had just taken over the governorship when he had to figure out how to balance the expectations of his rural supporters that he would restore the Massive Resistance era flag and the demands of corporate Republicans that he drop any effort that would paint Georgia as intolerant and backward looking.

Democrats must simultaneously maximize support among African Americans and avoid alienating moderate suburbanites, while limiting their losses in small towns and farmlands. Republicans have to motivate Christian conservatives with strong support for governmental restriction of social liberalism while appealing to libertarian instincts of gun owners and not driving away the "soccer moms" who represent a key swing constituency in many southern states.

Just as significantly, emerging debates on government taxing and spending policies are already creating deep divisions in both parties, but especially the emerging majority Republican Party. Our survey has revealed the deep division in Tennessee, where a Republican governor became a pariah by advocating a restructured tax system designed to raise money for enhanced state services. Alabama's Governor Bob Riley was handed a landslide defeat when he tried to convince voters to adopt a new tax system designed to raise $1.2 billion in additional state revenue. Virginia's Republican State Senate and House of Delegates engage in annual skirmishes over conflicting views of taxing and spending.

Increasingly, as urban areas press for more state funds to pay for traffic improvements, better quality schools, economic development, and enhanced environmental protection, regional schisms become more and more pronounced. The ability of the parties to respond to this new source of factionalism will help to determine the nature of party competition in the South in the decade to come.

At this point, the impact of factionalism in this new system is unclear. The evidence from this study suggests that factionalism will inherently appear in parties that are dynamic and growing and in systems where party competition is vital. It does not appear to create major problems for parties in maintaining the active support of even those who represent a minority viewpoint within the party, but it does suggest that those who find themselves increasingly isolated within the organization may exit its ranks.

CHAPTER

8

Mass-Elite Linkages and Partisan Change in the South

Barbara A. Patrick, Stephen D. Shaffer, Patrick R. Cotter, and Samuel H. Fisher III

National politics today is intensely competitive. In terms of the number of party identifiers, presidential votes received, and congressional seats held, the Democratic and Republican Parties are closely matched. A major factor contributing to the nation's current political competitiveness, which stands in contrast to the eras of one-party dominance that have characterized much of American history, is the presence of genuine two-party politics in the South. As a result, while politics in the South has always been important, the outcome of the region's elections has become an even more vital component of the nation's electoral politics (Black and Black 1992, 2002). The "vital" role of the contemporary South is illustrated by the importance of the region's Electoral College votes to Republican presidential candidates and the fact that since the 1960s the only Democrats to be elected president (Johnson, Carter, Clinton) have hailed from the South. Further, the Republicans' current narrow majority in Congress is greatly aided by its control over more than half of the seats from the South.

Chapter 1 explained how a competitive two-party system has finally arisen in the modern South. Yet, while Republicans hold a clear advantage in presidential elections, Democrats remain quite strong in state legislative and local contests across the region, providing a strong farm team of potential candidates for more visible offices. What explains this puzzling feature of "uneven" Republican electoral strength across the "vital" South (Aistrup 1996; Shaffer, Pierce, and Kohnke 2000)?

Perhaps the modern Republican Party in the South remains too ideologically conservative for the average voter. Mississippi's first Republican governor since Reconstruction, Kirk Fordice, was a construction company executive who had been active in the Republican Party organization since the Goldwater campaign in 1964. His outspoken and abrasive conservative philosophy was reflected in such actions as joking about calling out the national guard to prevent any judge from ordering a tax increase to better fund the historically black universities, declaring the United States a "Christian nation" at a national Republican governor's conference, and in his second term having his all white-male slate of College Board nominees rejected by the legislature. Needless to say, Democrats retained control of the Mississippi state legislature and even briefly regained the governorship after Fordice's term ended. Similarly, Alabama's Republican governor Fob James was probably best known for his conservative and controversial positions on social issues such as school prayer, abortion, and the public display of the Ten Commandments. His performance as governor, however, received generally negative reviews from most Alabama citizens. As a result, he was easily defeated in his 1998 reelection bid by Democrat Don Siegelman.

Today's southern Democratic Party may also be in the process of becoming ideologically out of touch with average voters, though in the opposite, liberal direction. In the 2003 state elections in Mississippi, Republicans won the governorship and three of the other seven statewide elected executive offices after a Democratic lieutenant governor switched parties, claiming that the national party had become too liberal and the state Democratic Party too partisan. Similarly, while Alabama's Don Siegelman achieved some success early in his administration, he was later linked to rumors of scandal and corruption. In the 2002 election, Siegelman narrowly lost his reelection bid to Republican Congressman Bob Riley.

In this chapter we examine the similarities and differences in policy beliefs between the South's party activists and voters to shed light onto this vital question of how well the political parties represent the views of average citizens. We also investigate whether the linkage between party activists and voters varies across types of issues or between different southern states. We employ unique data sources from the states of Alabama and Mississippi, as well as national survey data, to examine these critical linkage questions.

THEORETICAL CONCERNS FROM THE LITERATURE

The linkage between political elites and the voting masses has been an important theoretical concern of scholars of voting behavior. In *An Economic Theory of Democracy*, Anthony Downs (1957, 300) hypothesized that "parties act to maximize votes" and that "citizens behave rationally in politics." V. O. Key Jr.

(1966, 7–8) used national opinion polls to test this theory and concluded that "voters are not fools," as they are affected by "central and relevant questions of public policy, of governmental performance, and of executive personality." He pointed out, though, that the electorate was limited by the "clarity of the alternatives presented to it" (Key 1949, 7) by candidates. Scammon and Wattenberg (1970, 279) in *The Real Majority* argued that the average voter's policy preferences were essentially middle of the road, and that the "one essential political strategy" for parties and candidates was their "drive toward the center." Some party strategists learned this lesson the hard way, as Republicans saw their very conservative candidate Barry Goldwater losing the 1964 presidential election in a landslide and Democrats eight years later suffered a similar fate with their very liberal presidential hopeful George McGovern.

This important theoretical concern of mass-elite linkage on political issues has largely been studied at the national level and related to major party fortunes in federal elections. In their pioneering article, "Issue Conflict and Consensus among Party Leaders and Followers," McClosky, Hoffman, and O'Hara (1960) found that Republican national convention delegates in the 1950s were much more conservative than even their own party identifiers in the population, while Democratic delegates were much closer in views to average citizens, suggesting a mass-elite linkage explanation for Democratic Party dominance over federal elections since 1932. Other national studies using different definitions of partisan elites also found that Republican political elites were more out of touch with average citizens' policy views than were Democratic elites. Such was the case in the 1960s for campaign activists, those who wrote letters to the editor, and political activists in general (Nexon 1971; Converse, Clausen, and Miller 1965; Verba and Nie 1972).

With the leftward shift of national Democratic Party activists in the early 1970s era of George McGovern's presidential candidacy, national studies began to point out that either Democratic elites were more out of touch with the average citizen and average Democrats, or that both parties' elites were ideologically polarized and distant from the more moderate citizenry. Such was the case for college-educated party identifiers in the early 1970s, campaign activists throughout the 1970s, convention delegates in 1972 and 1988, and members of Congress in 1970 (Ladd and Hadley 1975; Nie, Verba, and Petrocik 1976; Shaffer 1980; Kirkpatrick 1975; Kagay 1991; Backstrom 1977). These studies essentially found that elites of the two major parties were more ideologically polarized than were more centrist average citizens identifying with the two parties. Many analysts argued that Democratic elites had now become more distant than Republican elites from their citizenry party, helping to explain why Democrats lost every presidential election except one for the twenty years beginning in 1968.

A related theoretical concern is the nature of belief systems in the mass and elite parties. Ideological polarization between the two parties' elites may reflect the generally "liberal" policy views of the Democratic elites and the largely "conservative" views of Republican elites, while the more centrist views of average citizens may reflect their cognitive shortcomings and inability to conceptualize politics in an ideological, unidimensional manner. Philip Converse's (1964) pioneering "The Nature of Belief Systems in Mass Publics" found little issue constraint (defined as views across public issues that are consistently "liberal" or "conservative") in the general population but more significant constraint among congressional candidates, as did Jennings (1992). Therefore, the general population was not ideologically consistent and was not divided into two hostile camps of ideological liberals and ideological conservatives. Stimson (1975) and Nie, Verba, and Petrocik (1976) point out that the cognitive abilities of citizens may influence the nature of the voters' belief systems. People who are more educated, who have more political information, or who are more interested in the campaign tend to view issues in a more unidimensional, "ideological" framework or in terms of a limited number of distinct issue areas. Those lacking such cognitive abilities tend to have belief systems that are less structured by a single ideology or by a limited number of policy areas.

Although there are a multitude of studies at the national level, few examine the mass-elite linkage on issues at the state level, even though electoral competition in the southern states has become increasingly fascinating. Using statewide public opinion polls from Alabama and Mississippi and county party organization surveys of the same states drawn from the 1991 Southern Grassroots Party Activists study, Breaux, Shaffer, and Cotter (1998) examined mass-elite belief systems and mass-elite differences on policy issues. Their findings supported studies conducted at the national level. Party elites had more sophisticated and constrained belief systems than did the masses, particularly those citizens having less cognitive ability. Issue differences between the party elites in 1991 were more pronounced than they were between the two citizenry parties. Democratic elites, though, were closer in views to average citizens than were Republicans, particularly in Alabama. The greater proximity between the Democratic elites and the masses was offered as a possible explanation for continued Democratic dominance of state and local offices in these Deep South states. The absence of longitudinal data precluded any conclusion regarding how ephemeral or long-lasting these mass-elite linkages were, a problem that is rectified with the current replication of this analysis. The absence of regionwide opinion polls precluded any generalization to the entire South, a limitation that is rectified with the current study that includes information from a national study with a significant sampling of southern voters.

THE METHODS OF OUR STUDY

This study of the similarities and differences in policy beliefs between the region's party leaders, party members, and voters is based primarily on data collected in two states in the Deep South—Alabama and Mississippi—though some regionwide information supplements our analysis. These two states were selected for an in-depth study for both theoretical and methodological reasons.

Theoretically, both states represent the curious nature of contemporary southern politics, where the Republican Party has made great electoral gains but remains a minority party in many state and local races. Except for the 1976 Carter election, both states have voted Republican for president since 1972. Gubernatorial elections can now be won by either party and have been intensely competitive since 1986 in Alabama and since 1987 in Mississippi. Statewide executive offices below governor have also become more competitive with Republicans holding at least half of these offices in Alabama since the 1994 Republican national tsunami and winning a historic high of three of seven executive offices in Mississippi in the 2003 state elections. Yet Democrats remain dominant in other state and local elections, controlling roughly 60 percent or more of the state legislative seats in both states. As late as 1999 in Mississippi, only 7 percent of county supervisors were Republicans, as were less than 10 percent of the state's county sheriffs, chancery clerks, circuit clerks, and tax assessors (Shaffer and Price 2001, 264–266).

Methodologically, extensive data are available in each state that permit numerous comparisons across samples of different kinds of people. Specifically, data used here to study the policy beliefs of party activists are based on the results of the 2001 SGPA survey, already described in chapter 1. Several of the policy items in that study were included in statewide public opinion surveys that are periodically conducted in Alabama and Mississippi by the chapter's authors. In Alabama, a random sample of five hundred adults was conducted by Southern Opinion Research in October 2001. In Mississippi, two representative surveys of adult residents were conducted by the Survey Research Unit of the Social Science Research Center at Mississippi State University with 613 respondents interviewed from April 3 to April 16, 2000, and 608 residents surveyed from April 1 to April 14, 2002. Since both the Alabama and Mississippi polls rely on telephone surveys that tend to underrepresent lower socioeconomic status households lacking phones, census data were used to weight them so that they were representative of key demographic groups such as education, race, and sex. A similar study of party activists and average citizens was conducted in Alabama and Mississippi in 1991 (Breaux, Shaffer, and Cotter 1998). Thus, with the available data it is possible to examine how the similarities and differences in policy beliefs between the region's party activists and voters have changed during the last decade.

We also included some information from the 2000 National Election Study (NES), which permitted a comparison between party activists in the entire South and the subset of average southerners in the NES study.[1] Three agree-disagree items regarding the death penalty, affirmative action, and gay employment rights, as well as six federal spending items, were worded virtually identically in both the NES and the SGPA study, permitting some interesting regionwide comparisons between masses and elites. Other items in the NES and other national studies were either worded differently from the SGPA items or used different response categories, preventing the more in-depth analyses that the Mississippi and Alabama public surveys permitted (see Bishop, Tuchfarber, and Oldendick 1978 for validity problems involving items with noncomparable question wordings or response categories).

The Alabama and Mississippi mass and elite surveys included numerous policy questions, but we focus here on those questions that were asked in both states and in both the mass and elite surveys, in order to be able to make direct comparisons between the masses and elites in both states. We also focus on questions that were asked in both the 1991 mass-elite study and the current study, in order to study change in the southern party system over the last turbulent decade. This results in ten issue items that reflect a diverse range of policy concerns from social spending programs to divisive lifestyle or cultural issues and includes issues of special concern to African Americans and women. Eight of these issue items were asked in identical form in the 1991 study (except for one item omitted from the 1991 Mississippi public survey). In addition, ideological self-identification was asked in all surveys in both years, except for the 2001 Alabama public survey.

The exact wording of these issue questions is provided in the appendix. The issues are also examined in greater detail in chapter 5. All issue items for the Mississippi and Alabama comparisons are coded or recoded so that they range from 1 for most liberal to 4 for most conservative (5 for ideology), as in the 1991 study. In the regionwide comparisons using NES data, the three issue agreement items are coded the same way, but the six federal spending items are coded to range from 1 for those wanting to spend less to 3 for those favoring more spending. We decided not to attempt to recode these spending items so that they had the same ideological direction because of the difficulty of identifying the ideological nature of at least one of the issues. For instance, while fighting crime is normally regarded as a "conservative" issue, some conservatives oppose increased government spending in general or believe that most issues including public order should be left to the states. In addition, some liberals may favor more *federal* spending on "dealing with crime," if the money goes to prevention and rehabilitation programs, such as summer jobs programs for inner-city youths or prison work training programs.

Two other general points follow: Whether activists are Democrats or Republicans is based on their membership in the party organization. The partisanship of the public is identified with the common party identification question used in our discipline. Independents who admit that they think of themselves as "closer" to one of the parties are classified as identifying with that party, since studies have found that such independent leaners have a similar voting pattern to strong and weak partisans. This also helps to maximize the sample size and minimize the sample error of our study. A second point is that we use some terms interchangeably, such as elites and activists, and masses and voters. The general theoretical concern is over policy differences between elites and masses, and our particular elites and masses are party activists and potential voters. We regard all adults sampled as potential voters and caution the reader that not all of these adults are actual voters. Identifying actual voters is beyond the scope of our study and would require violating our respondents' anonymity in order to ascertain whether they actually did vote on election day, and even then one must define how frequently people should vote in order to be regarded as a voter. In any event, since party organizations make a major effort to convert historic nonvoters to voters favoring their party's candidates, it makes more theoretical sense to define voters as potential voters.

The belief systems of the elites and of the masses of different cognitive levels were identified with factor analysis using principal components and varimax rotation. For the Mississippi public, only the 2002 survey was used in the factor analysis, since the 2000 survey excluded the death penalty and gun control issue items. Ideological self-identification was excluded from these factor analyses, since it was not included in the Alabama public survey. Among possible indicators of cognitive ability, education was employed since it was asked in identical form in all surveys. The public samples were divided into residents having a high-school degree or less and those having some college or more education. The current study is a methodological improvement over the 1991 study, since we employ all ten identically worded issue items in all six factor analyses.

We now turn to comparisons of the policy views of masses and elites, which rely on means, a well-established statistic employed in previous mass-elite studies. It merely identifies the issue orientation of the "average" potential voter and the average party activist and makes it quite easy to compare issue viewpoints across different groups of people.

ISSUE PROXIMITY BETWEEN PARTY ELITES AND MASSES IN TWO DEEP SOUTH STATES

It is quite clear from our data that the average voter in Alabama and Mississippi is not an ideologue of either the left or the right, reflecting national studies (Scammon and Wattenberg 1970). Instead, most voters are conservative on some issues but progressive or liberal on other issues (using 2.5, the midpoint of each issue item's scale, as the basic dividing point). The average voter in both states is more conservative on such cultural issues as school prayer, abortion, affirmative action, and the death penalty (table 8.1 and table 8.2: column A). On the other hand, the average voter is liberal on social service spending programs such as health and education, jobs, and programs benefiting the economic and social status of women and African Americans. These findings support studies at the national level

Table 8.1 Policy Views of Mississippians

Issues	*All Voters* *A*	*Democratic Voters* *B*	*Republican Voters* *C*	*Democratic Party Activists* *D*	*Republican Party Activists* *E*
Government aid for women	1.98	1.78	2.25	1.86	2.76
Abortion	2.68	2.53	2.89	2.20	3.05
Government services/spending	2.36	2.29	2.47	1.87	3.02
School prayer	3.47	3.44	3.51	3.27	3.53
Government aid to minorities	2.13	1.82	2.48	1.88	2.85
Guaranteed job and living standard	2.20	1.90	2.60	2.50	3.43
Equal role for women	1.69	1.65	1.74	1.60	1.86
Hiring preferences for blacks	2.79	2.43	3.20	2.76	3.64
Death penalty	2.85	2.62	3.12	2.56	3.19
Handgun control	2.35	2.07	2.68	1.89	3.22
Ideological self-identification	3.29	2.94	3.77	2.69	4.45
(Average *N* Size)	(1,050)	(485)	(426)	(355)	(449)

Note: Cell entries are means with scales ranging from 1 for most liberal to 4 for most conservative, except for ideology where 5 is most conservative. The ideological self-identification question is worded as follows: "What about your political beliefs? Do you consider yourself: Very liberal, Somewhat liberal, Middle of the road/moderate, Somewhat conservative, Very conservative?" For the wording of each issue item, see the copy of the questionnaire in the appendix.

that conclude that "most citizens do not engage in the ideological thinking of the sort found among political elites" (Erikson and Tedin 2003, 74; this book provides an informative review of the literature in this area).

Partisans in the general population also have differing views depending on different types of issues, though they appear a little more ideologically distinct than voters as a whole (who include political Independents). Democratic voters in both states are somewhat more liberal than all voters on every issue, while Republican voters are generally more conservative (table 8.1 and table 8.2: column B and column C). Indeed, on the cultural issues of affirmative action and abortion, where voters generally are more conservative, Democratic voters are moderate or slightly left of center. On the social service spending items of health and education and jobs, where voters are generally more liberal, Republican voters are essentially moderate or slightly to the right of center.

Table 8.2 Policy Views of Alabamians

Issues	*All Voters* *A*	*Democratic Voters* *B*	*Republican Voters* *C*	*Democratic Party Activists* *D*	*Republican Party Activists* *E*
Government aid for women	2.02	1.79	2.16	1.85	2.69
Abortion	2.59	2.26	2.90	1.89	3.09
Government services/spending	2.34	2.26	2.47	1.75	2.88
School prayer	3.43	3.39	3.45	3.07	3.52
Government aid to minorities	2.05	1.80	2.28	1.96	2.73
Guaranteed job and living standard	2.30	2.05	2.54	2.57	3.44
Equal role for women	1.71	1.69	1.65	1.49	1.73
Hiring preferences for blacks	2.78	2.54	3.02	2.93	3.58
Death penalty	2.89	2.75	3.05	2.61	3.17
Handgun control	2.33	2.02	2.68	1.93	3.22
Ideological self-identification	NA	NA	NA	2.55	4.44
(Average *N* Size)	(474)	(200)	(205)	(385)	(436)

Note: Cell entries are means with scales ranging from 1 for most liberal to 4 for most conservative, except for ideology where 5 is most conservative. NA indicates that the question was not asked in the 2001 public survey. For the wording of each issue item, see the copy of the questionnaire in the appendix.

Compared to voters, activists of both parties are more ideologically consistent, particularly Republican Party activists (table 8.1 and table 8.2: column D and column E). Liberals and even moderates are a dying breed in today's Republican Party, as the typical activist is midway between "somewhat" and "very" conservative in terms of ideological self-identification. Republican activists in both states are conservative on every issue except for equal rights for women. Democrats have a broader tent, with the average activist self-identifying as somewhere between moderate and "somewhat liberal" but closer to moderate. Democratic activists are often more liberal or conservative than the issue item midpoints depending on the issue's popularity among average voters, being more liberal on social services such as health and education and on improving the social and economic situations of women and blacks, and more conservative on such cultural issues as school prayer, affirmative action, and the death penalty. Unlike the more centrist or conservative views of most voters, however, Democratic activists in both states are essentially liberal on some cultural issues that are emotional ones for key voting groups, such as abortion and gun control.

Table 8.3 Changes in Policy Views of Mississippians, 1991–2001

Issues	*All Voters* *A*	*Democratic Voters* *B*	*Republican Voters* *C*	*Democratic Party Activists* *D*	*Republican Party Activists* *E*
Government aid for women	−.08	−.14	−.02	.01	.35
Abortion	.12	.04	.28	−.09	.27
Government services/spending	.08	.11	.06	−.20	−.01
School prayer	NA	NA	NA	−.09	.01
Government aid to minorities	−.05	−.09	−.04	−.25	−.04
Guaranteed job and living standard	.00	−.05	.03	.10	.21
Equal role for women	−.15	−.20	−.17	−.24	−.21
Hiring preferences for blacks	−.15	−.18	−.07	−.03	.07
Ideological self-identification	−.20	−.40	.07	−.22	.26

Source: Breaux, Shaffer, and Cotter (1998) provide the 1991 information.

Note: Entries are the difference between 2001 mean values and 1991 mean values. Positive values indicate that the group listed at the top became more conservative over the years on the issue listed at the left, while negative values indicate that the group became more liberal. NA indicates that the question was not asked in the 1991 public survey.

While Republicans are more ideologically homogeneous than are Democrats, both parties' activists appear to be growing more ideologically distinct, with the average Democrat becoming more liberal and the average Republican more conservative. In both Alabama and Mississippi, Democratic activists have grown somewhat more liberal over the last decade on abortion, school prayer, and affirmative action, and noticeably more liberal on social services, black socioeconomic improvements, women's equality, and ideological self-identification (table 8.3 and table 8.4: column D and column E). Only on public jobs have Democratic activists grown slightly more conservative. Republican activists in both states have become slightly more conservative since 1991 on school prayer and affirmative action and noticeably more conservative on women socioeconomic improvements, abortion, jobs and living standards, and ideological self-identification. Republican activists have not moved in as uniform an ideological direction as have Democrats, however. Republican activists have become slightly more liberal on social services and black socioeconomic improvements and noticeably more liberal on women's equality.

These patterns of growing ideological polarization between party activists may reflect different processes at work within the two states' citi-

Table 8.4 Changes in Policy Views of Alabamians, 1991–2001

Issues	*All Voters* *A*	*Democratic Voters* *B*	*Republican Voters* *C*	*Democratic Party Activists* *D*	*Republican Party Activists* *E*
Government aid for women	.07	−.03	.13	−.09	.22
Abortion	.19	−.10	.47	−.32	.28
Government services/spending	.21	.21	.28	−.40	−.03
School prayer	.16	.06	.18	−.24	.06
Government aid to minorities	−.21	−.27	−.09	−.42	−.13
Guaranteed job and living standard	−.12	−.13	.01	.07	.25
Equal role for women	−.19	−.19	−.20	−.44	−.34
Hiring preferences for blacks	−.17	−.12	−.15	−.21	.01
Ideological self-identification	NA	NA	NA	−.52	.23

Source: Breaux, Shaffer, and Cotter (1998) provide the 1991 information.

Note: Entries are the difference between 2001 mean values and 1991 mean values. Positive values indicate that the group listed at the top became more conservative over the years on the issue listed at the left, while negative values indicate that the group became more liberal. NA indicates that the question was not asked in the 2001 public survey.

zenry parties—a growing liberalism of Democratic voters, but no consistent shifts in the views of Republican voters. In both states Democratic voters have become somewhat more liberal on public jobs and a variety of issues relating to women and African Americans—women and black socioeconomic improvements, women's equality, and affirmative action (table 8.3 and table 8.4: column B and column C). Only on social services have Democratic voters become slightly more conservative over time. Republican voters in both states exhibit more contradictory and unclear patterns, becoming clearly more conservative over the years on abortion; slightly more conservative on social services and jobs; and slightly more liberal on women's equality, black socioeconomic improvement, and affirmative action. These conflicting shifts in partisan voters over time therefore yield few consistent attitude shifts among aggregated Alabama and Mississippi voters since 1991. Democrats, Independents, and Republicans combined in these two states are slightly more liberal on affirmative action, black socioeconomic improvement, and women's equality, but also slightly more conservative on abortion and social services.

The result of growing ideological polarization between the elite parties is that Democratic and Republican Party officials are frequently found on opposite sides of policy issues. In both states, on the issues of government efforts to improve the social and economic positions of women and African Americans, social service spending, abortion, gun control, and ideological self-identification, Democratic activists are to the left of the scale midpoints, while Republican activists are to the right (table 8.1 and table 8.2: column D and column E). Even on issues where both party activists are on the same ideological side (liberal on equal rights for women and conservative on school prayer, affirmative action, and the death penalty), Republicans are consistently more conservative than are Democrats.

Not only are Republican activists consistently more conservative than Democratic activists, but also this polarization between the two parties' elites is greater on every issue than are differences between the parties in the general population (table 8.5 and table 8.6: first two columns). Indeed, the greater polarization between elites compared to masses has become more noticeable since 1991 in both states on women and black socioeconomic improvement, social services, and jobs, and growing polarization is evident in Alabama on school prayer, affirmative action, and women's equality and in Mississippi on abortion (compare tables with Breaux, Shaffer, and Cotter 1998, table 10.4 and table 10.5). Obviously, the day when candidates could claim like George Wallace that there wasn't "a dime's worth of difference between the two major parties" is long past, as the southern party organizations are increasingly becoming as ideologically distinct as the national parties have been for over half a century. Such an ideological gulf between party officials can lead to increasingly bitter and divisive political debate among political leaders, as we saw in national politics with the impeachment of President Clinton and the increasingly negative rhetoric directed by Democratic presidential hopefuls against President Bush.

With both party organizations becoming even more ideologically distinct than they were ten years ago and possibly moving away from the more centrist views of average citizens, it is important to examine which party's elite is more in touch with its own partisans in the general population. If a political party is so ideologically extreme that it cannot even retain the support of its own party loyalists among voters, it has almost no hope of reaching out to independents and supporters of the other party in an effort to elect its candidates to office. Given the opposing ideological movements by Democratic and Republican activists, the net change among activists has failed to change the situation of mass-elite differences within each party that existed ten years ago. Once again, Republican activists are more conservative than are Republican voters on all public issues and in both southern states (table 8.5 and table 8.6: third and fourth columns).

Democratic activists in both states, on the other hand, are sometimes more conservative than Democratic voters but often more liberal than Democratic

Table 8.5 Differences in Policy Views between Mississippi Groups

	Polarization		*Proximity to Partisan Voters*		*Proximity to Average Voter*	
Issue	*Rep. Voters vs. Dem. Voters C–E*	*Rep. Activists vs. Dem. Activists E–D*	*Dem. Activists vs. Dem. Voters D–B*	*Rep. Activists vs. Rep. Voters E–C*	*Dem. Activists vs. All Voters D–A*	*Rep. Activists vs. All Voters E–A*
Government aid for women	.47	.90	.08	.51	−.12	.78
Abortion	.36	.85	−.33	.16	−.48	.37
Government services/ spending	.18	1.15	−.42	.55	−.49	.66
School prayer	.07	.26	−.17	.02	−.20	.06
Government aid to minorities	.66	.97	.06	.37	−.25	.72
Guaranteed job and living standard	.70	.93	.60	.83	.30	1.23
Equal role for women	.09	.26	−.05	.12	−.09	.17
Hiring preferences for blacks	.77	.88	.33	.44	−.03	.85
Death penalty	.50	.63	−.06	.07	−.29	.34
Handgun control	.61	1.33	−.18	.54	−.46	.87
Ideological self-identification	.83	1.76	−.25	.68	−.60	1.16

Note: Cell entries are differences between group means. The pairs of columns are identified by capital letters that correspond to the columns in table 8.1. Positive scores indicate that the first group is more conservative than the second group. Negative scores indicate that the first group is more liberal than the second group.

Table 8.6 Differences in Policy Views between Alabama Groups

	Polarization		*Proximity to Partisan Voters*		*Proximity to Average Voter*	
Issue	*Rep. Voters vs. Dem. Voters C–B*	*Rep. Activists vs. Dem. Activists E–D*	*Dem. Activists vs. Dem. Voters D–B*	*Rep. Activists vs. Rep. Voters E–C*	*Dem. Activists vs. All Voters D–A*	*Rep. Activists vs. All Voters E–A*
Government aid for women	.37	.84	.06	.53	−.17	.67
Abortion	.64	1.20	−.37	.19	−.70	.50
Government services/ spending	.21	1.13	−.51	.41	−.59	.54
School prayer	.06	.45	−.32	.07	−.36	.09
Government aid to minorities	.48	.77	.16	.45	−.09	.68
Guaranteed job and living standard	.49	.87	.52	.90	.27	1.14
Equal role for women	−.04	.24	−.20	.08	−.22	.02
Hiring preferences for blacks	.48	.65	.39	.56	.15	.80
Death penalty	.30	.56	−.14	.12	−.28	.28
Handgun control	.66	1.29	−.09	.54	−.40	.89
Ideological self-identification	NA	1.89	NA	NA	NA	NA

Note: Cell entries are differences between group means. The pairs of columns are identified by capital letters that correspond to the columns in table 8.1. Positive scores indicate that the first group is more conservative than the second group. Negative scores indicate that the first group is more liberal than the second group.

voters. On balance, as was found at the national level in the 1950s and 1960s, Democratic Party elites are more in touch with their party's masses than are Republican Party elites. Only on the cultural issues of abortion and school prayer are Republican activists in both states closer to their party's voters than are Democratic activists close to their voters. Both party activists are about equidistant from their respective voters on social services, women's equality, and the death penalty. Democratic activists in both states are closer to their party's voters on women and black social and economic improvements, affirmative action, gun control, public jobs, and (in Mississippi) ideological self-identification.

The central question remains—which party's elites are closer to the average voter, not just to their own party identifiers in the general population but also to the other party's identifiers and to independents? The answer is similar to what it was in Alabama and Mississippi ten years ago—the ideologically inclusive, biracial Democratic Party. Only on the issues of abortion and school prayer are Republican activists in both states closer to average voters than are Democratic activists (table 8.5 and table 8.6: last two columns). On women and black socioeconomic improvements, affirmative action, public jobs, gun control, and ideological self-identification (measured only in Mississippi), Democratic Party officials are closer to average voters than are Republicans. Indeed, Republicans are more conservative than the average voter on every issue.

Lest Democrats grow complacent over their greater proximity on issues to average voters, we point out that the growing liberalism of Democratic activists over the last decade has created a growing distance between themselves and average voters as well. Compared to the more mixed pattern found in our 1991 study, when Democratic activists were sometimes more conservative than average voters rather than more liberal, today's Democratic activists are more ideologically consistent. On all issues except public jobs and (in Alabama) affirmative action, Democratic activists today are more liberal than the average voter in both states. In other words, Democratic activists appear to be growing increasingly out of touch with average voters because of their party's greater liberalism than the general public's. The only reason that Democratic activists today remain closer to average citizens' policy positions is that Republican activists are even more out of touch with average voters (though in a more conservative direction).

ISSUE PROXIMITY BETWEEN PARTY ELITES AND MASSES IN ALL SOUTHERN STATES

In the Deep South states of Alabama and Mississippi, both party organizations have become more distinctive in terms of issue orientations with Democrats becoming a more left-of-center organization and Republicans becoming an even more clearly conservative group. Average voters who are less ideologically consistent on issues, being more conservative on cultural issues and more liberal on social program spending, are philosophically located between the two party organizations. Generally, voters are closer to Democratic organization members on issues than to Republicans, but an increasingly liberal Democratic organization threatens the historic image of the Democrats as being a broad tent party. We now examine whether these findings can be generalized to the South as a whole by matching the policy views of southern residents in the 2000 NES dataset with party activists in all eleven southern states.

As we found in Alabama and Mississippi, the average southern voter is not ideologically consistent. Voters of both parties are conservative (right of the issue item midpoints of 2.5 for the first three issues and 2 for the six spending items) on such cultural issues as affirmative action and the death penalty and on preferring that the federal government spend more on national defense but less on welfare (table 8.7: column B and column C). Both parties' voters are liberal on most social programs, backing more federal spending on Social Security, public schools, and the environment. Democratic voters are more concerned about protecting the employment rights of gays than are Republicans, while both parties' voters back more federal spending to deal with crime.

Party activists, on the other hand, have more ideologically distinctive views than do voters (table 8.7: column D and column E). Republican activists across the South take a conservative position on every issue except Social Security. The average Republican activist wishes to spend less money not only on welfare but also on such popular programs as public schools and protecting the environment. Democratic activists take a liberal position on every issue except affirmative action and on crime and defense where they prefer more federal spending. The average Democratic activist opposes the death penalty and favors current levels of spending on welfare, while most Democratic voters support the death penalty and wish to cut back slightly on welfare spending. The basic liberalism of Democratic activists and essential conservatism of Republican activists, compared to the more centrist views of voters, may heighten partisan conflict between Democratic and Republican public figures. On every issue except affirmative action, there is a greater distance between Democratic and Republican Party activists than there is between the two parties' voters (table 8.8: column 1 and column 2).

Republican activists appear to be particularly out of touch with voters, even voters of their own party, compared to Democratic activists. Taking differences between groups of a magnitude of .3 as an arbitrary rule of thumb for substantive significance, we find that Republican activists are more conservative than average voters on affirmative action and gay rights. Republican activists also prefer to spend more on national defense than average voters and are much more in favor of cutting federal spending on welfare, social security, the environment, and public schools. Indeed, Republican activists on every one of these issues except affirmative action are more conservative than even

Table 8.7 Policy Views of Southerners of All States

Issue Agreement or Spending Item	*All Voters* *A*	*Democratic Voters* B	*Republican Voters* C	*Democratic Party Activists* D	*Republican Party Activists* E
Issue agreement					
Death penalty	3.13	2.86	3.38	2.39	3.14
Hiring preferences for blacks	3.18	2.75	3.72	2.83	3.61
Gay job protections	2.31	2.02	2.63	2.06	3.20
Spending item					
Defense	2.38	2.21	2.55	2.11	2.79
Crime	2.65	2.69	2.62	2.44	2.26
Welfare	1.79	1.93	1.58	2.02	1.26
Social Security	2.65	2.80	2.47	2.64	2.06
Environment	2.44	2.63	2.23	2.62	1.80
Public schools	2.75	2.84	2.61	2.81	1.97
(Average *N* Size)	(516)	(236)	(206)	(3,477)	(3,469)

Note: Cell entries are means. The first three rows are agree-disagree items that have been recoded so that scores range from a 1 for most liberal to 4 for most conservative. The last six rows asked whether "federal spending should be increased, decreased, or kept the same for the following areas." These spending items are recoded so that scores range from 1 for spending less to 3 for spending more. The exact wording of these items is found in the appendix. Question wordings and response categories are virtually identical in both the 2001 SGPA study and the 2000 National Election Study.

voters of their own party (table 8.8: column 4 and column 6). Democratic activists are more liberal than average voters on the death penalty and affirmative action, but their preferences on federal spending programs are consistently more in line with the views of average voters than are those of Republican activists. Democratic activists are also pretty close to the views of Democratic voters on every issue except the death penalty, where activists are too liberal for party voters (table 8.8: column 3 and column 5).

The differing issue items used in this regional analysis compared to the two state studies do not permit a more direct comparison, but a common theme nevertheless emerges. The Republican Party organization in the South is a pretty conservative one, while the Democratic organization is becoming a somewhat left-of-center group. Indeed, the Republican Party is so conservative that it is generally more conservative than its own voters. As such, Democratic activists are closer on most issues to the average voter than are Republican activists. Yet, as other chapters of this book have pointed out, both parties' activists have become more polarized over the last decade, as Democrats have become more liberal while Republicans have become

Table 8.8 Differences in Policy Views between Southern Groups

	Polarization		*Proximity to Partisan Voters*		*Proximity to Average Voter*	
Issue Agreement or Spending Item	*Rep. Voters vs. Dem. Voters C–B*	*Rep. Activists vs. Dem. Activists E–D*	*Dem. Activists vs. Dem. Voters D–B*	*Rep. Activists vs. Rep. Voters E–C*	*Dem. Activists vs. All Voters D–A*	*Rep. Activists vs. All Voters E–A*
Issue agreement						
Death penalty	.52	.75	−.47	−.24	−.74	.01
Hiring preferences for blacks	.97	.78	.08	−.11	−.35	.43
Gay job discrimination	.61	1.14	.04	.57	−.25	.89
Spending item						
National defense	.34	.68	−.10	.24	−.27	.41
Crime	−.07	−.18	−.25	−.36	−.21	−.39
Welfare programs	−.35	−.76	.09	−.32	.23	−.53
Social Security	−.33	.58	−.16	−.41	−.01	−.59
Environment	−.40	−.82	−.01	−.43	.18	−.64
Public schools	−.23	−.84	−.03	−.64	.06	−.78

Note: Cell entries are differences between group means. The pairs of columns are identified by capital letters that correspond to the columns in table 8.7. The first three issue items are agree-disagree items coded from 1 for most liberal to 4 for most conservative. The last six items are federal spending items coded from 1 for spend less to 3 for spend more. For the wording of each issue item, see the copy of the questionnaire in the appendix. Positive scores for the three issue items indicate that the first group is more conservative than the second group; negative scores indicate the opposite. For the spending items, positive scores indicate that the first group wants to spend more than the second group; negative scores indicate the opposite.

more conservative. And there are some hot button issues, such as the death penalty, on which Democratic activists are more out of touch with voters than are Republicans.

THE BELIEF SYSTEMS OF SOUTHERN ELITES AND MASSES

Chapter 9 demonstrates how "purists" oriented toward promoting their policy preferences instead of seeking a winning candidate can be harmful to a party's electoral hopes by being less deeply involved in the party organization on a long-term basis. It also points out that conservative Republicans are particularly likely to be purists, while ideology is not related to a purist orientation among Democratic activists. Political activists live a life of politics and are more likely than average voters to view debate over public policy as a struggle between the ideologies of liberalism and conservatism. Such "gladiators" in political struggles may view people and issues as being arrayed along a single dimension with extreme liberals being on the far left of an ideology scale, extreme conservatives being on the far right, and moderates being in the center of the scale. They may believe that every issue, every political leader, and nearly every voter can be placed at a unique point on that single ideological scale. Such a simplistic interpretation of politics can lead to electoral disaster. Barry Goldwater supporters argued that eligible voters could be arrayed along a single ideological dimension and that most Americans were conservative but that few conservatives voted because the major parties did not offer a candidate who was a "real conservative." The Republican Party in 1964 was convinced to rectify that situation by nominating conservative Barry Goldwater, and the party lost the presidential race in a landslide (Converse, Clausen, and Miller 1965).

One of our clearest findings regarding the belief system of today's southerner is the absence of a simple unidimensional, liberal-conservative ideology that encompasses a diverse range of public policy issues. Members of the Alabama public require three dimensions (factors) to organize their preferences on public issues, and even then only 52 percent to 56 percent of the variance in all ten issue items is explained by these three dimensions (table 8.9). Members of the Mississippi public require four dimensions to organize their issue attitudes, though a higher percentage of 64 percent to 68 percent of the variance in all ten items is explained by them. Even each state's elites fail to organize their views into a single "ideology" dimension. Mississippi's party elites require two dimensions, which explain 57 percent of the overall variance in all issue items, while Alabama's party elites require three dimensions, which explain a higher 65 percent of the overall variance. Clearly, any political candidates who rely on a strictly

Table 8.9 Factor Analysis of Mass and Elite Policy Views in Two Southern States

Sample Examined	*No. of Factors Emerging*	*Percentage of Variance in All 10 Issue Items Explained by All Factors*	*Percentage of Variance in All 10 Issue Items Explained by Factor 1*	*No. of Issue Items Loading Most Highly on Factor 1*	*Average Person Correlation Among Items Loading Most Highly on Factor 1*
Alabama					
Voters, high school or less	3	52	22	5	.29
Voters, some college & above	3	56	28	5	.44
Party activists	3	65	34	6	.50
Mississippi					
Voters, high school or less	4	64	29	5	.43
Voters, some college & above	4	68	25	4	.43
Party activists	2	57	39	6	.56

"liberal" or "conservative" campaign appeal run the risk of being irrelevant to a public that views issues in a multidimensional manner.

Party activists in Alabama and Mississippi have belief systems that are organized in terms of either fewer dimensions than voters or into dimensions that include a primary dimension that is a more central one than it is to voters. In Mississippi, only two factors emerge to organize activists' issue attitudes, while the masses require four dimensions (table 8.9). Furthermore, that first factor is a more dominant dimension than it is for voters. It incorporates a greater number of issues (which load on it, being more highly related to it than to any other factor), and responses on those items are more highly intercorrelated than they are for voters (activists tend to take similar or consistent positions on these issues). Alabama activists organize issues into the same number of dimensions as voters, but the first dimension is also a more dominant dimension incorporating issues on which activists have more interrelated or consistent views than do voters. This slightly greater centralized organization of issue beliefs among activists compared to voters nevertheless falls far short of constituting a single, ideological dimension that organizes all public issues. A single ideological dimension organizing all issue opinions would theoretically explain 100 percent of the variance in activists' issue attitudes. In reality, this primary factor explains only 34 percent of the variance in all issue attitudes of Alabama activists and only 39 percent of the variance in Mississippi activists' issue orientations.

Table 8.10 Factor Numbers that Issue Items Are Most Highly Loaded On

Issue	*Alab. Voters (H.S.)*	*Alab. Voters (Coll.)*	*Alab. Activists*	*Miss. Voters (H.S.)*	*Miss. Voters (Coll.)*	*Miss. Activists*
Government aid for women	1	1	1	1	2	1
Abortion	2	2	3	4	2	2
Government services/spending	2*	3*	1	4	4	1
School prayer	3	2	2	3	3	2
Government aid to minorities	1	1	1	1	1	1
Guaranteed job and living standard	2	1	1	1	1	1
Equal role for women	1	2	3	2	2	2
Hiring preferences for blacks	1	1	1	1	1	1
Death penalty	3	3	2	2*	3	2
Handgun control	1	1	1	1	1	1
(*N* size)	(178)	(169)	(720)	(202)	(188)	(709)

Note: Respondents were asked whether they strongly agree, agree, disagree, or strongly disagree with these statements. All issues are coded so that they range from a 1 for most liberal to 4 for most conservative. For the wording of each issue item, see the copy of the questionnaire in the appendix. The designation "H.S." and "Coll." for the voters distinguishes between those with only a high-school education and those with some college education.

*Indicates that the issue item loaded on the factor in a negative direction; all other items loaded on factors in a positive direction.

The lack of a unidimensional, ideological framework that organizes the belief systems of southerners today is reflected in the difficulty of labeling each of the six groups' issue dimensions. The Mississippi elite's belief system appears most understandable, as there are only two factors and one is pretty clearly a social spending dimension and the other is a cultural dimension, but even here some confusion is introduced by affirmative action and gun control loading most highly on the social spending dimension (table 8.10). The Alabama elite belief system is even farther from a unidimensional ideological framework than is the Mississippi elite because of the introduction of a third "women's" dimension. This women's dimension incorporates the two women's issues from factor 2 of the Mississippi elite belief system, leaving a second cultural dimension that includes only school prayer and the death penalty.

Voters have belief systems that are even more complicated and farther removed from a single ideological dimension. Indeed, Alabama college-educated voters even possess a third factor on which social services and the death penalty are loaded in opposite directions, reflecting the existence of death penalty supporters who wish to spend more on social services (table 8.10). Mississippi college-educated voters possess a first dimension that includes diverse economic, race, and cultural issues; a second factor pertaining to women's rights; and a third factor reflecting people who favor school prayer but also the death penalty. High-school-educated Alabamians and Mississippians possess even more confusing belief systems that are unstructured by any single ideological dimension.

CONCLUSIONS

We find that the belief systems of Alabama and Mississippi voters are not sophisticated in a unidimensional, ideological manner but are instead multidimensional and focused around groups of substantively related issues. Rather than being consistently conservative or liberal, many southern voters are conservative on cultural issues such as school prayer and the death penalty but progressive or even "liberal" on social spending programs such as education and health care. Party activists, however, have belief systems that are less multidimensional and more organized around a dominant dimension that includes a diverse range of issues. Activists also have more ideologically homogeneous views than voters, with Democrats being somewhat to the left of center on most issues and Republican activists being a pretty conservative group.

A decade ago the Deep South states of Alabama and Mississippi possessed a political system where Republican Party activists were not only more conservative than the average voter but also more conservative than their own partisans in the general population. Hence, the biracial, ideologically inclusive Democratic Party was clearly closer to the issue preferences of average voters. Since then party activists in both states have become more polarized on issues, with Republican activists becoming even more conservative and Democratic activists becoming more liberal than they previously were. As Republicans have closed the gap in party identification in the general population, a numerically smaller Democratic Party among eligible voters has become a more liberal one (Shaffer and Johnson 1996). Therefore, the Democratic Party organization remains less distant from its party in the electorate, compared to the Republican Party's generally greater distance from its own party electorate.

The result of the growing ideological polarization of the party elites in the modern Deep South states of Alabama and Mississippi is that both party organizations today are somewhat out of touch with the more centrist voter.

Democratic elites are generally more liberal than the average voter, while Republican elites are consistently more conservative than voters. Republican elites, however, as was the case ten years ago, are even farther from the average voter than are Democratic elites. The same situation exists in the South as a whole, as Democratic activists are more liberal than average voters on nearly every public issue, while Republican activists are more conservative on every issue studied, often quite substantially.

The greater overall issue distance between Republican Party elites and average citizens helps explain why the Democratic Party continues to dominate state and local offices in many southern states. However, the leftward shift of Democratic activists found in Alabama and Mississippi, reflecting the party's diminishing base of identifiers in the general population, may help the Republican Party mask its own very conservative nature. Hence, increasing Democratic elite liberalism may eventually enable Republicans to make more gains in state and local offices in various southern states. Moreover, our finding that the overall Democratic advantage does not exist on some cultural (and, in general, more nationally oriented) issues such as abortion and school prayer in Alabama and Mississippi and the death penalty in other states helps explain Republican successes in presidential and congressional elections.

During recent years, American national politics have included several occurrences—involving subjects such as gays in the military, health reform, efforts to cut the budgets of popular social programs, and impeachment—that suggest that today's political party leaders are out of touch with average Americans. Our finding that in both Alabama and Mississippi Democratic and Republican Party elites have become more polarized than their loyal voters and farther removed from the average voter suggests that such occurrences may increasingly characterize southern politics.

Contemporary Mississippi politics illustrates some of these sharp ideological differences and partisan bickering between the parties. Despite a national recession generating declining tax revenues, Democratic Governor Ronnie Musgrove increased state spending to enact an expensive multiyear teacher pay raise, to enhance programs at the state's historically black universities, and to expand the health care coverage of low income children, producing a massive budget deficit. In a special election, voters trounced his "politically correct" move to remove a Confederate symbol from the state flag. Republicans in the 2003 state elections nominated as their gubernatorial challenger wealthy Washington, D.C., lobbyist Haley Barbour, a "hero" of the right wing because of his position as RNC Chair during the 1994 national Republican tsunami. The conservative Barbour proceeded to label government as "the beast" and to oppose any tax increase that would simply "feed the beast" and encourage more government spending. Both campaigns turned negative with one Musgrove television ad even accusing Barbour of lobbying for tobacco companies that "poison our kids." Voters chose Barbour as the lesser of the evils as he garnered 53 percent of the popular vote. After being criticized by the state press for racial insensitivity and for wearing an emblem of the state flag during his campaign, Barbour appointed a biracial transition team and pledged to appoint Democrats and African Americans to his administration.

Ideological and partisan bickering also dominated the Mississippi campaign for lieutenant governor and events leading up to it. Lieutenant Governor Amy Tuck, a centrist elected in 1999, found herself unwelcome in a Democratic Party increasingly influenced by liberal activists. Despite her support for Musgrove's expensive education programs, partisan liberal Democratic activists blasted her stance on congressional redistricting. Tuck had followed the desires of local communities to maintain geographically distinct congressional districts rather than create a district that benefited an incumbent Democrat facing a Republican incumbent (a situation necessitated by the state's loss of one House seat after the 2000 Census). With the Democratic congressman's electoral defeat in 2002 and Tuck's support for enacting limited tort reform, she found it prudent to switch to the Republican Party. The state Democratic Party chair's parting words were to characterize her loss to their party as being like a patient getting rid of "cancer."

After Democrats in 2003 nominated an African American state senator (Barbara Blackmon) to challenge her, Tuck blasted her opponent's liberal legislative record, mentioning the abortion issue. Blackmon responded that she had two children of her own and would not publicly state her "public" position on abortion until the divorced lieutenant governor signed an affidavit proving that she had never had an abortion in her "personal" life. Meanwhile, Tuck ran an ad where she was driving a car stuck in the mud, claiming that "Mississippi's economy is stuck in the mud, so that's why we need more tort reform," prompting Blackmon to charge that the Republican lieutenant governor had herself driven the state's economy into the mud. While most political observers credited Blackmon's landslide defeat to her liberalism and her "getting personal" on the abortion issue, the Democratic candidate and state party chair claimed that many whites were not yet willing to vote for an African American. A second African American Democrat, Gary Anderson, had also lost to a white in the treasurer's race, but some political observers pointed out that Anderson performed well by outpolling Democratic governor Musgrove by 1 percent of the popular vote despite being greatly outspent by his Republican opponent.

Both parties face significant challenges from the more ideologically extreme activists within their own membership, challenges that unless dealt with may produce parties that are increasingly irrelevant to more centrist voters. Further, such a condition poses serious problems to state and local governments within the region. Perhaps the best hope is that pragmatic, centrist-ruling officeholders will emerge once elected to office. Even with such officeholders, however, success is not assured. In 2003, Alabama's Republican governor Bob Riley fought for a tax reform plan that would benefit lower income people and greatly increase funding for the public schools. Riley's efforts placed him on the cover of *Governing* magazine as a Public Official of the Year who provided a real-life Profile in Courage (Gurwitt 2003). However, his tax proposal was soundly rejected by the state's voters. A major factor contributing to this defeat was opposition from Riley's fellow Republicans. Still, pragmatic leadership efforts by elected officials in the South likely remain the best approach for blunting the challenges posed by the region's partisan ideologues.

NOTE

1. The NES data were made available by the ICPSR, which bears no responsibility for the analyses or interpretations presented in this chapter.

CHAPTER

9

Purist versus Pragmatist Orientations among Southern Political Party Activists

Charles L. Prysby

What kinds of people choose to be active in political party organizations? This simple question has been the focus of considerable research. Attention has been given to this topic because many political analysts believe that the nature of the party organization is affected by the characteristics of its active members. In particular, both commentators and scholars have voiced concerns about the problems created by uncompromising ideologues who emphasize ideological purity rather than electoral victory. Some observers view such activists as a force that can impede electoral success by making the party too ideologically rigid. Others argue that the concerns over this new breed of party activist are unjustified. Regardless of which viewpoint is correct, the extent of purist orientations among party activists is a relevant feature of party organizations.

This study analyzes county-level political party activists in the South, drawing on the SGPA data described ealier in this book. The focus of this study is on the purist-pragmatist orientations of these grassroots activists, with the aim of (1) determining how purist or pragmatic contemporary activists are, (2) examining how these attitudes differ across party lines, (3) analyzing the sources of these orientations, (4) examining the consequences of these attitudes for party activity, and (5) analyzing change over time in the levels of these purist-pragmatist orientations in each party. As we discussed in chapter 1, local political party organizations are worthy of study, and analyzing them in the contemporary South is particularly worthwhile given the substantial recent political change in the region. The results of this investigation therefore should be of interest to both scholars interested in political party organizations and scholars concerned about southern politics.

PURIST VERSUS PRAGMATIST ORIENTATIONS

The concept of purism, as used in this study, is a simple one. It refers to the relative emphasis that a party activist places on policy issues versus electoral success. It is an attitude toward candidate and party behavior, and it can be conceptualized as a continuum. At one end of the continuum are extreme purists, who would not have the party or its candidates compromise at all on issues in order to win more votes. These purists favor ideological correctness regardless of its electoral consequences. At the other end of the continuum are extreme pragmatists. They are concerned solely with victory and care nothing about ideological correctness. For them, positions on policy issues are simply a means by which the party's candidates win votes. Few if any activists will be complete purists or pragmatists. Almost all will fall somewhere between these two extremes. But activists can be distinguished by their degree of purism or pragmatism, and those differences are the focus of this study. As a shorthand notation, we can refer to this concept as purism or as purist orientations, recognizing that being low on purism means being more pragmatic.

Scholarly interest in purist orientations was stimulated by Wilson's (1962) study of what he termed "amateur" versus "professional" activists in local Democratic Party organizations. Many subsequent studies focused on this distinction (Conway and Feigert 1968; Dodson 1990; Hitlin and Jackson 1977; Hofstetter 1973; Ippolito 1969; Maggiotto and Weber 1986; Roback 1975; Soule and Clarke 1970). Wilson's concept was multidimensional, including not only purism but also incentives for involvement and attitudes toward party democracy (Hofstetter 1971). This multidimensional nature of Wilson's concept has complicated research on this topic, as some studies have focused on one dimension of the amateur-professional distinction, while other research has focused on other dimensions. For this reason, it seems preferable to use the term purism in this study, as it clearly identifies the dimension that we are examining here. Another aspect of Wilson's concept, the incentives for involvement, is discussed in chapter 10, and the findings of that chapter nicely complement the conclusions of this chapter.

Existing research has focused on several aspects of purism or related concepts. Perhaps the question that has received the most attention is how purism is related to ideology. The general hypothesis is that those who are high in purism are more likely to be ideological extremists, meaning strong liberals among Democrats and strong conservatives among Republicans. This relationship has been found by a number of studies (Abramowitz and Stone

1984; Clarke, Elliott, and Roback 1991; Hitlin and Jackson 1977; Soule and McGrath 1975).

The rise of purist activists who also are ideologically more extreme led some researchers to predict dire consequences for the parties (Kirkpatrick 1976; Ranney 1975; Soule and McGrath 1975; Wildavsky 1965). Much of this research was conducted during the 1960s and 1970s. Subsequent research has taken a different view, finding that even though activists may be more purist, they remain concerned with winning and constrained by strong party loyalties (Abramowitz, McGlennon, and Rapoport 1983; Hauss and Maisel 1986; Maggiotto and Weber 1986; Stone and Abramowitz 1983). Even if earlier concerns about purist activists were overblown, the potential consequences of purist orientations remain a relevant topic. As we shall see from the following analysis, there is reason to believe that these attitudes could have consequences for the behavior of activists.

MEASURING PURIST ORIENTATIONS

Several items in the 2001 SGPA questionnaire were aimed at measuring purist orientations; all of the items are similar to ones used in previous research (Abramowitz and Stone 1984; Prysby 1998b). The question wording and distribution of responses for these items are in table 9.1. All have a good balance between those in agreement and those in disagreement. The most lopsided responses were to the last item, but even here there is about a 60/40 split. Moreover, for each item, those simply agreeing and disagreeing outnumber those strongly agreeing and disagreeing, respectively, so that the distributions are roughly similar across the items. The four items in table 9.1 were used to construct an index of purism, which is simply the mean score on the four items for all respondents who answered at least three of the items.[1] Nearly all of the respondents did answer at least three of the four items, so there is very little missing data on this item. For each item, disagreeing represented the more purist orientation, so scores on the purism index run from 1.0 to 4.0, with the high score representing the most purist orientation.

The distribution of scores on the purism index is displayed in figure 9.1. As we can see, scores are bunched in the middle, with only a small proportion of respondents at either end of the continuum. However, there is substantial variation on this item. About 31 percent of the activists have scores of 3.0 or higher, and around 23 percent have scores of 2.0 or lower. A score of 3.0 would result from disagreeing (but not strongly disagreeing) with each item, and a score of 2.0 would result from agreeing (but not strongly agreeing) with each item.[2] The difference between these two scores seems meaningful. It also is worth noting that nearly one-half of the activists have purism index scores between 2.25 and 2.75, indicating that their responses to the index component items were a mixture of agreement and disagreement.

Table 9.1 Purist-Pragmatist Attitudes among Southern Political Party Activists, 2001

	Percent Responding As:				*Mean*
Question	*SA*	*A*	*D*	*SD*	*Score*
Good party workers support any candidate nominated by the party, even if they basically disagree with the candidate.	14.2	38.3	37.1	10.4	2.44
Party organization and unity are more important than free and total discussion of issues, which may divide the party.	13.0	28.8	45.9	12.3	2.57
Controversial positions should be avoided in party platforms to ensure party unity.	11.3	31.5	45.5	11.7	2.58
Broad electoral appeal is more important than a consistent ideology.	9.5	29.4	48.4	12.7	2.64

Note: The "percent responding" entries are the percent of respondents who strongly agreed (SA), agreed (A), disagreed (D), or strongly disagreed (SD) with the item. These percentages sum to 100 percent by row. The mean score for each item is computed using a four-point scale, with SA = 1 and SD = 4. The Ns for each item run from 6,777 to 7,012.

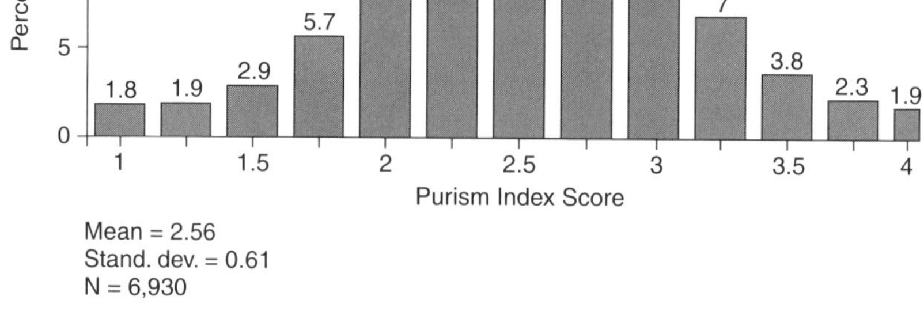

Figure 9.1 Distribution of Purism Index Scores for Southern Political Party Activists, 2001.

Existing research on southern political party activists has found that Republicans tend to be more purist and more motivated by policy issues (Moreland 1990a; Prysby 1998b; Shaffer and Breaux 1998). The same finding emerges from these data. Figure 9.2 shows the distribution of scores on the purism index for Democrats and Republicans. The differences are not enormous, but Republicans do fall more to the right on the bar chart, with a mean score of 2.64, compared to 2.47 for Democrats. Moreover, there are some significant cumulative differences in the distributions. About 36 percent of Republican activists have purism index scores of 3.0 or higher, compared to only about one-fourth of the Democrats. Similarly, around 28 percent of Democrats have purism index scores of 2.0 or lower, whereas less than one-fifth of Republicans have such scores.

PURISM AND IDEOLOGY

The higher levels of purism among Republican activists in the South would seem to follow from the fact that they are more ideologically extreme, at least in comparison to southern Democrats, a pattern discussed in more detail in chapter 5. The consistently conservative position of Republican activists is not surprising, as the growth of the party in the region has been based in large part on a clear conservative message. Democrats, on the other hand, have been a

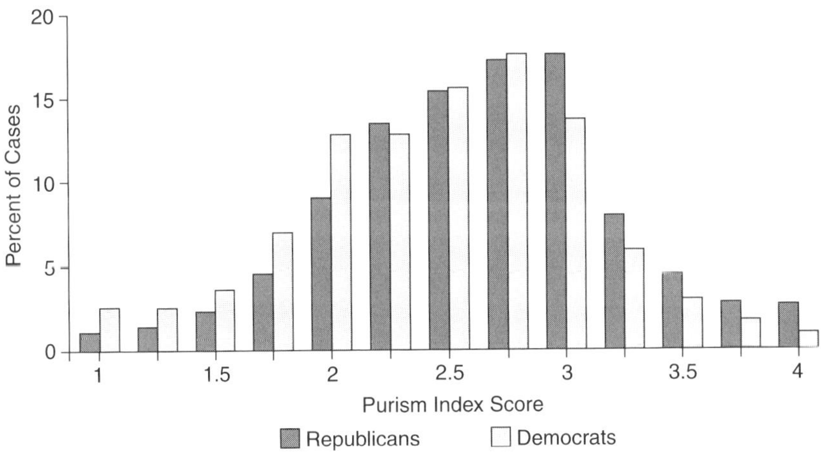

	Democrats	Republicans
Percent 1.0–2.0 (low purism) =	28.4	18.3
Percent 3.0–4.0 (high purism) =	25.7	35.7
Mean purism index score =	2.47	2.64

Figure 9.2 Distribution of Purism Index Scores by Party for Southern Political Party Activists, 2001.

diverse party, encompassing a wide range of ideological groups. In 1991, for example, Republican activists were solidly conservative, whereas Democrats were spread across the ideological spectrum, with a substantial number identifying as conservative (McGlennon 1998b; Steed 1998). In 2001, Republicans were even more conservative, with over 90 percent identifying as such and over one-half calling themselves strongly conservative. Democrats moved to the left over this ten-year period, so that by 2001 close to 60 percent called themselves liberal, although only about one-fifth claimed to be strongly liberal, and many identified themselves as moderate or even conservative (see chapter 5 for more detail on the ideological identifications of activists). If purism is related to ideological extremism, this would seem to explain why Republican activists display higher levels of purism, as compared to Democrats.

In order to test this explanation, we can examine purism levels by ideological position. The relevant data are in table 9.2. Among Republicans, purism is related to ideology. Those identifying as strongly conservative have the highest mean purist score, and the moderates have the lowest. However, the same pattern is not present for Democrats. The "very liberal" Democrats have purism scores that are only slightly greater than the moderate Democrats, and the "somewhat conservative" Democrats have purism scores that are slightly greater than those displayed by the "very liberal" Democrats. Finally, purism scores for Republican activists are higher even when corresponding ideological groups are compared. For example, the "very conservative" Republicans are substantially more purist than are the "very liberal" Democrats. If we measure ideology by using the respondent's responses to specific issues rather than the respondent's self-classification, we get much the same results (Prysby 2003).[3]

Table 9.2 Purist-Pragmatist Attitudes by Ideology and Party for Southern Political Party Activists, 2001

Ideological Classification	*Democrats*	*Republicans*
Very liberal	2.50	*
	[713]	
Somewhat liberal	2.47	2.61
	[1,213]	[51]
Moderate	2.44	2.51
	[948]	[247]
Somewhat conservative	2.55	2.54
	[381]	[1,375]
Very conservative	2.50	2.74
	[99]	[1,742]

Note: The entries are mean scores on the purism index by party and ideological classification. *N*s are in brackets.

*The *N* for very liberal Republicans is so low that these few respondents were combined with those in the "somewhat liberal" category.

Overall, these data suggest three conclusions. First, purism is related to ideological extremism, but the relationship is much stronger for Republicans than for Democrats. Second, the greater ideological extremism of Republican activists is only a partial explanation for their greater purism, as highly conservative Republicans tend to be more purist than highly liberal Democrats. Third, while ideology and purism are related, the connection between these two factors is far from perfect. There are moderates in both parties who are strongly purist, and pragmatists can be found among the very liberal Democrats and the very conservative Republicans.

INTRAPARTY DIVISIONS AND PURISM

In order to better understand the relationship between purism and general ideological orientation, it may be helpful to look at significant cleavages within each party. Among southern Republicans, the split between conservative Christians and others is the division most cited by scholars of southern politics (Baker 1990; Baker, Steed, and Moreland 1998; Green 2002; Layman 1999; Rozell and Wilcox 1996). The emergence of the Christian Right as a political force in southern politics is discussed in more detail in chapter 2. Here we will simply note that in many places, a division emerged between more traditional Republicans, who are concerned with economic issues, and religious conservatives, who emphasize social issues. A common perception is that these conservative Christians form a more ideologically extreme and more purist group within Republican ranks, one that in the eyes of some may hamper Republican electoral success by creating an extremist image for the party.

Table 9.3 presents data on the relationship of purism to religious orientations among Republican activists. Two measures discussed in chapter 2 are used here to identify religious orientations: (a) church attendance and (b) reported closeness to the Christian Right. In both cases, the relationships are clear. Purism increases with more frequent church attendance and with increasing closeness to the Christian Right (except that there is a slight increase in purism among those who feel very distant from the Christian Right). Those who say that they attend church more than once a week and those who feel very close to the Christian Right display particularly high purism scores compared to other Republican activists. In fact, these two groups have purism scores that are substantially greater than the scores of those who selected the next closest response on these two items, that is, those who attend church weekly (but not more than once per week) and those who feel close (but not very close) to the Christian Right.

The relationship between purism and religious conservatism suggests that certain social issues may be especially related to purism among Republican activists. Advancing conservative positions on such social issues as abortion, gay rights, and school prayer are key components of the Christian Right

Table 9.3 Purist-Pragmatist Attitudes by Religious Orientations for Republican Southern Political Party Activists, 2001

	Purism Index		
	Mean	(SD)	[N]
Church attendance			
More than once a week	2.79	(.63)	[904]
Once a week	2.61	(.57)	[1,100]
Almost every week	2.63	(.56)	[422]
Once or twice a month	2.53	(.53)	[357]
Few times a year	2.56	(.60)	[541]
Never	2.53	(.66)	[130]
Closeness to Christian Right			
Very close	2.85	(.64)	[562]
Close	2.70	(.60)	[962]
Neutral	2.54	(.56)	[1,204]
Far	2.54	(.53)	[369]
Very far	2.59	(.59)	[329]

Note: The entries are mean scores on the purism index. *N*s are in brackets. Only Republican activists are included in this table.

political agenda. To investigate the impact of specific issue orientations on purism, the thirteen policy issue items that were used to form the issue orientation index discussed earlier were examined separately. For almost every issue, Republican activists who hold the most conservative position are above average in purism. There are several issues where this tendency is particularly strong: abortion, government action to improve the status of women, gay job discrimination, gun control, aid to minorities, and government services and spending. With the exception of the last issue, all are social issues, and the first three are issues that traditionally have been emphasized by the Christian Right. These findings support the conclusion that high purism scores among Republican activists result much more from strong conservative positions on social issues, especially those stressed by the Christian Right, than from attitudes on economic or social welfare issues. It is important, however, not to exaggerate the connection between purism and religious conservatism among Republican activists. It would oversimplify reality to characterize all southern Republican activists who have strong purist orientations as supporters of the Christian Right or to assume that all supporters of the Christian Right are strong purists.

Among southern Democrats, race is generally considered to be the most divisive issue (Bullock and Rozell 2003b; Glaser 1996; Hadley and Stanley 1998; Moreland, Steed, and Baker 1987). Holding together the biracial coalition that is necessary for victory is a difficult task, a topic discussed in chapter 3. A number of race-related issues potentially can divide this coalition, including questions of affirmative action, aid to minorities, welfare programs, and redistricting. While race may be the dominant cleavage among southern Democrats, it is not strongly related to purism. White southern Democratic activists have a somewhat higher purism score than do their black counterparts (2.50 versus 2.35). More important, on the issue of affirmative action, those who are more supportive are no more purist than those in opposition. Also, those who strongly support government aid to minorities are not higher in purism. In general, purist orientations among Democratic activists are not as clearly tied to issue orientations as they are among Republicans. There are some issues for which more liberal Democratic activists tend to be those who are more purist (e.g., gay job discrimination, school prayer, capital punishment), but there are many other issues where there is little or even no connection between purism and issue position (e.g., abortion, school vouchers, government services and spending, affirmative action, aid to minorities, regulation of managed health care, flat income tax). This, of course, is consistent with the earlier finding that ideological orientation is more weakly related to purism among Democratic activists than among Republican activists.

SHIFTS IN PURISM OVER TIME

The 1991 SGPA survey contained similar items relating to purism. The findings from that study also found that southern Republican activists were more purist than were Democrats (Prysby 1998b). With the benefit of data at two points in time, we can examine shifts in the level of purism for each set of party activists. Table 9.4 presents mean purism scores broken down by year, party, and party position. The party position breakdown is simply between county chairs and other members of the county executive committees. County chairs tend to be more pragmatic than the other activists, either because more pragmatic individuals are selected to be chairs or because the position of chair entails responsibilities that encourage greater pragmatism. Since county chairs comprised a greater proportion of the 2001 sample than they did in 1991, a more accurate picture of changes in purism is obtained by including this breakdown in the analysis.

The patterns of change are interesting. Among Republicans, purism declined somewhat, at least among those who were not county chairs. This decline is not what we would have expected given the earlier observation about how purism is related to ideology. Between 1991 and 2001, Republicans became even more conservative, as reported earlier. This rightward movement in ideological orientations did not produce more purist orientations, a very interesting development.

Among Democrats, the opposite development has taken place. Southern Democratic activists became more purist between 1991 and 2001. During this

Table 9.4 Purist-Pragmatist Attitudes by Party and Organizational Position for Southern Political Party Activists, 1991 and 2001

	1991	*2001*
Democrats		
County chairs	2.28	2.38
	(.64)	(.60)
	[588]	[575]
County exec. comm. members	2.43	2.49
	(.69)	(.61)
	[4,509]	[2,886]
Republicans		
County chairs	2.62	2.60
	(.61)	(.57)
	[584]	[702]
County exec. comm. members	2.73	2.65
	(.64)	(.60)
	[4,023]	[2,767]

Note: The entries are mean scores on the purism index by party and organizational position for 1991 and 2001. Standard deviations are in parentheses. *N*s are in brackets.

period, Democratic activists also moved to the left ideologically, becoming more clearly liberal in 2001 than they were ten years earlier. However, it would be hard to attribute the increase in purism among Democratic activists to the ideological shift because, as we have seen in the preceding analysis, purism is not particularly related to ideology among Democrats.

In order to better understand the sources of these shifts in purism in both parties, a cohort analysis of purism scores in 1991 and 2001 is helpful. Such an analysis allows us to examine two competing explanations for these changes. One possibility is that the shifts in purism result from individuals becoming more or less purist with more years of involvement. Another possibility is that generational (or other) replacement is responsible for the changes. Those who became active after 1991 may have different purist orientations than those who ceased to be active after 1991.

Table 9.5 presents purism scores by year, party, and cohort group (defined by years of activity). By reading along each row, one can see how each cohort group changed between 1991 and 2001. By examining each column, one can see the relationship between years of activity and purism for each point in time. By comparing the 1991 entry with the 2001 entry on the preceding row, one can compare actives with the same years of experience at two points in time.

Table 9.5 Purist-Pragmatist Attitudes by Length of Activity and Party for Southern Political Party Activists, 1991 and 2002

Years Active In:		*Democrats*		*Republicans*	
1991	*2001*	*1991*	*2001*	*1991*	*2001*
—	1–10	—	2.60	—	2.72
			[625]		[892]
1–10	11–20	2.52	2.47	2.80	2.69
		[1,078]	[655]	[1,422]	[758]
11–20	21–30	2.47	2.48	2.72	2.56
		[1,512]	[660]	[1,339]	[619]
21+	31+	2.32	2.36	2.65	2.51
		[2,387]	[762]	[1,755]	[664]

Note: Entries are mean scores on the purism index. *N*s are in brackets.

Among Democrats, there is little change in any cohort over the ten-year period. For example, those who had between eleven and twenty years of activity in 1991, and therefore would have between twenty-one and thirty years of activity in 2001, had a mean purism score that was almost the same at both points in time (2.47 in 1991 versus 2.48 in 2001). Furthermore, purism is related to length of activity. Those with fewer years of activity tend to be more purist. Those who had no more than ten years of activity in 2001 (i.e., those who became active after 1991) have the highest purist score (2.60). This pattern indicates that replacement is the source of the increase in purism among Democratic activists. Those who had been active the longest in 1991 were the most pragmatic. Many of them were no longer active in 2001 (the *N*s indicate a very substantial drop-off), and they were replaced by activists with significantly more purist orientations.

Republicans have a pattern that differs from that for Democrats. Among Republican activists, we see a decline in purism within each cohort. For example, those who had been active from one to ten years in 1991 went from a purism score of 2.80 in 1991 down to 2.69 in 2001. Slightly greater declines took place in the other groups. Moreover, although higher purism is associated with fewer years of activity among Republicans, the 2001 purism score for those who became active after 1991 is only slightly higher than the 1991 purism score for the group with the most years of activity. Replacement is not the source of the decline in purism among Republican activists; the decline is due to changes among existing activists. The small replacement effect actually worked against a decline in purism.

In sum, different processes operated within each party to produce the shifts in purism.[4] Why did individual change lower purism among Republicans while replacement heightened purism among Democrats? We can only speculate on the answer to this question. It does seem that among Democratic activists, those who in 1991 had been active for a very long time were a very pragmatic group. The very low levels of purism among the oldest Democratic activists may have resulted from the very heterogeneous nature of the party in earlier decades. Before Republicans became competitive up and down the ballot, southern Democrats represented a wide range of ideological positions. This fact may have made it very difficult for strong purist orientations to emerge among those who were active at that time. As many of these older local party leaders ceased to be active in the following ten years, it was not surprising that their younger replacements would be more purist. Having grown up in an era during which the Democrats were becoming more ideologically distinct, they inevitably would be more purist. What is interesting, however, is that those who were active in 1991 do not appear to have changed their purist orientations in the subsequent ten years, even though the party was changing its ideological character.

We also can speculate about the reasons for the patterns of change among Republicans. The lack of a generational effect may simply be due to the fact that the older Republican activists were fairly strongly purist already. These were individuals who were motivated to be involved in party politics by issues and who believed in a strong conservative message. The more interesting point is that those who were active in 1991 tended to become less purist by the end of the decade. This change in the orientations of existing activists might be a response to the improvement in electoral fortunes for Republicans, especially farther down the ballot. Having captured majority control of Congress and a majority of the southern congressional seats during the 1990s may have given Republican activists a different perspective. With more Republicans in office and with the prospect of even more gains, such as in state legislative races, Republican activists may have become more concerned about electoral appeal than they were a decade ago. If this is the case, it shows an evolution of the party that was produced by the improved electoral situation, which might in turn suggest further change if the party makes substantial gains in state legislative elections during the next decade.

CONSEQUENCES OF PURISM

Purist orientations may influence how activists are involved in party activities. One hypothesis is that those with more purist orientations are less likely to be involved in party activity. This hypothesis follows from the view that purists will work hard for candidates whom they truly believe in but may be unwilling to be active on behalf of candidates who do not excite them. Purists may be less willing to remain active in the party year in and year out and less willing to devote time to routine aspects of party maintenance. This relationship has not been thoroughly investigated, but some recent research into southern political party activists has found support for this hypothesis (Feigert and Todd 1998b; Prysby 1998b; Shaffer and Breaux 1998).

To investigate this hypothesis, we can examine the relationship between purism and two different measures of party involvement. The first measure is based on respondent reports of the extent of campaign activity, behavior that is covered in more detail in chapter 11. Respondents were asked how active they had been in national, state, and local campaigns (responses were on a four-point scale, from very active to not at all active). A second measure is based on respondent reports of intraparty communication, discussed in chapter 12. A set of eight questions asked the respondents how often they communicated with other individuals or groups in the party (responses were on a four-point scale, from very often to never). An index of party communication was formed by taking the mean score on these items.[5]

Table 9.6 shows how purism is related to these two measures of party involvement for Republican and Democratic activists. Because county chairs tend to be both more active in their party and less purist, as was noted

Table 9.6 Relationship between Purist Orientations and Party Activity by Party for Southern Political Party Activists, 2001

	Purism Level			*Gamma*	
	Low	*Medium*	*High*	*or* r	[N]
Democrats					
Percent very active in:					
Local election campaigns	68	57	51	.17	[2,860]
State election campaigns	56	46	40	.16	[2,838]
National election campaigns	52	45	41	.11	[2,843]
Party communication index score	2.28	2.18	2.12	.14	[2,835]
Republicans					
Percent very active in:					
Local election campaigns	63	55	48	.16	[2,747]
State election campaigns	56	48	44	.11	[2,750]
National election campaigns	57	53	49	.09	[2,750]
Party communication index score	2.43	2.33	2.24	.16	[2,749]

Note: Entries in the first three columns are percentages (for campaign activities) or mean scores (for party communication). For displaying percentages or mean scores, the purism index is trichotomized. The fourth column reports the gamma (for campaign activities) or the correlation coefficient (for the communication index) between the full thirteen-point purism index and the full set of responses to each of the dependent variables. All gammas and correlation coefficients are significant at the .01 level. See the text for details on the individual items. *N*s are in brackets. County chairs have been excluded from this table for reasons discussed in the text.

earlier, they are not included in the following analysis. Their inclusion would tend to inflate the relationship. For ease of presentation, scores on the purist index have been trichotomized into low, medium, and high purism. However, the measures of association reported in the tables (gamma for the campaign activity measures; correlation coefficients for the communication index) are based on the full thirteen-point purism index and the full set of responses to each of the measures of party activity or involvement.

Among Democrats, activists with higher purism scores are less likely to report high levels of campaign activity. The differences here seem meaningful; for example, two-thirds of the Democrats with low purism scores report being very active in local elections, whereas only one-half of those with high purism scores report such activity. Also, those with higher purism scores are less likely to report high levels of communication with others in the party, indicating that their lower level of party involvement and activity is not limited to election campaigns. The pattern for Republican activists is very much the same. Republican activists with high levels of purism are less likely to be very active in campaigns at all levels, and they also are less likely to communicate with others in the party. Moreover, the strength of these relationships, as measured by gamma or *r*, is fairly similar for both Democrats and Republicans.

The consistency of the findings across several measures of party involvement and across party lines indicates that purist orientations do have consequences for the parties. A high concentration of activists with high levels of purism is likely to result in more activists who are involved on a selective basis. The party organization naturally would prefer fully committed activists who will be highly involved on a sustained basis. On this basis, high levels of purism would be regarded as less desirable by party leaders. However, we should note that the impact of purism on involvement is not enormous, and current levels of purism in either party do not seem to present a serious problem. In particular, the higher levels of purism among Republican activists do not seem to result in their being less active than their Democratic counterparts.

CONCLUSIONS

The findings of this study should be of interest to scholars concerned about political party organizations. The analysis shows that there are substantial differences in the purist-pragmatist orientations of grassroots activists. Furthermore, these purist-pragmatist orientations are related to ideology, with more purist activists holding more extreme ideological positions. However, the relationship of purism to ideology is much stronger among Republicans than among Democrats, indicating that the link between these two variables is not as clear and direct as some might think. Purist orientations have potential consequences for party organizational activity. Purists are less likely to be deeply involved in the party organization on a sustained basis, indicating a potential problem if purist orientations rise to a high level. Finally, there was a decline in purism among Republican activists during the 1990s, a change that may indicate that purism is influenced by the environment; more favorable electoral situations may lead activists to become less purist in their attitudes.

This study also has something to say about southern politics. Southern Republican activists tend to be more purist than southern Democratic activists. However, the difference in purism now is less than it was in the early 1990s. While Republicans have become somewhat less purist, Democrats have become a little more purist. This development has occurred even though the parties are ideologically farther apart now than they were a decade ago. Despite the fact that southern Republicans became more strongly conservative, they became less purist, just the opposite of what we might have expected. Among southern Republican activists, purism is related to ideology; strong conservatives are the most purist. In particular, high levels of purism are centered among supporters of the Christian Right and among those who hold strongly conservative positions on social issues, although these are not the only Republicans who have strong purist attitudes. Given the potential divisiveness of Christian Right activists in the party, the decline in purism surely is pleasing to Republicans who emphasize electoral success. Among Democrats, strong purist orientations are not clearly linked to an identifiable group of activists. Contrary to what we might expect, the Democratic activists who are strong purists are not much more liberal than those who are more pragmatic. For this reason, the increase in purism among Democratic activists is not likely to present a problem for the party. In fact, the increase in purism stems largely from the loss of older activists who were very pragmatic in their attitudes. The newer and younger Democratic activists are more purist than the activists whom they are replacing, but they still are less purist than the newer and younger Republican activists.

NOTES

1. The individual items all had four-point response scales (strongly agree, agree, disagree, and strongly disagree). In each case, strongly disagree was the most purist response. Each item was scored to range from 1 (strongly agree) to 4 (strongly disagree), so that a higher mean score on the index would indicate a higher level of purism. The four items have intercorrelations that range from .23 to .48.

2. Of course, disagreeing with each of the four items is not the only way to obtain a 3.0 index score. One could have agreed with two items and strongly disagreed with two others, for example.

3. An index was formed from thirteen questions on specific issues. The thirteen items dealt with a flat income tax, the desirable level of government services and

spending, government action to ensure jobs and good living standards, government regulation of managed health care, affirmative action, government aid to minority groups, government efforts to improve the situation of women, job discrimination against gays, handgun control, capital punishment, school vouchers, abortion, and school prayer. The individual items all had four-point response scales (strongly agree, agree, disagree, and strongly disagree). Each item was scored to range from 1 (most liberal response) to 4 (most conservative response), so that a higher mean score on the index would indicate a more conservative orientation on the issues. For a more detailed report of this analysis, see Prysby (2003).

4. There are some limitations to these data. The only measure of length of party activity was a question that asked respondents how long they had been active in politics beyond just voting. Of course, such political activity might represent campaign work for candidates, or it might represent involvement in a political party but not at the level of executive committee membership. Thus, those who said in 2001 that they had been active in politics for over twenty years might not have been a member of a county party executive committee in 1991. For this reason, our cohorts are not exactly comparable groups, but this measure of the length of involvement in party activity should be close enough to suffice. Moreover, a complementary analysis yields similar results. Instead of defining the cohort groups in terms of years of activity, we can define them by age. An analysis similar to that reported in table 9.5 but using age cohort groups was conducted, and the results of that analysis support the conclusions drawn from table 9.5. Among Democrats, there is very little change in purism for any age cohort between 1991 and 2001; their over-increase in purism during this ten-year period is not a result of increasing purism of existing activists. On the other hand, purism steadily declines with age in both 1991 and 2001, so the younger Democratic activists in 2001 were substantially more purist than the older activists whom they were replacing. Republican activists have a different pattern. Each of the age cohorts declined in purism between 1991 and 2001. Generational replacement contributed nothing to this decline; the youngest Republican activists in 2001 are slightly more purist than the oldest activists in 1991. See Prysby (2003) for a more detailed report of this analysis.

5. The eight items asked respondents whether they communicated very often, often, seldom, or never with different party members (e.g., county chair, county executive committee members) or elected officials (e.g., local officials, state officials). See the questionnaire for more details on these items. The items were scored from 4.0 (very often) to 1.0 (never), so that a higher mean score indicates more communication.

CHAPTER

10

Motives for Involvement among Grassroots Party Activists in the Modern South

James Newman, Stephen D. Shaffer, and David A. Breaux

A timeless concern of scholars studying political party organizations has been to identify what motivates people to join and become active in the organization. Researchers have identified three major incentives that precipitate joining the organization—to attain a material benefit, to influence the making of good public policy, and to enjoy socializing with other people. People motivated by differing incentives can exert an important effect over the direction of the political party. An organization heavily dominated by ideologues who wish to enact their extreme versions of good public policy could see its hopes of electing candidates diminished by the nomination of candidates who are too ideologically extreme for the average voter. On the other hand, an organization dominated by those seeking material benefits may quickly atrophy as members soon discover that the party organization has limited rewards to distribute to its members.

It is particularly important to study how these incentives motivate people to join the party organizations in the modern American South. The South today is a truly critical region in determining the future of two-party competition in the United States. Since the mid-1960s, every American president who was a Democratic Party member hailed from the South. In the 1994 congressional midterm elections, the Republican Party finally captured a majority of U.S. House seats from the eleven southern states, which was instrumental in making the Republican Party the majority party in the U.S. House of Representatives for the first time since 1954. What motivates people to join the party organizations in the South may shed light on the types of candidates that the parties offer in future years and how competitive the parties will be. Our chapter focusing on incentives for being members of the organizations complements the study of the purist and pragmatic orientations of party organization members in chapter 9, which provides a fascinating analysis of differences between the parties and changes in orientations over the past decade, with clear implications for electoral competition in the modern South.

The study of incentives for activism in the party organizations of the new South has become even more timely over the past decade, as the Republican Party continues to make electoral gains over the historically dominant Democrats. By the year 2003, Republicans controlled both state legislative chambers in Florida, Virginia, Texas, and South Carolina; controlled the state senate in Georgia; tied the Democrats in the state house in North Carolina; held 45 percent of the seats in both Tennessee chambers; and, for the first time since Reconstruction, reached the 40 percent mark in the Alabama house and the Mississippi senate (Shaffer, Pierce, and Kohnke 2000; updated by authors). Our current analysis is further enlightened by a comparison with a similar study conducted ten years ago, as we can assess how the party organizations have changed over this most recent, turbulent decade (Shaffer and Breaux 1998).

PAST STUDIES OF MOTIVATIONAL INCENTIVES FOR ACTIVISM

In the modern era of multimillion-dollar campaigns, party workers remain the "foot soldiers" who work to get the party's supporters to the polls to elect candidates to office. Given the considerable burden on a person's time and peace of mind that such heavy responsibilities may place on the individual party organization member, one must ask why anyone would want to join a party organization. In other words, "What's in it for me?" The answer to this question is vital in sustaining political party organizations that are essential to American democracy. It is also important in explaining how American democracy operates and what kinds of choices it offers to voters.

Our theoretical framework is that of incentive systems in organizations more generally, a pioneering theory developed by Peter B. Clark and James Q. Wilson over forty years ago. Clark and Wilson (1961) argued that political and nonpolitical organizations were distinguished by the different kinds of incentives that explained why people became members. They also pointed out that shortages in the availability of some incentives would force the organization leader to seek out other ways of attracting members, and that chief executives of organizations could rely on a diversity of incentives rather than just one.

Clark and Wilson proposed that incentives could be classified into three broad types: material, solidary, and purposive. Material incentives were tangible rewards that could be translated into a monetary value. Examples of organizations employing material incentives were a taxpayer's association that sought to reduce the taxes of its members and a neighborhood improvement group that sought beautification projects that raised the property values of its members. Historically, urban political machines, such as Mayor Richard Daley's in Chicago, that rewarded their members with patronage jobs and government contracts were clearly relying on material incentives to attract party workers. Solidary incentives were intangible rewards lacking monetary value but instead were based on personal satisfactions derived from the act of associating with other people. Individuals might join a group because they found it enjoyable to socialize with the other people in the group, or because they had a sense of identification with the group, or because they derived some social status from being a group member. Such incentives for joining the group were not dependent on the outcome of what the group actually accomplished; therefore, members were typically flexible about the goals of the group. An example of a solidary organization offered by Clark and Wilson was a women's luncheon group that members found to be sociable and fun. Purposive incentives also provided intangible rewards, but unlike solidary incentives these rewards were derived from the outcomes of group membership instead of merely the act of being a member. Organizations might seek such goals as eliminating corruption and inefficiency in government or some other change in public policy. Examples of purposive organizations provided by Clark and Wilson were reform and social protest groups, such as the NAACP.

While Clark and Wilson provided an invaluable theoretical framework, it was left to other scholars to apply this theory to modern political party organizations by systematically collecting information about party workers and scientifically testing this incentives theory with real-world data. Studying party organizations in a rural Illinois county and a suburban Maryland county, Conway and Feigert (1968) learned that people sought precinct leadership positions primarily for purposive reasons, such as a belief that it was their civic duty or because of a desire to influence public policy. Studying political party precinct and ward chairs in five communities in North Carolina and Massachusetts, Bowman, Ippolito, and Donaldson (1969) found purposive incentives most important, solidary incentives second in importance, and material incentives least important reasons for why these organization leaders were active in politics.

A related question is not merely why people join a party organization but whether their motivations change over time. Some studies suggest an evolution away from purposive incentives over time, as organization members find material and purposive goals difficult to achieve and increasingly enjoy such solidary rewards as social contacts and intense party loyalty that organizational membership provides (Conway and Feigert 1968; Bowman, Ippolito and Donaldson 1969). Other studies suggest a greater stability of incentives over time, with purposive incentives generally being most important in motivating people to first become politically active and remaining the key motivation keeping people politically involved as the years go by (Ippolito 1969; Hedges 1984; Miller, Jewell, and Sigelman 1987).

While a number of scholars have focused on why people join or remain in a party organization, very few have examined what may motivate people to rely on a particular type of incentive. For instance, why are some people more motivated by solidary incentives to join a party, while others are motivated by purposive incentives? Bowman and Boynton (1966a) found that party leaders in their five communities often came from politically active families and that they were more likely to have been encouraged by other party members to seek the party leadership post rather than to have taken the initiative by themselves. In a study of party delegates attending the 1972 and 1976 Republican national convention, Roback (1980) found that the two most important reasons that delegates first became interested in politics were socialization by their family and their own interest in issues or social movements. Neither study specifically examined why one person may be motivated by one incentive to become active in politics while another person may be motivated by a different incentive.

In the previous Southern Grassroots Party Activists Project, Steed and Bowman (1998) found that party members coming from politically active families and who have been active in the party organizations for a longer time were more likely to be consistently strong partisans (feeling intensely identified with and close to their party at both the national and state levels) than other organization members. Unlike the other studies cited, Steed and Bowman also specifically examined a possible source of purposive, solidary, and material incentives. They found that strong partisans were motivated to become involved in party work by all three types of incentives, while weak partisans rated purposive, solidary, and material incentives as less important motivations.

Given the importance of the solidary-material-purposive incentives theoretical framework to the study of political party organizations, it is somewhat surprising that so few studies have sought to examine what impact these different incentives may have on the behavior of the organization. One pioneering work is by Conway and Feigert (1974), who found that the effect of purposive motivations on task performance of party workers in two counties studied depended on the environment. In the county having the higher socioeconomic level, party members motivated by purposive incentives relied more on communicating the party's principles to voters, while in the lower socioeconomic county, party members motivated by the same incentive focused more on increasing voter turnout. The impact of incentives, particularly purposive incentives, on support for presidential candidates has been more extensively studied, as political activists motivated by purposive incentives are particularly likely to favor more ideologically extreme candidates who mirror their own issue orientations (Roback 1980; Abramowitz, McGlennon, and Rapoport 1983; Hedges 1984).

A more comprehensive examination of the sources as well as the effects of solidary, purposive, and material incentives was the previous 1991 study of county executive committee members of the Democratic and Republican Parties in the eleven southern states (Shaffer and Breaux 1998). Southern grassroots party activists as a whole were motivated more by purposive incentives than by solidary or material incentives. Republicans were more motivated than Democrats by purposive incentives, while Democrats were reliant more on solidary and material rewards. Incentives were also found to be related to party members' issue orientations and to whether their stylistic orientation was pragmatic or purist. All three incentives appeared to motivate party members to be more actively involved in political campaigns at local, state, and national levels, an intriguing finding that suggests that a diverse range of personal motivations, even potentially divisive purposive incentives, may contribute to the vitality of party organizations.

INCENTIVE DIFFERENCES BETWEEN THE SOUTHERN PARTIES AND OVER THE YEARS

We now turn to an analysis of the 2001 SGPA data, a data source described in chapter 1. Examining all sixteen questionnaire items that measured solidary, material, purposive, and other reasons for seeking one's current party position, we find that the motives cited as "very" important are candidate-centered, purposive, and party-oriented motivations. Nearly three-fourths of workers of both parties sought their current party positions to support a candidate they believed in or because of a concern over issues, and over 50 percent cited party attachment or viewing party and campaign work as a vehicle for influencing government. Examining each group of incentives separately for the two parties combined, purposive incentives were most frequently cited, with over 50 percent of aggregated party workers rating each of the three purposive indicators as very important (table 10.1: last column). Solidary incentives were second in importance, cited as very important by 19 percent to 58 percent of party activists. Material incentives were least important, rated as very important less than 20 percent of the time. The relative importance of these incentives for seeking one's current party position is very similar to what it was among southern grassroots party activists

Table 10.1 Incentives for Seeking Current Party Position

Incentive	*Democrats*	*Republicans*	*All*
Solidary			
Political work is part of a way of life	43.0	34.8***	38.9
Strong attachment to party	61.0	54.9**	57.9
Friendship/social contact	32.6	25.9***	29.2
Family's involvement in politics	23.2	14.3***	18.7
Excitement of campaign	31.5	25.9***	28.7
Material			
Building a personal position in politics	10.7	9.2*	9.9
Being close to important people	22.8	13.9***	18.3
Making business contacts	6.0	2.7***	4.4
Obtaining community recognition	12.7	7.8***	10.2
Purposive			
Campaigns influence government	51.2	55.2***	53.3
Parties influence government	53.8	60.6***	57.3
Concern with public issues	70.9	75.2***	73.0
Other			
Friendship with a candidate	17.6	13.1***	15.3
Friendship with a party official	22.3	20.6*	21.5
Community obligation	42.3	34.7***	38.5
Belief in particular candidates	73.0	73.7	73.3

Note: The instruction given was "Rate each of the following in terms of its importance in your personal decision to seek your current party position." Entries are the percent rating the item as very important. Complete wordings of these incentive questions can be found in the questionnaire in the appendix of this book.

***t-test for differences between Democratic and Republican means significant <.001
**t-test for differences between Democratic and Republican means significant <.01
*t-test for differences between Democratic and Republican means significant <.05

ten years ago and to what was found in previous studies (Shaffer and Breaux 1998; Bowman, Ippolito, and Donaldson 1969; Hedges 1984).

Despite this commonality of incentive rankings among Democrats and Republicans, there is a difference in emphasis on incentives between the two parties. Republicans are somewhat more likely than Democrats to rate all three items measuring purposive incentives as very important, while Democrats are more likely than Republicans to rate all five solidary items and all four material items as very important (table 10.1). These results were also found among southern grassroots party activists ten years ago, and they suggest a rational response by the two southern parties to their political environment. Southern Republicans who found an ideologically compatible home in a national Republican Party that was basically conservative were therefore motivated by issue-oriented purposive incentives to join their state or local

Table 10.2 Change in Incentives for Seeking Current Party Position

Incentive	*Democrats*	*Republicans*	*All*
Solidary			
Political work is part of a way of life	0	−2	−1
Strong attachment to party	4	2	3
Friendship/social contact	2	5	3
Family's involvement in politics	2	0	1
Excitement of campaign	3	4	3
Material			
Building a personal position in politics	1	1	1
Being close to important people	−3	−2	−3
Making business contacts	0	0	−1
Obtaining community recognition	−1	1	−1
Purposive			
Campaign influence government	6	0	4
Parties influence government	7	0	3
Concern with public issues	8	5	7
Other			
Friendship with a candidate	0	−1	−1
Friendship with a party official	0	1	1
Community obligation	0	1	1
Belief in particular candidates	11	9	10

Note: Entries are the change between 1991 and 2001 in the percent who rated the incentive as very important. Positive cell entries indicate how much the incentive became *more* important over time, while negative cell entries indicate how much the incentive became *less* important since 1991.

party organization, while Southern Democrats who were often out of touch with their "liberal" national party found themselves relying more on interpersonal solidary or self-seeking material incentives that were divorced from policy concerns. One potential problem for the southern Republican Party stemming from its members' greater focus on purposive incentives is conflict within the organization, as heated disputes over the goals of the party may cause significant divisions among party members. Divisions within each party's membership in terms of "pragmatic" versus ideological "purist" goals, and how these conflicting orientations may affect the party's candidates chances of getting elected, were examined in chapter 9.

The essential stability of incentives among southern grassroots party activists over the past ten years is illustrated in table 10.2, which directly compares responses on each questionnaire item between 1991 and 2001. Change among all activists (table 10.2: last column) was within four percentage points on every item except candidate support and a concern with issues, two items that workers in both parties cited as increasingly important to them. A more careful examination of change over time for the three incentive groups yields some interesting patterns. Solidary incentives appeared to become slightly more important to both parties' activists since 1991, suggesting an increasing relevance of the political parties to southerners as organizations that provide intangible rewards resulting from socializing with other people. Yet purposive incentives also became increasingly important over the years, particularly among Democrats, suggesting a slight change in the nature of the southern Democratic Party into a more ideologically concerned organization. Today's Democratic activists are beginning to mirror the more issue-oriented nature of the southern Republican Party, though in an opposing ideological direction. These results are consistent with the findings in chapter 9 that Democrats have become somewhat more purist over the past decade and that both parties have become more ideologically polarized.

In the remainder of this chapter, we examine how party members having these solidary, material, or purposive incentives for joining the organization may differ in other ways from members lacking such motivations, and how these incentives may shape party workers' activities. We employ a data reduction technique called principal components factor analysis with varimax rotation, which combines all sixteen incentive items into three major scales (factors) that correspond to the solidary, material, and purposive incentives. These three factors accounted for 47 percent of the variation in the sixteen items' intercorrelations, and the questionnaire items loading (related or correlated to) most highly on each factor are identical to how the items are grouped together in table 10.1 and table 10.2. Four other items either loaded on a minor "personal friendship" factor or loaded on more than one factor and for theoretical reasons are omitted from our analyses.

For ease of interpretation before performing the factor analysis, we recoded each of the motivational incentives to range from a low score of 1 for the incentive being not important at all to a high of 4 for the incentive being very important. Therefore, in all succeeding analyses, groups having the *higher* mean factor scores rate that incentive as *more* important than groups with a lower mean factor score. For instance, Republicans, who have a mean purposive factor score of .12, rate purposive incentives as more important than Democrats, who have a mean purposive factor score of −.12. Solidary incentives are more important to Democrats (mean solidary scale score of .13) than to Republicans (mean solidary scale score of −.13). Finally, material incentives are also more important to Democrats (mean material scale score of .08) than to Republicans (mean score of −.08).

In each of the following three sections, we determine through multiple regression whether differences in the means of the incentives across theoretically relevant groups are substantively significant. This advanced methodological technique permits us to rule out other possible explanations for why membership in a group is related to an incentive being cited as important.

POSSIBLE SOURCES OF MOTIVATIONAL INCENTIVES

The considerable literature on political socialization points out the importance of parents as a key source of the average citizen's political orientations, though fewer studies have examined whether parents affect the socialization of political party activists. Bowman and Boynton (1966a) and Roback (1980) are notable exceptions, though their finding that party officials and national convention delegates often come from politically active families does not explain *why* or *how* the family is an important motivating factor. Steed and Bowman (1998) find that having a politically active family can result in party organization members being consistent and intense partisans, though they also are not able to identify specifically why or how the family is influential over their offspring. We examine two important attributes of parents—their political activity levels and their party identifications—with questionnaire items asking respondents to recall whether their "parents or other relatives" had "ever been active in politics beyond merely voting" and to recall each parent's "party affiliation at the time you were growing up." Parents were either active or not active in politics, and we combined each parent's party identification item into one scale of parental partisanship that measured whether both parents held the same party as their offspring or whether one or both parents adhered to a different party.

Only the solidary incentive scale was related to having politically active parents, as respondents with more politically active parents rated solidary incentives as more important than those with politically inactive parents, as one might expect from the interpersonal nature of the solidary incentive that includes the family as one personal influence (table 10.3). Patterns varied depending on whether respondents shared their parents' partisanship. Party workers who kept the same partisanship as their parents may have been socialized by their families to value solidary incentives, which included attachment to a political party, as such incentives were more important to activists sharing their parents' partisan orientations than they were to respondents who disagreed with their parents' partisanship. On the other hand, party workers who disagreed with their parents' party identifications rated purposive incentives as more important than did those having the same party as their parents. This suggests that the ideological views of some respondents may have led them to choose to adopt a political party different from their family. For instance, conservative Republicans whose parents had been Democrats were likely motivated by their concern over issues to defect and to join the modern Republican Party.

Party organizations must have members in order to exist and to carry out their functions. They either actively seek out new members or decide whether to admit people who take the initiative to join their group. Bowman

Table 10.3 Incentives and Possible Sources of Activism

Predictor	*Solidary Scale Score*	*Material Scale Score*	*Purposive Scale Score*
Parents active in politics	.22*	.01	.01
Parents not active politically	−.22	−.01	.00
Both parents same party as self	.15*	.05	−.08*
One or both parents different party	−.15	−.05	.08
Self-starter in 1st partisan activity	.02	.03	.11*
Others urged 1st partisan activity	−.08	−.07	−.26
Self-starter seeking current posit.	.03	.10*	.10
Others urged current position	−.07	−.11	−.12
No position previously held	−.13*	−.01	−.09*
One position previously held	−.02	.11	.04
Two positions previously held	.22	−.01	.17
County chair holder	.10	−.01	.09
County committee member	−.02	.00	−.02

Note: Table entries are means for the solidary, material, and purposive scales for each of the groups listed at the left. All *N* sizes are a minimum of 839, and usually much higher.

*Multiple regression coefficient is significant at the .001 level. All six sets of predictors listed in the table were included in three multiple regression equations that predicted party workers' scores on the solidary, material, and purposive scales.

and Boynton (1966a) found that most local party officials were recruited by other party members rather than self-recruited, while Hulbary and Bowman (1998) found that both mechanisms were important in recruiting southern grassroots party activists to their party office. Generally unexamined by the literature is how these differing recruitment mechanisms may be related to the incentives that motivate party members, though Hulbary and Bowman's (1998) discovery that purposive and material incentives are more related to self-recruitment while solidary incentives are more linked to recruitment by others is a notable exception.

We examined the differences between being a self-starter or being recruited by others for two separate decisions—the decision to "first become involved in party politics" and the decision to "seek your current party position." For both questionnaire items, those who responded that a major consideration was that they had decided "to participate/run pretty much on my own" were classified as self-starters, while other party members were regarded as being more influenced by other people, such as party or elected officials. Interestingly enough, while we also find that being a self-starter is related to material and purposive incentives, these incentives are related to differing decisions. Being a self-starter in the initial decision to become involved in party politics is related only to purposive incentives, while being a self-starter in the later decision to seek a party position is significantly related only to material incentives (table 10.3). Those urged by other people to become active in party politics and to seek a party position rate purposive and material incentives as less important than self-starters, and there are no significant differences in solidary incentives between self-starters and those urged by other people to be active.

Other studies have generally agreed that purposive incentives are particularly important in motivating people to become active in partisan politics, while disagreeing over whether purposive or solidary incentives are most important in keeping people active as the years go on (Ippolito 1969; Hedges 1984; Miller, Jewell, and Sigelman 1987; Conway and Feigert 1968; Bowman, Ippolito and Donaldson 1969). Our chapter suggests that there may indeed be an evolution in one's motivations as one gains more experience in party politics, but that change is most likely to occur among self-starters. Self-starters may first become active in party politics for the idealistic and perhaps naïve belief that they can really "make a difference" in public policy, but as time goes on their realization of their limited impact on governmental policies may cause some to seek out more tangible material rewards for seeking a party office. It is intriguing that while other studies have argued that material incentives are so scarce that party members rely more on solidary incentives as reasons to remain in the organization, we find in the modern South that material rewards remain important incentives, as least for self-starters.

Since previous studies found that purposive or solidary incentives were especially important motivations for remaining active in a party organization and we found that material incentives were important to one group of activists, it is logical to expect that incentives may be related to two likely rewards for years of party experience—becoming a county party chair instead of remaining a mere county committee member, and having previously held party or appointed public office positions. Whether respondents were county chairs or county committee members was one of the items collected by the survey; we created a scale from three questionnaire items to measure the number of previous party or appointed public office positions held. We found that incentives were related to leadership experience in the party organizational activity, though not to the current occupation of a leadership position.

Those reported to have previously held two or more party positions or appointed public offices rated purposive and solidary incentives as more important incentives, compared to those who had held no previous party or public position (table 10.3). Furthermore, differences in the importance of purposive and solidary incentives between those having and those lacking previous positions remained after controlling for other possible correlates of incentives. Holding previous political positions was significantly related to solidary and purposive motivations, even when taking into account other factors such as having politically active parents with the same partisanship as their own, being self-starters in the decisions to first become active in party politics and to seek one's current position, and being a county chair or committee member. Such was not the case for currently being a county party chair instead of a committee member. While county chairs rated purposive and solidary incentives as more important compared to mere county committee members, this distinction disappeared after multivariate controls for all of the other predictors listed in table 10.3. A likely explanation is that county chairs tended to hold more previous party/public positions than did county committee members, and number of previous positions was the more important of the two factors in shaping reliance on solidary and purposive incentives.

To summarize, each of the three incentives for occupying one's current party position are related to social background and experience factors in different ways. Having politically active parents may socialize party workers into the importance of solidary reasons for being active in a party organization. Those who continue to hold the same party identification as their parents are even more motivated by solidary incentives, while those who have switched from their parents' partisanship are more motivated by issue-oriented purposive incentives. Issues often motivate a person to take the initiative to first become involved in party politics, as self-starters rate purposive incentives as more important than do other party workers. As time goes on, party workers find multiple reasons for remaining active in the organization. Those holding two or more previous party or public positions, for example, rate solidary and purposive incentives as more important than do those in their first party position. In addition, those who took the initiative to seek their current party position regard material incentives as more important motivations than those who weren't self-starters.

INCENTIVES AND ISSUES, PARTISANSHIP, AND PURISTS VERSUS PRAGMATISTS

It is important to examine how incentives are related to party workers' issue orientations, their partisan intensity, and their purist versus pragmatic orientations toward party work for two major reasons. First, it sheds light on why people become and remain active in a party organization, a vital question for the very existence of the organization. For instance, what would induce a liberal or even a moderate person to be active in a party as conservative as is today's southern Republican organization? Second, how issues or partisanship are related to motivational incentives can have important implications for the operation and electoral success of the party. If people motivated by a purposive orientation to join a political party are also more ideologically extreme than other party members, and if their decisions as party members are motivated more by a desire to promote their ideological goals rather than by a more pragmatic desire for their party to win at any cost, then they may support candidates who are so distant from the average citizen that they are unelectable.

The literature disagrees over whether people view policy issues in a unidimensional manner consistent with a liberal-conservative framework, or in a multidimensional framework reflecting different issue areas (see chapter 8 for a review of this controversy). With fourteen agree-disagree issue items, seven federal spending on programs items, and one ideological self-identification question in our questionnaire (see the appendix for the specific items), we addressed this controversy and simplified the data by conducting a principal components factor analysis with varimax rotation. Two factors explained 51 percent of the variance in the items' inter-correlations, with cultural issue items loading most highly on the first factor and domestic economic spending items loading most highly on the second factor. After examining two correlation matrices of the items loading most highly on the first and second factors, we determined that agree-disagree items on school prayer, the death penalty, and defense spending best measured cultural issues and that federal spending on the public schools, social security, and health care best measured domestic economic issues. The economic and cultural issue scales were created through simple summation, as the codes of items within each issue area ranged in the same ideological directions, and each scale was trichotomized so that each category contained virtually the same number of categories. The resulting scales resulted in more cultural conservatives (53 percent) than economic conservatives (11 percent), and more economic liberals (50 percent) than cultural liberals (13 percent), as one would anticipate from the policy views of average southerners (Breaux, Shaffer, and Cotter 1998).

The relevance of incentives to party activists, particularly purposive incentives, clearly depends on the dominant ideology of the national party. Among Democrats, both economic and cultural liberals were more motivated by purposive incentives to seek their current party position than were economic or cultural moderates or conservatives (table 10.4). Among Republicans, economic conservatives were more motivated by purposive incentives than were economic moderates or liberals (table 10.5). A similar pattern existed in the 1991 study, illustrating how contemporary southerners who are motivated by issues to be active in the party organizations are able to sort themselves out into the party that best reflects their policy preferences—liberals joining the Democratic Party and conservatives joining the Republican Party (Shaffer and Breaux 1998). Other studies have also pointed out how party sorting by ideology is going on in the modern, two-party South but have not examined the role that incentives play in this process (Steed 1998).

Issue differences in material and solidary incentives are less clear. Material incentives do appear to provide some motivation for ideological deviants to remain in a party organization where they are in the philosophical

Table 10.4 Incentives and Issues, Partisan Intensity, and Purist-Pragmatist Attitudes among Democrats (Means of Incentive Scales)

Predictor	*Solidary Scale Score*	*Material Scale Score*	*Purposive Scale Score*
Economic liberal	.22*	.09	−.06*
Economic moderate	−.19	.05	−.36
Economic conservative	NA	NA	NA
Cultural liberal	.18	−.24*	.22*
Cultural moderate	.18	.07	−.19
Cultural conservative	.04	.37	−.27
Inconsistent partisan	−.48*	.28*	−.43*
Consistent partisan	.30	.03	−.04
Low purism index score	.39*	.31*	−.26*
Medium purism index score	.14	.02	−.08
High purism index score	−.13	−.07	−.02

Note: Table entries are means for the solidary, material, and purposive scales for each of the groups listed at the left. All *N* sizes are a minimum of 512, and usually much higher. NA indicates an insufficiently large *N* size for analysis, as there were only fifteen economically conservative Democrats in the sample.

* The multiple regression coefficient is significant at the .001 level. All four sets of predictors listed in this table and the six predictors in table 10.3 were included in three multiple regression equations that predicted Democratic Party workers' scores on the solidary, material, and purposive scales.

minority. Thus, culturally conservative Democrats rate material incentives as more important than do culturally liberal or moderate party colleagues, while economically liberal Republicans rely more on material incentives than do economically moderate or conservative Republicans. However, material incentives are unrelated to economic issues among Democrats or to cultural issues among Republicans. Solidary incentives may bear some relationship to issue orientations for Democrats, as economic liberals rate these incentives as more important than do nonliberals, though cultural issues are not significantly related to solidary incentives among Democrats. The relationship between solidary incentives and issue orientations among Republicans is contradictory, as economic liberals and cultural conservatives rate solidary incentives as more important than do other issue groupings. In conclusion, while purposive incentives help activists sort themselves out into the party that best represents their positions on issues, material incentives operate to ensure that the parties are broader tents than they otherwise would be. Such broader tents retain at least some ideological dissenters, thereby enhancing the party's electoral hopes of attracting more middle-of-the-road voters.

Table 10.5 Incentives and Issues, Partisan Intensity, and Purist-Pragmatist Attitudes among Republicans (Means of Incentive Scales)

Predictor	*Solidary Scale Score*	*Material Scale Score*	*Purposive Scale Score*
Economic liberal	.04*	.18*	−.08*
Economic moderate	−.08	−.09	.08
Economic conservative	−.40	−.25	.37
Cultural liberal	NA	NA	NA
Cultural moderate	−.28	−.02	.04
Cultural conservative	−.06	−.09	.14
Inconsistent partisan	−.58*	.15*	−.09*
Consistent partisan	.03	−.13	.16
Low purism index score	.21*	.20*	−.01*
Medium purism index score	−.10	−.02	.07
High purism index score	−.32	−.27	.24

Note: Table entries are means for the solidary, material, and purposive scales for each of the groups listed at the left. All *N* sizes are a minimum of 529, and usually much higher. NA indicates an insufficiently large *N* size for analysis, as there were only twenty-one culturally liberal Republicans in the sample.

*Multiple regression coefficient is significant at the .001 level. All four sets of predictors listed in this table and the six predictors in table 10.3 were included in three multiple regression equations that predicted Republican Party workers' scores on the solidary, material, and purposive scales.

Intensity of one's partisanship can benefit a party by encouraging party members to actively support the organization (Steed and Bowman 1998) or by dampening the potentially divisive effects of ideologically extreme party activists in the nomination of candidates (Abramowitz, McGlennon, and Rapoport 1983). This topic is discussed in chapter 6. We defined intense or consistent partisans as those having strong identifications with their party at the national and state levels who also voted for their party's presidential candidates in 1996 and 2000, while all other party workers were classified as less intense or inconsistent partisans. Party workers' responses on all four of these questionnaire items were correlated at the Pearson *r* level of .95 or higher, justifying combining these items into a single scale.

We found that consistent partisans in both parties were more motivated by purposive and solidary incentives than were inconsistent partisans (table 10.4 and table 10.5), confirming Abramowitz, McGlennon, and Rapoport's (1983) argument that a purposive orientation does not conflict with one's psychological commitment to a party or with support for nominating an electable candidate. Inconsistent partisans in both parties were more motivated by material incentives compared to consistent partisans.

The 1991 study found that organization workers who were more partisan tended to have higher motivations on all three incentives than did less partisan workers. Therefore, the greater material motivation of inconsistent Democratic and Republican partisans today suggests that workers less psychologically committed to the party, as well as ideological dissidents, are able to find some tangible reason for remaining active members of their party.

To measure the concept of purist-pragmatist orientations, or the extent to which party workers value promoting ideological purity over party unity and a broad electoral appeal that helps to win elections, we employed the trichotomized index of purism discussed in chapter 9. Workers in both parties who were low on the purism index, and therefore more pragmatically geared toward "winning" elections, rated material and solidary incentives as more important than did other party workers. This was also the case in our 1991 study, suggesting that the pragmatic politician who avoids divisive issues remains an important element in party politics in the South. Members of both parties who were high on the purism index and therefore more geared toward seeking ideological purity, rated purposive incentives as more important than did other party members (table 10.4 and table 10.5). This is a change from the 1991 study, when purposive incentives were more important to purist Republicans but not to purist Democrats. It is also interesting to recall chapter 9's finding that Democrats today are a little more purist in orientation than they were in 1991. The emergence of purposive incentives as a motivating force for purist Democrats as well as Republicans suggests that the modern southern Democratic Party may be on its way to becoming as "ideological" an organization as the conservative southern Republican Party was in the latter years of the twentieth century.

Issue orientations, partisan consistency, and purist orientations are clearly interrelated with purposive, solidary, and material incentives among today's southern party activists. Activists who are from the ideologically dominant wing of their party, who are consistent partisans, and who are purists all rate purposive incentives as more important in their decisions to seek their current party positions, compared to other members of their party. In both party organizations, consistent partisans and pragmatists rate solidary incentives as more important than do inconsistent partisans and purists. More marginalized party members, such as inconsistent partisans and those in the ideological minorities of their parties, who also tend to be pragmatists, are motivated more by material incentives. These patterns persist even after controlling for other possible explanations for differences in incentives among issue, partisan, and purist groups of activists. Six multiple regression equations that predicted the solidary, material, and purposive scale scores for each party separately from the ten predictors in the preceding and current sections of this chapter yielded the statistical significance levels noted in table 10.4 and table 10.5.

THE BEHAVIORAL EFFECTS OF MOTIVATION INCENTIVES

Studies have shown how solidary, material, and purposive incentives can motivate people to become politically active and to join a party organization, but very few scholars have explored whether such incentives influence the activities of people after they join the organization. Conway and Feigert (1974) argued that party organization members who were motivated by purposive incentives stressed different campaign activities in differing environments, stressing communicating the party's principles to voters in higher socioeconomic environments and seeking to increase voter turnout in lower socioeconomic areas. Shaffer and Breaux (1998) discovered that all three incentives may play a role in motivating party members to generally be more involved in political campaigns at the local, state, and national levels than other party members, though they did not examine the specific ways that members became more active.

While not linking up specific activities with party members' solidary, material, or purposive incentives, previous studies do suggest what types of activities we should focus on. Bowman and Boynton (1966b) and Ippolito and Bowman (1969) found that local party officials viewed their roles in terms of the most important things that they did in their jobs, and those tasks were primarily campaign-related tasks and party organizational work. Bowman and Boynton (1966b) also explored the communication patterns of party officials, finding that party members were more likely to talk to local and state public officials about public problems than to national officials, though no study has attempted to link communication patterns with the three types of incentives.

We examined southern grassroots party activists' behaviors in their general role as party organization members, in their more specific roles as activists in political campaigns, and as members of an intraparty communications network. Party workers were asked how important each of fourteen different activities was in their "current party position," and whether they performed each of thirteen different activities in "recent election campaigns." They were also asked how frequently they communicated with the county and state party chairs; the county, state, and national executive committee members; and government officials at the local, state, and national levels. To identify conceptually distinct types of party and campaign activities and of communication patterns, we subjected all three sets of questions to three separate principal components factor analyses with varimax rotations.

Activities performed by party workers in their current party positions did indeed form two separate factors or dimensions—working with voters and maintaining the party organization. Activities performed in recent election campaigns formed three separate dimensions, which we labeled as working with media to get the candidate's message out, mobilizing voters, and supporting the candidate by distributing literature or raising money. Intraparty communication formed two separate dimensions—communications at the local level where 73 percent of activists fell into the high communications category, and communications at the state and national levels where only 17 percent fell into the high communication group. To relate these two communication scales, the two party position activity scales, and the three campaign scales to solidary, material, and purposive incentives, all seven of these scales were dichotomized into higher and lower activity groupings.

Our examination of a diverse range of party and campaign activities reinforces the conclusions of our 1991 study. Party members who were most motivated by all three types of incentives—material, purposive, and solidary—were more politically active than those less motivated by each type of incentive. Party activists who report that working with voters and maintaining the party organization were important activities that they performed in their current party positions have higher scores on the solidary, material, *and* purposive incentive scales, compared to party members who view these tasks as less important parts of their jobs (table 10.6).

Table 10.6 Incentives as Possible Sources of Activism (Means of Incentive Scales)

Predictor	*Solidary Scale Score*	*Material Scale Score*	*Purposive Scale Score*
Activities of current position			
High level of work with voters	.25*	.16*	.21*
Low level of work with voters	−.15	−.09	−.13
High level of organization work	.31*	.23*	.28*
Low level of organization work	−.19	−.12	−.15
Recent campaign activities			
Very active in candidate support	.18*	.00	.18*
Less active in candidate support	−.20	.00	−.21
Very active in voter mobilization	.20*	.14*	.16*
Less active in voter mobilization	−.09	−.07	−.07
Very active in media work	.15*	.13*	.13*
Less active in media work	−.09	−.07	−.07
Communication with other party members			
High communication with locals	.13*	.07*	.10*
Low communication with locals	−.36	−.17	−.30
High communication, state/national	.36*	.19*	.21*
Low communication, state/national	−.09	−.04	−.04

Note: Table entries are means for the solidary, material, and purposive scales for each of the groups listed at the left. All *N* sizes are a minimum of 1,036, and usually much higher.

*Multiple regression coefficient significant at .001 level. All of the predictors in table 10.7 were included in the multivariate analyses yielding these significance levels.

Furthermore, each incentive continues to exert direct effects on party work with voters and on organizational matters, even after controlling for the other two incentives and all other possible sources of party activism (the predictors included in table 10.3, table 10.4, and table 10.5). Purposive incentives appear to be the most important motivating force for both activities, while solidary incentives are second in importance, and material rewards are the least important incentive (table 10.7). Other factors exerted limited or inconsistent effects on activity levels, with county chairs and those previously holding party positions being more active than other party members on organizational maintenance tasks but not in working with voters,

Table 10.7 A Multivariate Analysis of Sources of Activism

	Activities of Current Position		*Recent Campaign Activity*			*Communications with Other Party Members*	
Predictor	*Voter Work*	*Organ. Work*	*Media Work*	*Voter Work*	*Candid. Support*	*Local Individuals*	*State/Nat'l Individuals*
1. Parents' political activity level	−.03*	−.01	.02	−.01	.04*	.06*	.05*
2. Parents same party as self	.03*	0.0	−.02	.02	−.04*	.05*	−.01
3. Self-starter in first partisan activity	−.05*	−.02	.03	−.01	.02	.01	−.02
4. Self-starter in seeking current party position	.05*	.01	.02	.02	−.01	.01	.01
5. No. of previous party or public positions	−.01	.07*	.18*	.10*	.10*	.15*	.15*
6. County chair or committee member	−.03*	.15*	.22*	.09*	.10*	.14*	.13*
7. Economic issues	−.17*	−.06*	.02	−.05*	.05*	.01	.02
8. Cultural issues	.09*	.10*	−.01	−.02	.01	.07*	.04*
9. Partisan consistency	.01	.01	.00	.04*	.07*	.06*	.07*
10. Purism index	−.03	−.06*	−.01	−.01	−.01	−.03*	−.03*
11. Material incentives	.11*	.15*	.11*	.12*	.02	.12*	.08*
12. Purposive incentives	.22*	.23*	.07*	.10*	.17*	.16*	.09*
13. Solidary incentives	.17*	.19*	.09*	.10*	.16*	.16*	.10*
Adjusted *R*-squared	.13	.18	.14	.07	.11	.16	.10

Note: Each column pertains to a different dependent variable. Cell entries are Betas or standardized regression coefficients. Variables are recoded so that high scores are as follows: all dependent variables have high activity levels; material, purposive, and solidary incentives are important; parents are politically active; parental party is same as respondent; self-starter in first partisan activity/current party position; held multiple previous positions; was a county chair; was a conservative on economic/cultural issues; is a consistent partisan; is high on purism index. Democrats and Republicans were combined in these multiple regression analyses because of the similar results obtained when each party was examined separately.

*Indicates statistical significance at the .05 level.

and liberals on economic issues but conservatives on cultural matters being slightly more active on both types of tasks.

Turning to acts performed in recent election campaigns, party organization members who are more active in working with the media or with voters during campaigns rate material, purposive, and solidary incentives as more important, compared to organization members who are less active in these types of campaign activities (table 10.6). Regarding direct support of candidates during a campaign, those more active rate purposive and solidary incentives as more important than do the less active, while no significant differences exist in terms of material incentives.

Once again, these patterns are unchanged after simultaneously controlling for all three incentives as well as all other possible explanations for campaign activity. Material rewards are the most important incentives for working with voters and with the media, but purposive and solidary incentives also directly stimulate these campaign activities (table 10.7). Purposive and solidary incentives are essentially equally important in encouraging candidate support activities, while material rewards do not affect the amount of this type of campaign activity. Political experience and leadership positions also affect campaign activity levels, as county chairs and those having previously held party/public positions were more active in all three types of campaign activities than were county committee members and those with less party experience. Indeed, these two nonincentive factors were more important than all three incentives in explaining campaign work with the media and were equally important as incentives in explaining campaign work with voters, though less important than purposive and solidary incentives in explaining candidate support.

Given the highly motivated nature of the more active members of the party organization, one might expect that those who have the most communication with other party and public officials are similarly motivated by a diverse set of incentives. Such is indeed the case, as party organization members who often communicate with local or state/national political figures rate material, purposive, and solidary incentives as more important than do organization members who seldom or never communicate with political figures (table 10.6).

Once again, each type of incentive remains a statistically significant predictor of both levels of intraparty communication, even after simultaneously controlling for the other two incentives and all other possible sources of communication activism. Purposive and solidary incentives are essentially equal in importance in shaping frequency of communications, while material incentives are slightly less important (table 10.7). Once again, leadership as a county chair and having previous party/public experience are also important factors, being virtually as important as the incentives in shaping frequency of local communication, and more important than the three incentives in shaping frequency of state and national communications. Parental socialization and party intensity/consistency may also play a role in interpersonal communication levels, as members whose parents were politically active and members who were intense and consistent partisans have more communications with local, state, and national figures than do less intense partisans having less active parents.

Our 1991 study suggested the intriguing possibility, unexamined by the literature, that such diverse motivations as purposive, solidary, and material incentives could *all* encourage organization members to be active workers for the party rather than to be party members in name only. This chapter provides strong evidence that all three incentives do indeed encourage party members to be active in a number of different ways. As party organization members, all three incentives encourage members to work with voters as well as to work on maintaining the party organization. These incentives also inspire party members to be active in political campaigns in many ways—directly supporting candidates, working to get the campaign's message out, and mobilizing voters. Even between campaigns, material, purposive, and solidary incentives stimulate party members to communicate with other party or governmental officials at the local, state, and national levels. Previous studies of southern grassroots activities have found that county chairs are more active than other party members on party maintenance activities and on campaign activities (Feigert and Todd 1998; Clark, Lockerbie, and Wielhouwer 1998). Rather than doing the work of the party entirely by themselves, today's county chairs and those who have previously served in such leadership posts can seek to motivate other members of their party to actively support the party's goals by relying on policy appeals, an appeal to material self-interest, and the appeal of working with others in a common cause.

CONCLUSIONS

Clark and Wilson (1961) theorized that people joined organizations in general to obtain material, purposive, or solidary incentives, while subsequent scholars applied the theory specifically to party activists and learned that they were particularly motivated by purposive and solidary incentives to be active in party organizations (Conway and Feigert 1968; Bowman, Ippolito, and Donaldson 1969; Ippolito 1969; Hedges 1984; Miller, Jewell, and Sigelman 1987). Our study finds that southern grassroots party activists are most motivated to seek their current party positions by purposive incentives and are also motivated by solidary rewards but are least influenced by material gains. We also find different emphases for the two major parties, as Republicans are somewhat more motivated by purposive incentives, while Democrats are generally more influenced by solidary and material rewards.

Fewer studies have sought to explain why different people are motivated by different incentives, or how those incentives may affect people after they become members of a party organization. One exception is Steed and

Bowman (1998), who found that strong partisans were motivated to become involved in party work by all three types of incentives, while weak partisans rated purposive, solidary, and material incentives as less important motivations. Other exceptions focus on the types of presidential candidates supported during the nomination process, as party activists motivated by purposive incentives were found to be more likely to back more ideologically extreme candidates (Roback 1980; Abramowitz, McGlennon, and Rapoport 1983). Our chapter finds that family socialization, being a self-starter, and being experienced in party matters affect what incentives most motivate a person to seek a party position. We also find that issue orientations, partisan intensity and consistency, and having a purist or pragmatic orientation affect reliance on particular incentives. Despite people having differing incentives for seeking a party position, all three incentives have a similar effect on how active one is as a party member. Relying on any of these incentives can stimulate an organization member to be active in maintaining the organization, communicating with other party members, and helping to elect the party's candidates to office.

Scholars debate over the effects of incentives on the vitality of an organization. Clark and Wilson (1961) claim that purposive incentives may be harmful by generating divisive debates over the goals of the organization. Abramowitz, McGlennon, and Rapoport (1983) point out that party activists motivated by purposive incentives may nevertheless be intensely committed to their party and that such intense partisan commitments may encourage support for electable candidates. We found that purposive incentives help to maintain organizational distinctiveness by sorting activists into the party that is most ideologically appropriate for them, as liberal Democrats and conservative Republicans were more motivated by purposive incentives than were their party colleagues. Material incentives helped to ensure that the party did not become too ideologically narrow, as ideological dissidents in both parties were motivated more by material rewards than were other party members.

While the operation of these incentives is generally positive for the vitality of a party organization, some developments suggest a more challenging future for the parties in the South. Purposive incentives—always important in the southern organizations—appear to have become even more important over the last ten years. While pragmatists rate solidary and material incentives as particularly important, purists are more motivated by issue-oriented purposive incentives. The increased importance of purposive incentives, as well as their association with an orientation that stresses ideological purity over nominating candidates who are electable, suggests that both parties may face some challenges in offering attractive candidates to the southern electorate in future years, a topic addressed in chapter 8.

CHAPTER

11

Party Activists in Election Campaigns

Robert E. Hogan

The central task of a political party is to elect its slate of candidates to positions of power within the government. To that end, party organizations perform a variety of different activities, from registering voters and raising money to recruiting candidates and waging get-out-the-vote drives. Previous studies demonstrate that these activities have many important consequences, not the least of which is an influence on election outcomes (Cotter et al. 1984; Frendreis, Gibson, and Vertz 1990). For these reasons, a close examination of campaign efforts by parties and the factors that motivate them are important to our overall assessment of party organizations in American politics.

The present analysis considers the role of grassroots party activists in campaigns and elections in southern states. In what ways do these party operatives participate in campaigns? Are some of the tasks they perform more common than others? What differences do we see between the two parties in terms of specific tasks performed as well as in overall effort? Have there been any changes in the extent of activity over the past decade? Given the movement toward two-party competition in most southern states, do we see any increase in activities by the parties?

In addition to questions of what party operatives do in campaigns, the analysis is also concerned with those factors responsible for shaping these activities. What characteristics associated with activists themselves are responsible for their degree of involvement? For example, how important is their position within the party (county chair or county committee member) to their overall participation? How do such factors compare with the perceptions of party strength and factionalism in affecting the extent of their campaign-related work?

Results of the analysis demonstrate that campaign and election activities by those at the grassroots have increased over the past decade, although the increase has been much greater among Democrats. When we hold constant a large number of variables, we find that Democratic activists are engaged in a larger number of campaign activities than their Republican counterparts. Whereas Democrats lagged behind in the early 1990s, by 2001 they appear to have caught up to the gains made by Republicans during the 1980s and early 1990s. These findings suggest the groundwork continues to be laid for a more competitive two-party system throughout the southern region.

POLITICAL PARTIES IN AMERICAN ELECTIONS

The role of political party organizations in U.S. elections has changed dramatically over the past century. The growth of primaries, the use of the secret ballot, and the diminished influence of political patronage have altered many of the traditional sources of party strength (e.g., Epstein 1986; Mayhew 1986; Reichley 1992). Parties are no longer the sole agents of candidate recruitment, and many of their grassroots functions have been supplanted by campaign professionals such as pollsters and media consultants versed in "new-style" electioneering practices (Agranoff 1976; Wattenberg 1994). Elected officials often create their own "permanent campaigns" (Blumenthal 1982) for the purposes of communicating directly with constituents from election to election. Overall, the party-centered era of politics has given way to a decidedly more candidate-centered environment (e.g., Menefee-Libey 2000; Salmore and Salmore 1989).

But such changes have not led to the demise of party organizations. As Paul Allen Beck (1997, 247) notes, "many have come to the conclusion that the traditional grassroots party organization has become technologically obsolete—that it has been superseded by newer, more efficient, and more timely avenues and techniques of campaigning . . . [b]ut this conclusion overlooks the great adaptability of the party organizations." Over time, the needs of candidates created a way for parties to assume a larger role in political campaigns. Beginning in the 1970s, a resurgence occurred in national and state parties, in part as organizations began to adopt a more service-oriented approach. As Bibby (1999b, 195) notes, "[m]ost state party organizations today bear scant resemblance to either the traditional party organization of early in this century or the weak organizations that were so characteristic of the 1950s and early 1960s." Parties on many different levels now provide a variety of services to candidates to aid in their election efforts including polling, fund-raising assistance, and media services (Aldrich 1995; Cotter et al. 1984; Reichley 1992). Thus, parties have embraced changes in campaign practices by carving out new sources of strength for their organizations.

Studies from a variety of perspectives demonstrate the important role played by parties in the election process. Studies of the past focused primarily on the grassroots and labor-intensive efforts of parties to get out the vote and found mixed results for these activities (e.g., Cutright and Rossi 1958; Katz and Eldersveld 1961; Kramer 1970). However, more recent work shows that party efforts can and do have important electoral consequences, (e.g., Cotter et al. 1984; Frendreis et al. 1990; Wielhouwer and Lockerbie 1994), particularly through their provision of services to candidates in congressional (Herrnson 1988) and state legislative elections (Hogan 2003). The present analysis continues this inquiry by examining party efforts from the perspective of those at the grassroots who are most often responsible for carrying out these activities.

Building on earlier work that examined such questions in the early 1990s, the goal is to understand the vitality of these organizations and perhaps gain a perspective on their role in elections. Such questions are particularly instructive in southern states where two-party competition continues to rise. Whereas previous studies found parties in southern states to be less active than in other parts of the county (Cotter et al. 1984; Mayhew 1986), results of an analysis in early 1991 found southern parties active in a number of campaign-related areas (Clark, Lockerbie, and Wielhouwer 1998). This study found that "most organizations are active in campaigns, and the emergent Republican activists tend to be more involved than their Democratic counterparts" (Clark, Lockerbie, and Wielhouwer 1998, 133). A decade later, do we find local parties playing a similarly active role? Have their activity levels increased, decreased, or stayed about the same? Are the factors that were once responsible for variations in party activity still having an important effect?

ACTIVITIES AT THE GRASSROOTS

What role do grassroots party activists play in campaigns and elections? Table 11.1 provides the percentages of county chairs and county committee members by political party who engage in thirteen different types of activities. Summary measures for overall activity levels (means and medians) are also reported for each group.

Some campaign activities are clearly more common than others. For example, nearly 70 percent or more of county chairs and committee members alike report distributing campaign literature, distributing posters or lawn signs, and contributing money to campaigns. However, very few activists report purchasing billboard space, utilizing public opinion surveys, or helping to maintain a campaign Web site. Thus, the most widely used techniques

Table 11.1 Campaign and Election Activities, 2001

	Democrats		*Republicans*	
	Chairs	*Members*	*Chairs*	*Members*
Organized door-to-door canvassing	39.3	32.8	36.8	33.5
Organized events	65.8	35.5	70.2	39.4
Arranged fund-raising activities	53.6	28.5	61.7	33.4
Sent mailings to voters	52.0	46.1	58.3	53.8
Distributed campaign literature	79.3	69.0	80.8	74.4
Organized telephoning	48.3	31.8	48.8	34.4
Purchased billboard space	9.2	3.3	9.4	3.8
Distributed posters or signs	84.4	70.2	90.2	75.1
Contributed money	78.5	67.9	86.2	77.2
Conducted voter registration drives	42.9	30.7	33.7	27.8
Utilized public opinion surveys	13.7	9.8	14.7	11.6
Dealt with media	53.2	18.3	60.0	23.2
Helped maintain or create Web site	8.8	4.3	11.3	5.6
Mean number of activities	6.2	4.3	6.5	4.7
Median number of activities	6	4	7	4

Note: Entries represent the percent who engaged in the activity, unless otherwise indicated.

are also some of the most traditional forms of electioneering. "New style" or "modern" techniques (opinion polls and Web sites especially) are used much less frequently. Such a finding is surprising given the attention in the literature to the increasing use of modern electioneering practices.

One clear pattern that emerges is the higher levels of involvement reported by county chairs compared to county committee members within each activity category. Among Democrats, chairs report an average of 6.2 forms of participation while members report only 4.3. For Republicans, a very similar picture emerges, where the average number of activities for chairs is 6.5, while for members the average is only 4.7. In addition to these overall trends, it is important to note that on some dimensions the difference between chairs and members is quite substantial. For example, nearly twice as many chairs than members report organizing campaign events and arranging fund-raising. Chairs are nearly three times more likely than members to report having "dealt with campaign media." Such higher rates of involvement reported by chairs are not surprising given that many of the differences are among activities that can be considered managerial in nature. Analyses of the 1991 data reported similar findings and noted that such differences represent a division of labor within the organization that may be interpreted as evidence of a relatively sophisticated organization (Clark, Lockerbie, and Wielhouwer 1998).

Another pattern emerging from table 11.1 involves the different levels of activity reported by Democrats and Republicans. The 1991 survey found that Republicans were more involved in a larger number of areas. Results

Table 11.2 Change in Campaign and Election Activities, 1991 to 2001

	Democrats		*Republicans*	
	Chairs	*Members*	*Chairs*	*Members*
Organized door-to-door canvassing	+9.6	+7.0	+4.9	+2.9
Organized events	−0.9	+5.6	+0.2	+5.6
Arranged fund-raising activities	−3.6	+3.1	+1.1	+5.3
Sent mailings to voters	+11.5	+13.1	+4.5	+6.7
Distributed literature	+6.4	+8.5	+2.1	+3.0
Organized telephoning	+2.7	+2.7	−8.0	−4.2
Purchased billboard space	+0.8	−1.2	+0.2	−1.6
Distributed posters or signs	+13.6	+18.0	+10.5	+9.8
Contributed money	+1.3	+8.1	+0.8	+4.3
Conducted voter registration drives	+7.8	+10.4	+0.1	+4.8
Utilized public opinion surveys	+0.9	+0.7	−1.8	−0.9
Dealt with media	+7.7	+0.3	−4.0	+0.6
Average number of activities, 1991	5.78	3.68	6.40	4.51
Average number of activities, 2001	6.20	4.28	6.51	4.66

Note: Entries represent the change between 1991 and 2001 in the percent who engaged in each activity.

from 2001 suggest that this pattern has not changed dramatically over the last decade. Among chairs, Republicans are more active than Democrats in eleven of the thirteen areas examined (among members they are more active in twelve areas). It is only for voter registration drives where Democratic chairs and members report higher levels of activity than their Republican counterparts. For the mean scores, Republicans chairs report an average of 6.5 activities, while Democratic chairs report 6.2. Among members, the mean is 4.7 for Republicans and 4.3 for Democrats. Overall, the Republican activists appear to utilize a wider assortment of campaign and election techniques.

A key question is whether or not campaign activities performed by party activists have changed over time. Given the continued rise of two-party competition in most southern states, we would expect to see increased rates of involvement by activists in both parties. It would seem that Republican activists would be working to continue establishing their party's presence while Democratic activists would be working to counteract these changes. To determine if such trends are present, table 11.2 shows the percentage point change in reported activist involvement (positive or negative) in the twelve areas where comparisons are possible.[1]

The results show convincingly that party activity increased over the last decade. While there were reductions in the use of some activities, for the vast majority of items, reported use grew over the time period. For some activities these changes were minor (e.g., organizing campaign events and public opinion surveys), but for others the increases were substantial (e.g., sending mailings and distributing posters or lawn signs). Comparing the average number of activities in each time period at the bottom of the table demonstrates changes in overall activity levels. While average increases are reported for all four categories of respondents, it is important to note that the largest increases occurred among Democrats (for both chairs and members). Such findings suggest that during the 1990s, the period of Republican growth in campaign activities began to plateau while Democratic activities grew, perhaps in response to Republican electoral gains.

Now that we have some sense of the types of campaign activities that are used by those at the grassroots, we now turn to factors that explain variations in overall party campaign activities. It will be interesting to see if the different levels of activity seen between chairs and members and between the two parties persist in multivariate analyses where controls are included for a variety of variables.

FACTORS RESPONSIBLE FOR VARIATION IN PARTY EFFORTS

Previous analyses have identified a number of variables responsible for variations in levels of campaign activity at the grassroots (Clark, Lockerbie, and Wielhouwer 1998). Many of these same factors are examined here along with several additional variables. Of particular concern is whether factors responsible for differences in activity in the early 1990s continue to have a similar effect. Ordinary least squares analysis is used to determine the relative impact of independent variables on overall levels of campaign activity. Such a statistical analysis enables us to gauge the independent impact of each variable while holding constant all the other effects. The dependent variable is a summary measure for the number of activities reported by each respondent. The activity scores range from a low of 0 to a high of 12.

Anticipated Effects

Perceptions of the local party organization are expected to play a large role in campaign involvement. Where local parties are strong, we expect to see those at the grassroots engaged in a larger number of activities. To gauge the level of party health, an index was created based upon responses to five questions about the local party's strength. Respondents were asked to use a five-point scale to indicate whether the local organization was stronger or weaker than a decade ago on several dimensions: overall strength, campaign effectiveness, ability to raise funding, the role in recruiting candidates for office, and efforts to develop the organizational skills of workers. Responses were combined into an index where values ranged from 0 to 20, with higher values indicating greater organizational strength. It is expected that where local parties are perceived to be stronger, more effort will be directed toward campaign and election activity.

Another feature of local parties likely to influence activity is the degree of factionalism within the party. From one perspective, one might expect that greater conflict within a party would reduce the organization's ability to engage heavily in campaign activities. It would seem that fractured parties would have difficulty deciding where to direct organizational effort and activists would simply participate at a lower rate. However, previous studies show that greater factionalism is, in fact, positively related to party activity. Clark, Lockerbie, and Wielhouwer (1998, 131) explain this finding from their examination of 1991 survey responses by saying that "rather than driving activists out through disenchantment, [factionalism] acts as a catalyst for increased activism, perhaps in a competition for control of that party." It will be interesting to see if this effect is present in 2001 or if the influence of factionalism has subsided over time. This variable is measured based upon responses to a question concerning perceptions of factionalism within the party on a four-point scale. The variable ranges from 0 (low factionalism) to 3 (very high factionalism).

A second set of factors expected to influence campaign activity involves the attitudes and beliefs of party members. A major component of belief structure relevant for understanding variation in campaign activity is the degree of pragmatism or purism expressed by a party member. Previous studies define purists as those concerned more with issues and ideological correctness while pragmatists are those interested primarily in political victory (see chapter 9 for a more detailed discussion of this concept). Research finds such attitudes are important in explaining a wide variety of other attitudes and behaviors among party activists (e.g., Abramowitz and Stone 1984; Prysby 1998b; Wilson 1962) as well as those specific to campaign activity (Clark, Lockerbie, and Wielhouwer 1998). Given these previous findings, we should see greater activity among pragmatists than among those who espouse a purist orientation. Here, the purism versus pragmatism continuum is operationalized as an index of party purism based upon responses to questions about the role of party organizations in elections. The index ranges from 1 to 4 with increasing values of the index representing greater support for the party purism position. If the results match our expectations, the coefficient in the multivariate analysis should be negative.[2]

Closely linked to the party purism dimension is political ideology. Do activists describe themselves as liberal, conservative, or moderate in their orientations? It would seem that those who are more extreme in their ideology would be motivated to engage in a larger number of campaign activities. Indeed, previous studies identify such a linkage—activists whose orientation is closer to that of their national party exhibit greater involvement (Clark, Lockerbie, and Wielhouwer 1998). This means that among Democrats, the liberals should be more active than moderates or conservatives, while among Republicans, conservatives should be more active than moderates or liberals.

A variable measuring activist ideological placement relative to the dominant orientation of his or her party is created based upon self-placement on a seven-point ideological scale. Higher values on this measure indicate greater agreement with the national party's base and should be positively related to the measure of campaign activity.

A final attitudinal factor likely to affect campaign activity involves the rationale that activists had for seeking their current political party position. For many activists, the desire to take part in campaigns is a major reason why they decided to become part of local organizational efforts in the first place. For these individuals, we would expect to see a much higher rate of campaign involvement. To determine if there is such an effect, the survey asked respondents to indicate how important a list of reasons were to the "personal decision to seek your current party position." Included among the many reasons was the following statement: "I see campaign work as a way to influence politics and government." It is expected that those who identify this as an important reason will be more likely to engage in a greater number of campaign activities. Answer options were on a four-point scale and were coded from low to high levels of importance.

The third set of factors likely to affect campaign activity is a party member's experience in holding public office. Activists who have served in an elected or appointed office probably have a higher level of practical knowledge concerning politics that can be brought to bear on their roles within the party. Activists with such experience are likely to have a greater stake in election outcomes and may have expertise that those involved in campaigns want to tap. For this reason, we expected that those who have held office are likely to be more involved in campaign activities, all other things being equal. Past office experience is measured using a dichotomous variable to indicate whether or not the activist reports having held an appointed or elected office.

In addition to past offices held, anticipated office holding is also examined as a possible explanation for level of campaign activity. Party members who report that they "expect to run for public office in the future" may be more inclined to take part in electoral activities since such experience may help them in their future endeavors. A dichotomous indicator is used to measure expectations about running in the future.

A final set of factors expected to influence participation in campaigns involves the characteristics of the activists themselves. Earlier it was shown that political party and position within the local organization (chair or member) affect the level of activity reported. In general, chairs are more active than members, and Republicans are more active than Democrats. Used as independent variables in a multivariate model, it will be interesting to see if these variables continue to have this effect.

Along with leadership position and political party, several other demographic characteristics of the activists are also examined. Age, gender, level of education, income, and racial characteristics are all included as independent variables. We know that voter participation is often affected by such features (Verba and Nie 1972; Rosenstone and Hansen 1993), and previous studies indicate that these factors often shape the involvement of party activists. For example, Clark, Lockerbie, and Wielhouwer (1998) found that females and those with higher family incomes consistently participated in a larger number of campaign activities. In addition, older party members participated in fewer activities, all other factors being held constant. Given the changing nature of party activists over the past decade, it will be interesting to see if such differences persist in 2001.

The effects of all these variables will be examined in equations separately for four categories of activists: Democrats, Republicans, chairs, and members. While all the variables are expected to have an influence within each category, the influence of many of the variables will probably play a larger role for members than for chairs. Because chairs of local organizations are already quite committed to their party's effort (given their leadership role), we would expect the effects of most variables to have their greatest impact on rank-and-file party members.

Multivariate Analyses

Table 11.3 provides the results of multivariate regression models separately by political party and by party position (chair and member) using data from the 2001 survey. These unstandardized regression coefficients represent the average change in number of activities performed by an activist for a one-unit increase in each independent variable. For example, among Democrats we find party chairs engaging in 1.594 more campaign activities than party members. Similarly we find among Democrats that a one-unit increase in the ideological score in the liberal direction (on the seven-point scale) results in a .285 increase in party activity (a little more than one-fourth of an activity). These coefficients allow us to determine the relative impact of the various factors.

As one can see, many of the variables have an influence in the manner that was anticipated. Among perceptions of the party, health has a positive influence on campaign activity. Where parties are viewed as strong, activists are more likely to take part in a larger number of functions. Party factionalism does not have a consistent effect across the categories of candidates. It is statistically significant for members and marginally so for Republican activists. However, its effects are in the opposite direction than what one might suppose. Such a finding is similar (although less strong) as that identified in previous analyses (Clark, Lockerbie, and Wielhouwer 1998). This result suggests that factionalism may stimulate some degree of competition for control of the party.

Among attitudes and beliefs, all three factors examined have an important effect on campaign activities. Those who became involved with party politics for the purpose of taking part in elections are, not surprisingly, more active in campaigns. The negative coefficient for party purism indicates that those with

Table 11.3 Factors Affecting the Extent of Campaign and Election Activities, by Party and Position, 2001

Variable	*Democrats*	*Republicans*	*Chairs*	*Members*
Perceptions of parties				
Party health	.061***	.106***	.171***	.060***
Party factionalism	.081	.103+	−.029	.114**
Attitudes and beliefs				
Reason for involvement	.749***	.655***	.534***	.734***
Party purism orientation	−.615***	−.490***	−.859***	−.491***
Ideology	.285***	−.032	.331**	.158***
Public office holding				
Held office	.354**	.476***	.184	.484***
Plan to run	.630***	.397**	.189	.567***
Characteristics of activists				
Chair	1.594***	1.604***	—	—
Party (Democrat)	—	—	.928***	.121
Age	−.017***	−.011**	−.015*	−.014***
Gender (female)	.208+	.532***	.295	.426***
Education	.209***	.114*	.198*	.171***
Income	.420***	.324***	.350*	.352***
African American	.229	−.627	−.288	.228+
Hispanic American	.724*	.062	−.522	.649*
Constant	2.732***	2.714***	3.517***	2.462***
Adjusted R^2	.20	.18	.16	.13
(*N*)	(2,488)	(2,703)	(996)	(4,195)

Note: Entries are unstandardized ordinary least squares coefficients.

$^{+}p < .10$, $^{*}p < .05$, $^{**}p < .01$, $^{***}p < .001$

a pragmatic outlook on party politics are the members more likely to engage in campaign efforts. Political ideology also has an effect mostly as expected—those members whose ideology is closer to the base of their national party are more active in three of the four equations. However, this effect is present only among Democrats; for Republicans the coefficient is statistically insignificant and in the opposite direction. Why would ideology have an effect for Democrats but not for Republicans? It is probably because Republican activists as a group are more ideologically homogeneous than Democratic activists. For example, 53 percent of Republican activists identified themselves as "very conservative," the most extreme ideological position on that side of the seven-point scale, whereas only 19 percent of Democrats put themselves in the corresponding extreme position ("very liberal"). In fact, 18 percent of Democrats said they were "somewhat conservative" or "very conservative" but only 1 percent of Republicans reported being in either "liberal" category.

The greater variation among Democratic activists simply means that ideology has a greater potential to have an effect on their campaign activity.

Moving on to holding public office, we find that both variables have an influence in three of the four equations. Only for party chairs do we not see an influence. Previous experience in public office increases the likelihood that members take part in election-related activities. In fact, just having a plan to one day run for office has a rather substantial effect on campaign activity. Perhaps these members are looking for practical experience that may assist them in their future campaigns.

Characteristics of party activists are also important predictors of campaign involvement. Given the earlier descriptive findings, it is not surprising that party chairs engage in a greater number of campaign activities. When holding constant so many variables, we find in both parties that chairs engage in about 1.5 more activities than members. What is surprising is that Republicans do not appear to be more active than Democrats. In fact, participation levels are actually higher for Democratic chairs than for Republican chairs (about one more activity reported on average). While such a result is surprising, it is consistent with multivariate findings from the 1991 survey that showed greater involvement for Democratic chairs. But the 1991 survey results also indicated that Republicans members were more active than Democratic members. In 2001 no such difference between party members is detected. Such differences suggest that Democrats have pulled even among members and stayed ahead among chairs in terms of overall campaign activities.

Several of the demographic features tested have an effect in a manner consistent with those found from the 1991 survey (Clark, Lockerbie, and Wielhouwer 1998). Similar to findings from a decade earlier, age is negatively associated with participation, while education, income, and gender (except among chairs) are all positively related. Whereas the 1991 findings showed lower involvement for African Americans in some areas, no such effect is identified in 2001. In fact, among party members, the coefficient for African Americans is marginally significant and positive, suggesting that African Americans may actually participate at higher rates than others.

To gain a better sense of the different effects of these variables across time, an analysis using all the cases is conducted separately for 1991 and 2001. Here, political party and party position (chair or member) are included as independent variables. The results presented in table 11.4 illustrate that most of the variables have a similar influence across the two time periods. For most of the variables, the coefficients are all statistically significant and in the same direction. The only exceptions are for the effects of party and racial characteristics. It is clear from this analysis that Democrats were generally less active than Republicans in 1991, but ten years later this pattern had reversed. The statistically significant coefficient for party in 2001 demonstrates that a Democratic activist engaged in about one-fourth of an activity more on average than the typical Republican activist. Finally, there

Table 11.4 Factors Affecting the Extent of Campaign and Election Activities, 1991 and 2001

Variable	*1991*	*2001*
Perceptions of parties		
Party health	.041***	.079***
Party factionalism	.240***	.089*
Attitudes and beliefs		
Reasons for involvement	.616***	.708***
Party purism orientation	−.449***	−.562***
Ideology	.224***	.188***
Public office holding		
Held office	.891***	.420***
Plan to run	.941***	.500***
Characteristics of activists		
Chair	1.515***	1.599***
Party (Democrat)	−.302***	.262**
Age	−.020***	−.014***
Gender (female)	.604***	.398***
Education	.126***	.175***
Income	.125+	.378***
African American	−.267*	.137
Hispanic American	.305	.449+
Constant	2.789***	2.395***
Adjusted R^2	.19	.19
(*N*)	(7,168)	(5,191)

Note: Entries are unstandardized ordinary least squares coefficients.

$^+p < .10$, $^*p < .05$, $^{**}p < .01$, $^{***}p < .001$

are also some differences over time for the effects of racial characteristics. Whereas African American activists engaged in fewer forms of campaign participation in 1991, by 2001 this difference had disappeared. And for Hispanic Americans where no differences in participation were found in 1991, by 2001 we see a positive effect for this variable (although the influence has only marginal statistical significance).

A final perspective on changes in campaign activity at the grassroots can be obtained by conducting a combined analysis that incorporates survey responses from both the 1991 and 2001 surveys (see table 11.5). By including a dichotomous variable for year (1 = 2001, 0 = 1991), we can assess how time has changed the level of campaign involvement by political party and party position (chair and members). The results of these models demonstrate that when holding all the other variables constant, time does have an influence for some categories of activists. For Democrats, participation

Table 11.5 Factors Affecting the Extent of Campaign and Election Activities, by Party and Position, 1991 and 2001 Combined

Variable	*Democrats*	*Republicans*	*Chairs*	*Members*
Perceptions of parties				
Party health	.036***	.084***	.164***	.039***
Party factionalism	.115**	.219***	.072	.188***
Attitudes and beliefs				
Reasons for involvement	.682***	.625***	.489***	.683***
Party purism orientation	−.504***	−.478***	−.761***	−.438***
Ideology	.284***	.056	.390***	.194***
Public office holding				
Held office	.666***	.715***	.499***	.715***
Plan to run	.768***	.700***	.315*	.814***
Characteristics of activists				
Chair	1.588***	1.581***	—	—
Party (Democrat)	—	—	.711***	−.186**
Age	−.023***	−.012***	−.017***	−.017***
Gender (female)	.338***	.635***	.429**	.542***
Education	.198***	.071*	.123+	.154***
Income	.200**	.267***	.156	.247***
African American	−.044	−.393	−.710*	.016
Hispanic American	.381	.285	−.759+	.563**
Year (2001)	.394***	.071	.186	.230***
Constant	2.735***	2.600***	3.392***	2.571***
Adjusted R^2	.21	.17	.16	.15
(*N*)	(6,148)	(6,212)	(1,904)	(10,456)

Note: Entries are unstandardized ordinary least squares coefficients.
$^+p < .10$, $^*p < .05$, $^{**}p < .01$, $^{***}p < .001$

clearly increased over time, while for Republicans, their overall levels of activity stayed the same. Activity levels were similar in both time periods for the party chairs while individual members participated more in 2001 than in 1991. Such findings would appear to corroborate the comparisons made of the separate analysis that Democratic activists appear to have caught up to, if not overtaken, Republicans in terms of overall campaign activity.

CONCLUSIONS

Grassroots activists are at the front lines of a party's efforts to win elections. This look at their role in political campaigns demonstrates that these workers engage in a wide variety of election-related activities. It is interesting to find that much of this effort involves the traditional party role in canvassing—distributing posters and literature, organizing telephone banks, and registering voters. In fact, much of the increase in activity over the past decade has been in such areas of traditional party work. These findings appear to contradict conventional wisdom that suggests modern forms of electioneering have become pervasive.

Many of the findings uncovered here are similar to those identified in data collected in the early 1990s (Clark, Lockerbie, and Wielhouwer 1998). Those who lead the local party efforts (county chairs) are far more involved than county committee members in most campaign-related activities, particularly those that can be considered managerial in nature. Also, many of the factors responsible for overall campaign effort are the same in 2001 as they were in 1991. For example, perceptions of party health and factionalism, attitudes about party purism, ideology, and many demographic variables have a similar influence across the two time periods.

However, some major differences were uncovered from the 1991 survey. Whereas Clark and his colleagues found levels of Republican activity to be greater than those of Democrats, by 2001 such differences had disappeared. In fact, among local chairs, Democrats were more active than their Republican counterparts. These findings suggest that Democrats responded to increased Republican efforts in the late 1980s and early 1990s with their own grassroots efforts to counter the successes of the Republican Party.

The findings presented here demonstrate that parties are alive and well on the local level and continue to play an important role in elections. The wide variety of activities engaged in by those at the grassroots will be a prominent part of the movement toward two-party politics in the South.

NOTES

1. The question concerning the construction and maintenance of a campaign Web site was not included in the 1991 survey instrument, so comparisons on this dimension cannot be made.

2. Activists were asked to respond on a five-point scale from "strongly agree" to "strongly disagree" to a series of statements about party activity. Four of the following statements were used in constructing the purism index: "Good party workers support any candidate nominated by the party even if they basically disagree with the candidate," "Party organization and unity are more important than free and total discussion of issues that may divide the party," "Controversial positions should be avoided in party platforms to ensure party unity," and "Good party workers should remain officially and unofficially neutral in primary contests even when they have a personal preference." Respondents expressing greater disagreement with each of these statements are considered "purists" while those expressing greater agreement are considered more "pragmatic" in their orientation. The response categories were coded 1 through 4 with 4 being the highest level of disagreement for each response. The measure was constructed by summing the responses and dividing by 4. The range of the resulting variable is from 1 to 4.

CHAPTER

12

Communication Patterns and Party Integration

John M. Bruce and John A. Clark

Observers of political parties often speak of "the party" as if it were a monolith, an organization that operated with a singular purpose. The reality is much different, at least in the American context, where the Democratic and Republican Parties are characterized by a remarkable level of decentralization (Epstein 1986). Individual party organizations may be strongest when they have a considerable degree of autonomy, but the party as a whole gains strength from cooperation among its constituent parts (Schlesinger 1985). Thus, we seek to examine the level of interaction between local party activists. Using contact between grassroots activists and other party and elected officials as a proxy for integration, we find that activists who are in frequent contact with other party leaders are more active and feel more connected to their party than those who have little contact. Those who are better integrated also are more likely to perceive that their organization is gaining in strength.

STRATA, NUCLEI, AND INTEGRATION IN LOCAL PARTIES

The relative levels of autonomy and cooperation between levels of U.S. parties have been categorized in very different ways by parties scholars. Eldersveld (1964) found low levels of contact between local party activists in the Detroit area. He termed this phenomenon "stratarchy" to emphasize the autonomy of the various levels (or strata) of the party. Unlike hierarchical organizations where control is administered from the top down, party leaders in Eldersveld's study seemed to have little control over—or even knowledge of—the workings of other organizational groupings.

An alternative perspective is offered by Joseph Schlesinger (1985). He conceptualized the various units of a party as nuclei. Though independent, various nuclei should agree to cooperate when their interests are threatened. Multinuclear parties are able to take advantage of economies of scale in their campaign activities. Since support generated for one of the party's candidates would likely spill over onto other candidates' campaigns, all can benefit from their cooperation with one another. Of course, in doing so some level of autonomy must be sacrificed. High levels of uncertainty over election outcomes would encourage multinuclear organizations to form, while various nuclei could retain their autonomy when the likelihood that they would win or lose was known.

The evidence available to test these competing theories suggests that parties have become increasingly centralized, and perhaps increasingly integrated, over time. Democratic centralization in the 1970s focused on the rules of the presidential nominating process, while Republicans opted to strengthen their national organization by making funds available to state and local organizations (Bibby 1981; Wekkin 1985). This latter approach was especially conducive to integration, as the financial rewards were often tied to party building activities that lent themselves to greater cooperation across organizations. Huckshorn and his colleagues (1986) found a relationship between state-national integration and state party organizational strength, which they attributed to the socialization of state party leaders more than the availability of resources for party building itself.

There is evidence of cooperation across party units within states, as well. The availability of "soft money" encouraged state parties to engage in such activities like fund-raising, computing services, and voter mobilization (Bibby 1999a, 72–75). For example, the frequency of joint registration drives and get-out-the-vote efforts increased dramatically in the early 1980s (Gibson, Frendreis, and Vertz 1989). More recently, local parties began to work more closely with individual candidates to provide campaign labor and sophisticated technologies (Frendreis and Gitelson 1999). In contrast to the stratarchy observed by Eldersveld, Schwartz (1990) described the level of integration among Illinois Republicans as a "robust" network of party leaders, elected officials, candidates, and affiliated interest groups.

PARTY INTEGRATION AND ITS CORRELATES

Previous researchers conceptualized integration as "a two-way pattern of interaction" between party units (Huckshorn et al. 1986, 978). The successful integration of disparate party units into a single, cohesive party requires at minimum communication between those units. For our purposes, the degree of this communication will be assessed by how often the county chairs and precinct committee members communicate with a range of other partisan figures. Greater communication frequency is, then, taken as an indicator of greater integration. The respondents were asked the following:

> Now we would like to ask you about your communication in the party organization. How often do you communicate with:
>
> county party chair?
> other county party members?
> state party chair?
> state party committee members?
> national committee members?
> local government officials?
> state government officials?
> national government officials?

The responses included "very often," "often," "seldom," and "never." While frequent communication may not guarantee meaningful integration, a lack of contact between party units would ensure a lack of integration.

The basic responses to this battery of questions is shown in table 12.1. Respondents are broken down by party and position. The entries in the table are the percentage of respondents who say they communicate "very often" or "often" with their fellow party officials, as well as elected officials. Four clear patterns are present in this table. First, the county chairs of each party report higher levels of communication than do precinct committee members on every single question (see also Clark and Lockerbie 1993; Brodsky and Brodsky 1998). While this is not surprising (a chair that does not communicate would

Table 12.1 Levels of Contact by County Chairs and Precinct Members

	Democrats		*Republicans*	
	Chairs	*Members*	*Chairs*	*Members*
Other party committee members	86.1	61.0	90.4	72.0
County party chair	89.3	60.1	95.3	69.1
State party chair	29.3	10.4	32.3	13.1
State party committee members	37.4	20.1	47.0	23.2
National committee members	10.1	8.6	13.3	9.5
Local government officials	83.1	63.6	84.0	68.6
State government officials	53.9	37.9	60.3	43.8
National government officials	18.8	17.5	33.4	22.9
(Minimum *N*)	(496)	(2,850)	(596)	(2,765)

Note: Cell entries are the percentage responding they had contact "very often" or "often" with the various individuals.

be an ineffective party leader), the magnitude of the differences is substantial. In both the Democratic and Republican cases, the difference between the mean for chairs and members is just over sixteen points. Second, Republican chairs report higher levels of communication than do Democratic chairs. On each of the eight communication items, Republican chairs have more reported contact. The mean response for Republican chairs is six points higher than that of the Democratic chairs. Third, on every question, Republican precinct committee members report more frequent communication than do their Democratic counterparts. The difference between the mean response for the two sets of committee members is 5.4. Fourth, the level of communication that takes places decreases as the partner in communication grows less proximate to the local level. The highest levels of communication are with other party committee members and county party chairs, with contact rates dropping sharply as the scope is broadened to the state party committee, the state chair, and national committee members. Likewise, contact with elected officials is highest at the local level and lowest at the national level.

When compared to 1991, these results reflect the increasing success of Republican candidates for local, state, and national offices across the South. At the time of the original SGPA study, Democratic leaders were much more likely to report contact with local and state government officials (Clark and Lockerbie 1993). Ten years later, Republicans had pulled even at the local level and surpassed the Democrats in contact with national government officials. Democrats, meanwhile, reported lower levels of contact with elected officials at all three levels compared to the earlier study.

To facilitate analysis across the remainder of this chapter, we have created an index of integration by adding the eight communication terms.[1] Responses to the eight questions were simply reversed to make high scores represent high integration, and then summed. The resulting scale runs from 8 (no contact at all) to 32 ("very often" in contact with all party units).

In the analysis that follows, the index was broken into thirds and activists were grouped accordingly to facilitate comparisons: low integration (8–15), moderate integration (16–24), and high integration (25–32). Among chairs, 18 percent of the Democrats were scored as highly integrated, with 21 percent of the Republicans being scored that way.[2] Approximately 11 percent of the Democratic chairs and 5 percent of the Republican chairs were scored as having low integration. Among precinct committee members, 7 percent of the Democrats and 9 percent of the Republicans were highly integrated, with 34 percent of the Democrats and 26 percent of the Republicans being scored as having low levels of integration. Figure 12.1 displays the relative size of each group.

While the web of effects that may exist around a fully integrated party are likely complex, identification of all effects is impossible. What we can expect to find is that grassroots activists working in a highly integrated environment will possess a different set of psychological perspectives than found among activists working in an environment with low levels of integration. We

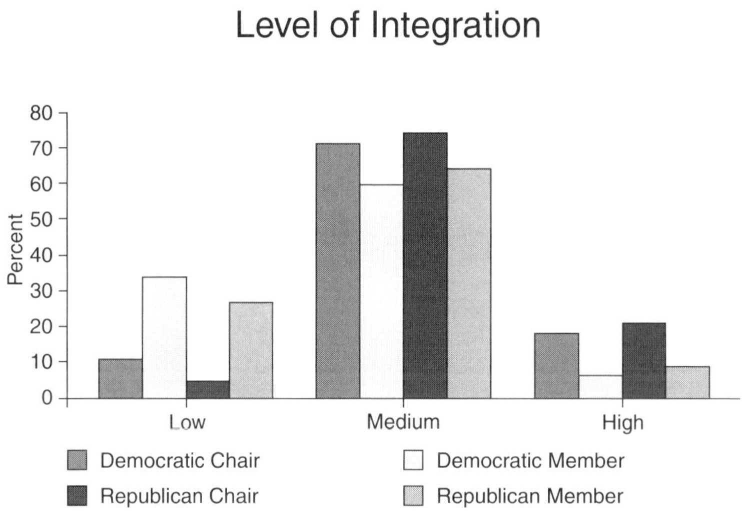

Figure 12.1 Levels of Party Integration by Party and Position.

thus compare those activists falling into the high and low integration categories across a range of items. We first look at the length of time they were active in politics and whether they had held office. We then examine their activity in various elections, their attitudes toward the party, and their perceptions of the strength of their organizations.

The survey instrument did not include large numbers of attitudinal measures. It did contain a battery of questions on party-related behavior, however, which we can safely assume would be, at least in part, influenced by a respondent's psychological standing in politics. Table 12.2 reports analysis on a range of political activities that should reflect the strength of attitudes among chairs and members. In terms of length of political activity, Democrats have a longer history than do Republicans (22.1 versus 19.3 years), and the county chairs of each party have longer average histories than do precinct committee members of that party (23.7 versus 20.4 for Democrats, 21.8 versus 19.1 for Republicans). Additional differences are found when these groups are broken down by levels of integration (the first set of numbers in table 12.2). Activists classified as having high integration have longer histories of activity, in some cases by sizable amounts. These same basic patterns hold across the range of activities listed in the table. There is no consistent pattern of difference between the two partisan groups, but chairs tend to be more active than members. Lower integration levels are also linked to sometimes dramatically lower activity rates. This is true for the respondents' history of office holding, level of campaign activity, and general activity in local, state, and national politics. The impact of integration extends to support for the parties' presidential candidates. Those with low integration were more likely to defect from their party's ticket, although the difference among Republican precinct members was quite small.

Table 12.2 Political Activity and Party Integration

	Democrats		*Republicans*	
	Chairs	*Members*	*Chairs*	*Members*
Mean years active in politics				
High integration	27.2	24.8	23.1	24.9
Low integration	22.0	18.8	14.9	15.4
Held political office				
High integration	45.8	45.2	49.2	49.1
Low integration	24.0	20.9	18.5	24.0
Voted for own party's presidential candidate in the 2000 election				
High integration	96.4	94.1	98.4	98.0
Low integration	78.0	86.5	88.9	95.4
Participated in 10–12 campaign activities				
High integration	32.5	23.5	34.5	27.1
Low integration	4.0	1.0	0.0	0.3
Very active–local				
High integration	92.7	91.4	84.4	78.8
Low integration	51.0	32.5	29.6	29.3
Very active—national				
High integration	87.8	80.2	89.3	81.4
Low integration	26.5	23.0	33.3	24.6
Very active—state				
High integration	82.9	73.3	83.5	75.8
Low integration	28.6	30.1	37.0	35.8
(Minimum *N:* high integration)	(82)	(177)	(121)	(245)
(Minimum *N:* low integration)	(49)	(896)	(27)	(703)

Note: Cell entries are the percentage of high and low integration respondents who meet each condition, except where otherwise indicated. Moderate integration respondents are not shown.

One set of party-specific attitudes we can assess within the context of integration involves partisanship and the degree to which the activists feel "close" to their party. Responses to four questions of this sort are shown in table 12.3. The first two questions deal with how close respondents feel to their national and state party. The entries in the table are the percentage who indicate they feel "extremely close" to the party in question. A couple of clear patterns are obvious. First, county chairs generally are more likely to feel extremely close to the party than are precinct committee members. Second, high integration respondents are far more likely to feel close to their party than are low integration

Table 12.3 Party Attitudes and Party Integration

	Democrats		*Republicans*	
	Chairs	*Members*	*Chairs*	*Members*
Feel extremely close to own national party				
High integration	43.4	41.3	55.0	50.2
Low integration	20.8	22.1	25.9	17.5
Feel extremely close to own state party				
High integration	69.5	54.2	69.5	64.5
Low integration	17.0	17.1	22.2	23.0
Strongly identify with own national party				
High integration	96.3	89.1	99.2	94.1
Low integration	72.9	78.6	76.9	84.5
Strongly identify with own state party				
High integration	97.6	92.8	99.2	95.5
Low integration	81.3	79.4	69.2	79.4
(Minimum *N:* high integration)	(82)	(173)	(118)	(240)
(Minimum *N:* low integration)	(44)	(779)	(25)	(665)

Note: Cell entries are the percentage of high and low integration respondents who meet each condition. Moderate integration respondents are not shown.

respondents from the same party and position group. Third, an interesting reversal appears when comparing how each party-position-integration level group feels about their state and national parties. High integration respondents in all four groups are more likely to feel close to the state party, while low integration respondents are more likely to feel close to the national party (albeit with both rates lower than their high integration counterparts).

The next two questions in the table are concerned with partisan intensity. The first observation to make is that all groups are clearly partisan. This is not unexpected since they were, after all, surveyed because of their party activity. Still, the level of partisanship is impressive. Among high integration respondents, the weakest set is the pool of Democratic precinct committee members, where *only* 89 percent are strong partisans in state politics. Among low integration respondents, the low mark is among Republican county chairs, with 69 percent reporting a strong partisan attachment to the state party. There is a slight likelihood for chairs to be more partisan than committee members and for high integration respondents to be more strongly partisan than low integration respondents. Also, Democratic respondents have a slight tendency to be more strongly attached to their state party, while Republicans report stronger attachments to their national party. While this difference may seem surprising in the light of the Republican Party's emphasis on state party building, it does seem perfectly compatible with the nature of politics in the South (see chapter 6; Clark and Lockerbie 1998). Local Democratic activists who have seen their political fortunes fade a bit may blame the decidedly nonsouthern agenda of the national party and its candidates. In contrast, many of the Republican activists may feel that their local situation has been improved by the rising tide of the national party. Unfortunately, there is no appropriate question in the survey that would allow us to directly test this plausible notion.

Another way to examine the relationship between integration and partisan attitudes is to explore the relative levels of purism and pragmatism among these grassroots activists (see chapter 9). Here, we simply replicate Prysby's measure of purism and consider it through the lens of party integration. Among Democrats, for both county chairs and committee members, those respondents who report the highest integration hold decidedly more pragmatic views. Those activists who are the most likely to value ideological purity over winning are the least likely to have communication with other elements of the party. The same is true for Republican committee members, but there is only a very slight difference between high and low integration Republican chairs. While an individual's view on the winning at all costs versus ideological purity trade-off is certainly not the only factor that shapes integration, it seems likely that an ideological purist is less likely to engage in communication and collaborative party work with a fellow partisan with whom there may be ideological disagreement. Indeed, perhaps the ideal local party leader is one that ranks party success as the primary goal, with any specific ideological or issue agenda falling somewhere down the list.

Consistent with the evidence presented so far, we would expect a relationship between the degree to which respondents report integration in the party and their views of the strength of their respective party. Others (e.g., Cotter et al. 1984) have shown a relationship between the organizational strength of the party and level of integration. While we do not have a full measure of organizational strength, we do have the activists' subjective assessments of how strong their party is on a variety of fronts, relative to their organization's strength ten years previously. That is to say, we have a measure of perceived change in party organizational strength. We expect that more highly integrated respondents will be more likely to feel positive about the changes in their party. We theorize that the central mechanism for this is the psychological effect of communication. All things equal, an activist that is in regular contact with other party officials is more likely to catch a sense of a dynamic party than is one who is in less frequent contact with others.

Respondents were asked to assess the strength of their party today, relative to ten years ago, in seven specific areas, as well as in terms of overall organization. The most dramatic results are in terms of integration (see table 12.4). Of the thirty-two possible within party-position comparisons in

Table 12.4 Assessments of Party Strength and Party Integration

	Democrats		Republicans	
	Chairs	*Members*	*Chairs*	*Members*
Campaign effectiveness				
High integration	24.1	22.4	60.3	49.2
Low integration	4.2	5.4	18.5	29.7
Raise funds				
High integration	21.7	21.5	48.3	48.4
Low integration	4.2	4.2	18.5	26.8
Party role in recruiting candidates				
High integration	17.3	10.6	42.1	40.1
Low integration	4.2	3.1	14.8	25.5
Party effort in organizing workers				
High integration	14.6	19.5	32.8	30.2
Low integration	2.1	3.6	7.4	15.6
Party use of media				
High integration	25.3	13.6	33.9	26.3
Low integration	2.1	4.5	3.8	13.6
Party use of opinion polls				
High integration	20.7	15.3	11.8	17.4
Low integration	2.1	2.4	0.0	10.4
Party use of computer technology				
High integration	43.9	43.0	50.4	58.3
Low integration	12.8	19.1	18.5	33.8
Overall organization				
High integration	25.3	23.6	74.4	55.9
Low integration	10.4	7.6	25.9	44.8
(Minimum *N*: high integration)	(81)	(174)	(115)	(235)
(Minimum *N*: low integration)	(47)	(804)	(26)	(658)

Note: Cell entries are the percentage of high and low integration respondents who rate their own party as significantly stronger than ten years ago on each aspect. Moderate integration respondents are not shown.

the table, respondents with higher levels of integration report their party as being significantly stronger more often than respondents with low levels of integration in all thirty-two. The differences are significant; in some instances the high integration response is ten times the low integration response. Clearly, respondents who are in more frequent contact with other party and elected officials are the most glowing in assessment of their party's strength. Several

Table 12.5 Electoral Competitiveness and Party Integration

	Democrats		*Republicans*	
	Chairs	*Members*	*Chairs*	*Members*
Average Democratic Presidential Vote				
High integration	45.1	45.2	43.0	42.4
Low integration	40.3	43.3	45.1	42.8
(*N*: high integration)	(82)	(174)	(122)	(246)
(*N*: low integration)	(46)	(897)	(27)	(711)

Note: Cell entries are the average vote for the Democratic nominee in the general elections of 1992, 1996, and 2000. Moderate integration respondents are not shown.

other trends are worthy of note. First, there is no systematic pattern of differences between county chairs and precinct committee members. There seems to be nothing in the role of county chair that colors the respondents' views in a unique way. Second, Republican activists are more likely to report their party being significantly stronger than are their Democratic counterparts in similar positions with similar integration. These partisan differences are not trivial. Indeed, in numerous cases the percentage of Republicans indicating significant growth is more than twice the percentage of Democratic respondents who do so. This is true for overall organization, as well as for six of the seven specific areas considered. In one, the party's use of public opinion polls, the Republican activists have unusually weak assessments of their party. While the differences by party are interesting, they are also expected. The ten-year period under consideration covers a time in which the Republican Party matured as an organization in the South. It would be surprising if Republicans did not see greater increases in strength than did the Democrats.

Assuming that parties demonstrate any strategic behavior, the degree to which different party elements are integrated should not be a random feature of the southern party system. Activists in hotly contested areas and those representing strong concentrations of the core constituency are more likely to be involved in active communication channels than are those who are a lost cause geographically (Schlesinger 1985; Trish 1994). While ascertaining the strategic intent of party communication is beyond our data, we do have an indirect method of tapping this possibility. We can use the Democratic vote share for president as a measure of the importance of the county to the party. The stronger the Democratic vote, the more integration we would expect among Democrats, with Republicans in the strongest Democratic locales being less likely to report high integration.

The results, shown in table 12.5, confirm these expectations.[3] Among Democrats, stronger support for Clinton (1992, 1996) and Gore (2000) is found among the high integration respondents, especially the chairs. Among Republicans, the reverse is true, with the Republican chairs reporting high levels of integration having the lowest levels of Democratic support (there is no difference among Republican committee members). While this is admittedly indirect evidence, it does suggest that parties do not "waste" communication efforts on activists in areas where the party has lower odds of success, or, alternatively, activists in counties where the odds of success are low may feel less need to be integrated.

CONCLUSIONS

Our analysis of communication patterns among southern grassroots party activists provides a first look at party integration within the region. Several findings are worth noting. First, Republican contact with elected officials increased over the decade of the 1990s, while Democratic contact decreased. This trend may reflect the success of Republican candidates across a wide range of elections. It may also exemplify the difficulty the Democrats have had in maintaining their multiracial, ideologically heterogeneous coalition in elections and in the party organization itself.

Second, levels of integration are related to a variety of behaviors and attitudes. Activists with higher levels of integration are more active in campaigns, feel closer to the party, and are more likely to believe that their party has gained strength.

Finally, there is a modest connection between the success of a party's presidential candidates and the integration of its activists. This relationship may reflect a strategic calculation on the part of party leaders. Alternatively, some activists may be energized by a particular candidate or campaign, leading them to become more involved in the party's affairs (Trish 1994).

Taken together, these results demonstrate the need to reexamine the traditional notion of U.S. party organizations as decentralized and largely autonomous from one another. County party chairs have considerable contact with those lower in the hierarchy, with other chairs, and with local elected officials. Paired with polarization in terms of ideology and issues (see chapter 5), a new type of party organization may be evolving in the South.

NOTES

1. One might question whether all the contact items fall along a single dimension. To answer this question, the responses were subjected to factor analysis. When all respondents are analyzed together, two distinct factors are apparent. The first, a "local politics" factor, includes communication with county party chairs, other precinct committee members, and local elected officials. The second factor is best considered

a "state-national politics" factor. Items loading primarily on this factor include communication with the state party chair, members of the state party committee, members of the national party committee, and state and national elected officials. The two factors, correlated at 0.46, combine to explain about 65 percent of the variance, with the nonlocal factor alone explaining 50 percent. We believe that combining them into a single scale is consistent with the broader focus on integration. The notion of meaningful integration requires communication across a full range of partisan entities. All things equal, more frequent communication—be it with elected officials, state party committee members, or other precinct committee members—means a greater likelihood of integrated party units. Analysis constraining the results to a single factor shows all terms have a substantial loading on the factor, and the model fit is consistent across the four party-position groups.

2. This represents a switch from the 1991 Southern Grassroots survey, which found Democratic chairs as having higher levels of integration. Clark and Lockerbie (1993) ranked 30 percent of the Democratic chairs as highly integrated, as were 25 percent of the Republican chairs. Only 4 percent of the Democratic chairs and 7 percent of the Republican chairs were scored as low. Among precinct members of both parties, less than one in ten were in the high integration range, while a third scored in the low integration category.

3. There is substantial variation in the Democratic vote in the counties that are represented in our surveys, with a high of 85 percent and a low of 13 percent. According to ANOVA analysis, the mean levels of Democratic presidential support are significantly different for the party-position-integration level combinations ($F = 28.19$).

CHAPTER

13

Conclusion

Patterns of Change between and within Party Organizations

Charles L. Prysby and John A. Clark

A half century of political change in the South has transformed the region into a competitive two-party area in which Republicans have an electoral edge, at least for presidential and congressional elections. This study helps us to understand one dimension of that change: how southern political party organizations have adapted in recent decades. This understanding, in turn, leads us to understand that the realignment in the South has involved more than just a shift in the electoral balance between the two parties. It also has involved a change in the nature of the political party organizations and the political party system in the South. Our data deal specifically with political party activists, who are only one aspect of the party system, but other studies report changes in other aspects of the southern party system that are consistent with the conclusions of this study. Thus, our findings, while based primarily on our analysis of party activists, lead to broader statements about the nature of the political party system in the South at the beginning of the twenty-first century.

Equally important, this study tells us something about the contemporary state of political parties in the United States, especially about local political party organization. Little systematic data on local party organizations exist. The systematic data that have been collected by previous studies of party organizations focus primarily on national and state organizations. County-level party organizations have often been the subject of case studies, but few scholars have attempted to systematically collect data on grassroots party organizations over a number of states. For this reason, the results of this study, even though they deal only with one region, are a useful addition to our knowledge about American party organizations. Also, while our study focuses only on grassroots party activists, the findings of many studies of American political parties suggest that other changes in party organizations are consistent with what we report. Our work therefore complements and contributes to the efforts of others to understand political party development in the contemporary United States.

The findings reported earlier in this study can be summarized and discussed from two perspectives: the responsible party perspective and the party renewal perspective. Each perspective has a conceptual framework, a set of theoretical concerns, and a number of conclusions about the state of American parties. These perspectives seem highly relevant for our study, as we believe that our findings indicate that southern political parties have moved in the direction of more responsible party organizations and have developed their organizational capacity in a manner that indicates substantial party renewal. Furthermore, we believe that by reviewing the conclusions of the earlier chapters in this book through these two perspectives, we are placing our empirical findings in a richer theoretical context. Such an approach should contribute more to our understanding of party organizational change in the South and elsewhere.

THE RESPONSIBLE PARTY PERSPECTIVE

Arguments for more responsible political parties in this country have been made for a long time. Over fifty years ago, the American Political Science Association's Committee on Political Parties issued a report that called for the development of a more responsible two-party system (Committee on Political Parties 1950). The report drew immediate attention from both critics and defenders, and it continues to stimulate debate even today (Green and Herrnson 2002). The report had several goals and contained a number of recommendations. The most important element of the report, however, was the conclusion that American political parties needed to be more programmatic. They needed to be more ideologically cohesive, and they needed to present voters with clear policy alternatives.

Criticisms of the report came from a variety of directions. One complaint was that the report envisioned a party government model that was unrealistic given the social and institutional characteristics of the country. These limiting characteristics include the large and heterogeneous nature of American society, the emphasis placed on the protection of minority rights at the expense of majoritarian democracy, and the presence of a separation of powers and a federal system (Herrnson 1992; Kirkpatrick 1971; Ranney 1951).

Another criticism was that highly cohesive ideological parties could be dysfunctional, creating divisions rather than reducing conflict in the political system (David 1992). Critics also argued that the report confused internal party responsibility with accountability between the parties (Ranney 1951; White 1992). Some even claimed that the report underestimated the extent to which the parties already were responsible (David 1992).

Despite all of the criticism leveled at the report, there does appear to be considerable support among political scientists and analysts for a more qualified position on this issue, one that simply argues that American political parties can and should be *more* responsible than they were in the 1950s—which, after all, was the title of the report. A number of prominent scholars and analysts have argued that stronger parties are needed for effective government in the United States (Broder 1971; Burnham 1982; Coleman 2003; David 1992; Pomper 1971; Price 1984; White 2001). Furthermore, there is a large literature on party renewal in this country, which argues that while parties are weaker in some ways than they were decades ago, they also are stronger in some important ways (Cohen, Fleisher, and Kantor 2001; Green and Farmer 2003; Green and Shea 1999; Kayden and Mahe 1985; Maisel 1998; Pomper 2003). Moreover, most of this literature either implicitly or explicitly suggests that party renewal is a desirable development, that the United States is better off with stronger parties, and that one aspect of stronger parties is greater party clarity and cohesiveness on major issues of public policy.

Our study of grassroots political party activists in the South indicates that the party organizations are more ideologically cohesive now than they were a few decades ago. Moreover, substantial change occurred during the 1990s. As chapter 5 clearly indicates, party activists already were fairly well divided in 1991. Still, party divisions widened considerably by 2001. Republican activists were clearly conservative in 1991, but they became even more so by 2001, as nearly all called themselves conservatives, with a majority claiming to be very conservative. Democratic activists in 1991 were definitely more liberal when compared to Republican activists, but many Democrats classified themselves as moderate or even conservative. The number of conservative Democratic activists was greatly reduced by 2001, with over 80 percent of the Democratic activists then calling themselves moderate or liberal. These ideological classifications of activists reflect real differences on issues of public policy. On every issue examined in chapter 5, Democrats are more liberal than Republicans. On many issues, the party differences are great. Moreover, the analysis indicates that party differences on specific policy issues expanded during the 1990s. Thus, the ideological and issue orientations of southern political party activists are more polarized along party lines than they were in the past. At least in terms of the party organizations, programmatic parties are a reality in the southern political landscape.

The growth in party distinctiveness has been accompanied by an increase in party cohesion. As already mentioned, Republican activists are now overwhelmingly conservative. Democrats are somewhat more ideologically heterogeneous, but they clearly are more cohesive now than in the recent past. A similar pattern of development exists for some, although not all, issues. For example, Republican activists were quite divided by abortion in 1991, but by 2001 there were far fewer pro-choice voices in the party. Democratic activists became more clearly liberal on abortion. The result is that now the two groups of activists clearly represent the two basic positions in the abortion debate.

Increased party cohesiveness exists not only in terms of ideological and issue orientations but also in terms of the attachments that activists have with their party at all levels. Chapter 6 shows that both Democrats and Republicans identify more strongly with their state and national parties now than they did a decade ago. The change is most notable for Democrats. In previous decades many Democrats did not have a strong attachment to their party, especially the national party. Even as late as 1991, there were sharp differences in the attachment of Democratic activists to their state and national parties. In 2001, the differences were very small. Republican activists remain more strongly committed to their party than do Democrats, but the gap has been greatly narrowed and both groups of activists now display stronger attachments.

While ideological differences between these two groups of party activists have increased and ideological cohesion within each group has decreased, both party organizations remain at least somewhat heterogeneous. Factionalism is down in both parties, as chapter 7 reports, but it is far from gone. Among Democratic activists, the most important division involves race and race-related issues, a topic discussed in chapter 3. African Americans have been a crucial element of the Democratic electoral coalition in every southern state for at least three decades, but their representation among party activists was relatively low for most of this time. Even as late as 1991, only about 14 percent of grassroots Democratic activists were black. Now over one-fifth of these activists are African American. This increased pressure could exacerbate tensions within the party organization, particularly on race-related issues, as the discussion in chapter 3 points out. Questions of affirmative action, for example, divide Democrats along racial lines. In fact, in terms of their attitudes on affirmative action issues, white Democratic activists actually are closer as a group to Republican activists than they are to black Democratic activists. On the other hand, it might be that the increased number of black Democratic activists will help to cement the Democratic biracial coalition by promoting more dialogue among black and white party activists.

Among Republican activists, religion stands out as the most important source of internal division, as chapter 2 emphasizes. About one-half of the Republican activists in our study identified themselves as supporters of the Christian Right. This group differs from those Republican activists who are not supporters of the Christian Right, with the differences most pronounced on some key social issues, such as abortion. On other issues, however, differences between these two groups are small. Nevertheless, the few issues on which substantial divisions exist can be the basis for bitter conflict. The danger is that Christian Right Republican activists will withhold support from candidates who do not fully agree with them on these crucial moral issues, a conflict that has divided the party in some places at some times. Still, as chapter 2 points out, while this is a danger, it is far from a reality across the South. Many Republican candidates have successfully united both groups of Republicans.

One of the concerns of the critics of the responsible government model is that highly cohesive ideological parties could be too divisive. If the parties become dominated by purist extremists, they may be unwilling to compromise. The result could be government inaction and an alienated electorate. Our analysis suggests that there is some potential for this problem to emerge. First, activists now are heavily motivated to be involved in party politics by issues and public policy rather than by social or material factors, a point discussed in detail in chapter 10. Second, both groups of activists are more ideologically polarized than are the voters for both parties, as chapter 8 explains. Democratic activists are to the left of Democratic voters, and Republican activists are to the right of Republican voters. Third, in both parties there is a sizable minority of activists who hold strong purist views, which is discussed in chapter 9. These purist activists are less willing to compromise on issues for the sake of electoral success. On all three dimensions, Republicans display more potential for disruptive behavior. They are more ideologically distant from the center of public opinion, more motivated by issues, and more purist in orientation. However, the differences between Democratic and Republican activists on these dimensions are less now than they were in 1991, largely because Democrats have moved to the left and become more purist.

A situation in which party activists are highly motivated by issues, more ideologically extreme than party voters, and uninterested in compromising on issues has the potential to be dysfunctional. At this point, the problem does not seem to be a critical one in either party. Both parties seem primarily concerned with winning. Pragmatists clearly outnumber purists among activists, especially among county chairs, who are particularly important grassroots activists. Both parties retain some ideological diversity among their activists, especially the Democrats. Furthermore, the candidates of both parties are likely to be more pragmatic and more interested in winning. While the activists in the party can influence the character of the party's candidates, there are many other influences as well; and differences among candidates, voters, and activists in a party can coexist without resulting in the party being uncompetitive (Jackson, Brown, and Bositis 1982; McClosky, Hoffman, and O'Hara 1960). Nevertheless, developments in this area among southern party activists in future years are worth monitoring.

The emergence of more responsible grassroots party organizations is matched by similar developments in other aspects of the southern political party system. Candidates and officeholders are now much more clearly distinguished along party lines. This is most evident among members of Congress, as their legislative voting records provide us with considerable data on their policy orientations. A number of studies have analyzed the changes in congressional voting patterns, and they all have found that southern Democratic members of Congress have moved closer to northern Democrats, creating a large gap between themselves and southern Republican members (Black and Black 2002; Berard 2001; Rohde 1991; Whitby and Gilliam 1991). These changes resulted in part from the replacement of conservative southern Democrats by more liberal Democrats, but they also were due to southern congressional Democrats changing their voting patterns, changes that can be attributed to changes in the composition of their districts (Berard 2001; Whitby and Gilliam 1991).

The development of clear policy differences between Democratic and Republican candidates and officeholders demonstrates an enormous shift in the character of southern politics. Party differences at the elite level were blurred in the Solid South. The Democratic Party may have been the party of white supremacy, but Republicans at that time hardly championed civil rights. There were some notable populists among southern Democrats, and some among mountain Republicans as well, but for the most part the Democrats and Republicans supported business interests equally well. The lack of pronounced policy differences between Democratic and Republican candidates and officeholders was a major reason why southern elections frequently were described as issueless (Key 1949).

The southern electorate also is more ideologically divided along party lines than in the past. Republicans identify themselves as conservatives much more than do Democrats (Black and Black 1987, 1992, 2002; Carmines and Stanley 1990; Cowden 2001). This new alignment of ideology and partisanship developed partly through conversion and partly through replacement (Carmines and Stanley 1990; Wattenberg 1991). Many conservative white voters ceased to identify as Democrats, becoming either independents or Republicans, a process of conversion that sometimes operated slowly. Younger voters entering the electorate in the post–civil rights era generally had less firmly established party loyalties and have been more likely to align along ideological lines than the older members of the electorate whom they were replacing. Even when older conservative white Democrats retained their party identification, they became unreliable Democratic voters (Black and Black 2002). Furthermore, the ideological differences between Democratic and Republican voters now involve the full range of policy issues—economic and social welfare issues, race-related issues, social issues, and even foreign policy and defense issues. The breakup of the Solid South may have been precipitated by civil rights issues, but the current party cleavages go far beyond that one dimension (Cowden 2001; Prysby 1989). Of course, partisanship undoubtedly is more clearly linked to issue orientations now because of the increased ideological differentiation of the candidates and the activists of the parties. The interrelationship of these emerging divisions among voters, candidates, and party activists indicates that we should not view changes in the party activists as isolated from other changes in the parties and the party system.

THE PARTY RENEWAL PERSPECTIVE

The party renewal perspective emerged in response to research indicating a decline in the importance of parties in the 1970s. Journalist David Broder (1972) noted that parties had become less capable of offering meaningful choices to the electorate and then delivering policies consistent with those choices. Others focused on changes in the presidential nominating system that led to a diminution of the role of organizational leaders (Kirkpatrick 1976) or the disappearance of urban party machines (Ware 1985). Still others identified weakened ties to party in the electorate or a lack of party voting in Congress as evidence of the decline in parties more generally (Wattenberg 1994; Crotty and Jacobson 1980).

The presence of these trends was hardly in dispute, although some of them have reversed direction since then. Instead, critics of the decline school focused on one area where parties seemed to be getting stronger: their organizations. At the national level, once moribund organizations developed new vitality. Both parties grew increasingly professionalized and developed permanent headquarters and stable staff resources (Cotter and Bibby 1980). Republicans led the way in the use of financial incentives to spur organizational development and to support candidates at all levels, and Democrats quickly followed suit (Bibby 1980, 1998; Herrnson 1988). Boosted by infusions of cash from the national parties, state parties soon became stronger, too (Cotter et al. 1984). State parties in the South, once the weakest organizationally, were among the strongest by 1999 (Aldrich 2000). The organizations that evolved are oriented toward providing services to candidates to help them in their election efforts. Some went so far as to suggest that decline in partisan attachments contributed to stronger organizations as party leaders sought to compensate for changes in the electorate (Schlesinger 1985).

While state and national party organizations are stronger now than in the past, the condition of local party organizations is less clear. To be sure, the decline of big city party machines indicates weakening in some places, yet these organizations were more exceptional than their prominence in the literature would suggest. John Bibby (1998, 151) notes that, in the post-war era, "Most local organizations did engage in party building and candidate support activities, but these organizations were operated in an improvising mode by volunteers and were characterized by organizational slack." There is less systematic data on the strength and vitality of local parties, yet some studies indicate party renewal at this level as well (Cotter et al. 1984; Gibson, Frendreis, and Vertz 1989). In particular, they focused on activity levels during and between campaigns, levels of communication among party officials, and the general bureaucratic development of the organizations.

Urban machines may have been anomalies in most parts of the country, yet even their weaker counterparts were largely missing in the South until fairly recently. Without competition in the formerly "Solid South," there was little reason for either Democrats or Republicans to organize. In many places across the region, local Democratic Party organizations existed to run primary elections rather than to actively campaign on behalf of the party's candidates, serving more as election boards than political entities (see, for example, Clark 1997). Republicans simply were not organized other than in a few mountainous regions (Key 1949).

Given this weak baseline, virtually any evidence of local party activity in the southern states would seem to be evidence for party renewal. Our findings go well beyond that minimal baseline. We find that the parties are active at the local level in the South. While not approaching the threshold of the old machine, they are clearly more of a presence than they were half a century ago.

One way that grassroots party activists make their presence known is through campaign activities. As chapter 11 shows, the amount of campaign activity has increased or at least remained constant over the last decade. We lack the data to draw conclusions about how the current activity levels compare to what existed in the 1950s and 1960s, although obviously there has been a big improvement for the formerly unorganized Republicans. But the fact that our survey of activists shows that they are at least as involved now as they were in 1991 provides support for the conclusion that there has been party renewal at the local level. Also, the fact that Democrats closed the activity gap that existed in 1991 indicates that party organizations can and do respond to changes in their competitive environment. A competitive South likely means that we will have more organized and active parties that contest elections at all levels (Key 1949; Schlesinger 1985; Aldrich 2000).

In the not-too-distant past, some analysts predicted that media and money would overtake the labor-intensive activities best handled by local parties (e.g., Kayden and Mahe 1985). Our data show that grassroots activists still perform traditional campaign activities, such as getting out the vote, at high levels. These activities are especially useful for candidates for lower-level offices, such as state legislator or county commissioner (Frendreis and Gitelson 1999; Hogan 2003).

Activists are involved between election campaigns as well as during them (Feigert and Todd 1998b). The respondents in our survey rate as important a range of noncampaign activities. County chairs naturally are more involved than others, but there are few differences across parties. While direct comparisons are difficult due to slight changes in the response codes, it appears that the importance of performing each activity reported by these activists has increased since 1991 on all six party maintenance items: participating in party meetings, raising money, recruiting and organizing workers, increasing political information for party workers, policy formation, and county party organizational work.

The party renewal thesis implies that party organizations will become increasingly integrated with one another as they work together (Bibby 1998). As chapter 12 shows, grassroots activists in 2001 report an increase in levels of communication with other party officials. This is especially true for Republican contacts with elected officials, no doubt due to the increased success of GOP candidates across the decade. Democrats, in contrast, had less contact with elected officials, which in turn affected their overall levels of integration. Robust communications networks are shown to have implications for campaign activity and support for the party as a whole.

Finally, we asked activists to evaluate the change over the last five to ten years in the condition of their organizations on several dimensions of organizational vitality. We recognize that their responses are suspect for a variety of reasons. For example, they may overestimate improvement to justify their effectiveness as leaders, or they may not have an appropriate baseline for comparison. Nevertheless, the patterns we find are telling. Large majorities of Republican activists report substantial improvement on every dimension but the use of public opinion polls. Democratic activists were less positive in their assessments. Only once did a majority of Democrats report improvement in their local organizations (increased use of computer technology). On several questions, more said their party was weaker than it had been in the past. While slight variations may be found from state to state, the overall pattern is consistent across the region (Clark and Prysby 2003). These trajectories spell trouble for the Democratic Party, although they could represent Republicans catching up.

Taken together, the findings we present seem to give credence to the party renewal thesis. Several trends bear watching, however. For one thing, the activists surveyed in 2001 tended to be older than was true in 1991. It could be the case that the parties are maturing into stable organizations with longer apprenticeships before moving into positions of leadership. On the other hand, this trend might reflect a difficulty in recruiting new workers into party activity. Should the latter explanation hold, evidence of increased activity and communication could be swept away by a wave of retirements.

A second trend has to do with the increased polarization of the parties. The willingness of individuals to be involved in party organizations at a time when political and civic engagement is generally in decline nationally may be stimulated by the fact that the parties in the South have become much more ideologically distinct. Liberal activists may feel that it is even more important now to be involved in the Democratic Party. Conservatives may have similar feelings toward the Republican Party.

The increasing cohesiveness of the parties also may make participation more enjoyable and rewarding. As factional clashes diminish in intensity (see chapter 7), participation becomes more pleasant. The social aspects of involvement should not be ignored. As chapter 10 shows, people become active in party politics not only to influence government but also for personal reasons. If activists find more areas of agreement over issues, they may derive greater satisfaction from the social side of their activity. Solidary rewards may keep them active after the fires of issues have waned.

Although it is consistent with the responsible parties perspective, ideological purity may run counter to the goals of pragmatic, institutionalized party organizations (Gibson, Frendreis, and Vertz 1989). The organizational principles espoused by Ray Bliss and Bill Brock, who chaired the Republican National Committee in the 1960s and 1970s, respectively, focused on electability rather than policy. At the present time, pragmatic orientations are widely held by the activists in our survey, yet this trend also deserves watching.

CONCLUSIONS

The findings of this study indicate that the attitudes of grassroots party activists in the South are much closer to the responsible party model than they were a few decades ago. Indeed, there has been significant development in this direction even in the last ten years. Democratic and Republican activists are more ideologically distinct and more ideologically cohesive than before. They are more strongly attached to their parties than before. They are more motivated by issues than before. These developments in the character of the party activists parallel developments among candidates and voters. The result is that the current political party system in the South is not only a much more competitive one but also one with more cohesive and distinct parties, a development that supporters of the responsible party model would applaud. To some extent the party activists may have contributed to this development rather than just be a reflection of it. The interesting question is whether there will be further ideological differentiation of the parties and, if so, what consequences will flow from such a development.

Likewise, our findings offer support for the party renewal thesis. Local party activists have increased their involvement during the campaign season. They devote more attention to the party's operation between elections. They communicate regularly with those most proximate to them in the organizational hierarchy. Many of them perceive their parties to be stronger than in the past, especially Republicans.

This brief overview masks the fact that there is substantial variation among activists within the South. The contributors to this volume account for some of that variation by examining patterns of religion, race, and migration, for example. Additional research remains to be done, and we applaud those who pursue that path. In addition to following trends identified here, others may wish to examine how party organizations respond to the opportunities and setbacks that befall them (Appleton and Ward 1994; Klinkner 1994). Can electoral success be translated into organizational development? Will parties adapt to slow a decline in electoral fortunes?

A second open question involves how party organizations adapt to changes in the way campaigns are conducted. For decades, state and local parties were the beneficiaries of soft money largess. How will they respond to a different campaign finance regime that may restrict their ability to raise funds (La Raja 2003)? Will party organizations be able to take advantage of new innovations in campaign technology without losing the vitality of people who staff them between elections?

The decade of the 1990s brought increased partisan conflict and other changes to local party organizations in the South. The contributors to this volume have attempted to catalog these changes and place them into the context of the scholarship on political parties. The focus of our attention is, we should note, a moving target. This volume, therefore, represents a baseline from which to measure changes into the twenty-first century.

APPENDIX

SGPA 2001

Description of the Sampling Plan and Response Rates

The SGPA 2001 project aimed at surveying county-level political party activists from both the Democratic and Republican Parties in each of the eleven southern states. The target population varied somewhat from state to state and even between parties in the same state, due to differences in party organization and differences in the availability of names. In every case, the intent was to interview county chairs and other members of the county executive committees. The sampling plan for each state and party is described in the following sections. The number of individuals initially selected, the number of valid addresses, and the number of returned questionnaires for each state are all provided in the table at the end of this description.

ALABAMA

Democrats: The sample included all 67 county chairs, as well as county committee members from 41 of the 67 counties. These were the 41 counties that provided lists of county committee members and they included all of the state's largest counties. The lists were provided by the county chairs and included 1,241 county committee members. From these, a systematic random sample of 926 individuals was selected. The final sampling list included the 67 county chairs plus the 926 county committee members.

Republicans: The sample included all 67 county chairs, as well as county committee members from 31 of the 67 counties, all of which were asked to provide lists. A list of all state Republican Party executive committee members was also obtained, all of which were shown to also be members of the county committee, and this list was merged with the 31 county lists. The merged list contained 922 county committee members. The final sampling list included the 67 county chairs plus the 922 county committee members.

ARKANSAS

Democrats: The sample was drawn from the list of all county chairs and all county committee members for each of the 75 counties. The size of the county committees differs dramatically from county to county. These names and addresses were provided by the state party headquarters. For each county, the proportionate number of individuals was randomly drawn from the committee to develop an overall sample size of 711 for the state.

Republicans: The sample was drawn from county chairs, as well as including all state Republican committee members, county Republican Women chairs, and College Republican chairs (all of whom also serve as county committee members). The names and addresses were provided by the state party headquarters. The list included 291 names.

FLORIDA

Democrats: The sample included all county chairs for each of the 67 counties. At the time of mailing the questionnaires, 9 counties had a vacant chair. The Florida Democratic Party did not have a central listing of members of executive committee members for each county. Consequently, requests were made for a list of members from each county chair. This information was provided by 38 counties. An initial respondent list of 800 committee members and chairs was drawn. Given the concentration of Florida's population in seven urban counties, 300 names were taken from Broward, Dade, Duval, Hillsborough, Leon, and Orange counties (Pinellas county was missing), and the remaining 500 from all the other counties.

Republicans: The sample included all county chairs and state committee members for each of the 67 counties. At the time of mailing the questionnaires, 6 counties had a vacant chair and 9 state committee positions were also vacant. The Republican Party of Florida chose not to release their listing of members of executive committee members for each county.

Consequently, requests were made for a list of members from each county chair. This information was provided by 44 counties. An initial respondent list of 800 committee members and chairs was drawn. Given the concentration of Florida's population in seven urban counties, 300 names were taken from Broward, Dade, Duval, Hillsborough, and Orange counties (Leon and Pinellas counties were missing), and the remaining 500 from all the other counties.

GEORGIA

Democrats: The sample included county chairs only. The lists of county chairs were obtained through the office of the executive director of the state Democratic Party. Attempts were made to obtain the names and addresses of other grassroots activists, such as precinct chairs, but these efforts were unsuccessful. As a result, the sample was limited to the county chairs.

Republicans: The sample included county chairs and other activists. The lists of county chairs were obtained through the Web site of the state Republican Party. In addition to the 191 county chairs or co-chairs, a list of 134 other activists was obtained. The final sample included both groups.

LOUISIANA

Democrats: The sample included all members of the Democratic Parish Executive Committees from Louisiana's 64 parishes. These officials were elected on March 14, 2000 and serve for four-year terms. The Louisiana Secretary of State's Office provided names and addresses of these committee members. The chair of each parish executive committee is elected from among the membership of the committee following the election. The state Democratic Party supplied a partial list of chairs that was completed by telephone calls placed to respondents from the missing parishes.

Republicans: The sample included all members of the Republican Parish Executive Committees from Louisiana's 64 parishes. These officials were elected on March 14, 2000 and serve for four-year terms. The Louisiana Secretary of State's Office provided names and addresses of these committee members. The chair of each parish executive committee is elected from among the membership of the committee following the election. A listing of the chairs was provided by the state Republican Party.

MISSISSIPPI

Democrats: The sample included all county chairs and all county executive committee members from counties where we were able to obtain lists. Fifteen of the state's 82 counties did not have a current chair according to state party records, and despite repeated contacts with the state party and with each county chair, lists of county executive members were not obtained from 37 of the 82 counties. The sample thus consisted of 67 county chairs and 1,072 executive committee members from 45 counties. This sample appears representative of Democratic activists in the state as a whole. Using the 1991 Mississippi Democratic sample from the first NSF Grassroots Party Activists project, differences in such key factors as education level, factionalism amount, ideological self-identification, race, sex, and state campaign activity between sampled counties and those not sampled were minute and consistently lacked statistical significance.

Republicans: The sample included all county chairs, as well as a representative sample of all county executive committee members. These lists were comprehensive and were obtained from the state party headquarters. Five of the state's 82 counties did not have a current chair according to their records. The total number of county executive committee members in the state are 1,257, from which a random sample of 981 was chosen, so each member had a .78 chance of inclusion in the sample. All 77 county chairs were sent questionnaires, as was this sample of 981 county executive committee members.

NORTH CAROLINA

Democrats: The sample included all county chairs and other elected county executive committee members for each of the 100 counties. In addition to the county chair, there are five other elected members of the county executive committee—three vice chairs, a secretary, and a treasurer. However, not all of these positions were filled for each county, so there were considerably fewer than 600 elected members of the county executive committees (508 names, 483 names with valid addresses). These names were provided by the state party headquarters. This list was supplemented by a sample of precinct chairs from the seven counties containing a major city (212 names, 207 valid addresses). These names were obtained by contacting the county chairs in these seven counties. The addition of the precinct chairs from the urban counties provides additional respondents from the most populous counties and makes the proportion of respondents from these counties roughly proportional to their share of the population of the state.

Republicans: The sampling included all county chairs and other elected county executive committee members for each of the 100 counties. In addition to the county chair, there are three other elected members of the county executive committee—a vice chair, a secretary, and a treasurer.

However, not all of these positions were filled for each county, so there were somewhat fewer than 400 elected members of the county executive committees (370 names, 351 names with valid addresses). These names were provided by the state party headquarters. As with the Democrats, this list was supplemented by a sample of precinct chairs from the counties containing a major city (146 names, 144 valid addresses). However, two of these seven counties, Mecklenburg (Charlotte) and Forsyth (Winston-Salem), did not supply a list of precinct chairs, so these two counties are represented in the sample only by the elected members of the county executive committee. As with the Democrats, the addition of the precinct chairs from the urban counties provides additional respondents from the most populous counties and makes the proportion of respondents from these counties roughly proportional to their share of the population of the state.

SOUTH CAROLINA

Democrats: The sample included all county chairs and randomly selected precinct presidents and county executive committee members from each organized precinct in the state. These lists were provided by the state party headquarters. A number of counties were not included in the state lists, so the county chairs in those counties were contacted to request their precinct organizational lists. Precinct lists from nine counties were not obtained either because the county had not organized at the precinct level in the past three years or because they simply did not have the precinct lists available (or would not make them available; it is not entirely clear in all cases). Moreover, any response that indicated that the respondent was not a precinct official in spite of being listed as such on the party records was excluded from the sample. Unfortunately, two major urban counties, Spartanburg and Richland counties, are underrepresented in the sample because neither county provided precinct organizational lists. The lists from the state party headquarters included a handful of precinct officials from each of these counties, but they were clearly incomplete.

Republicans: The sample included all county chairs and randomly selected precinct presidents and county executive committee members from each organized precinct in the state. These lists were provided by the state party headquarters. As with the Democrats, not all counties were organized at the precinct level, so the sample did not include all 46 counties (except for the county chairs). Moreover, as with the Democrats, any response that indicated that the respondent was not a precinct official in spite of being listed as such on the party records was excluded from the sample.

TENNESSEE

Democrats: The sample included all members of the executive committees of each of the 95 counties in Tennessee, including party chairs in each county. The number of members on executive committees varied considerably from county to county, much more so than among Republicans. The state Democratic Party provided names and addresses for 780 county party leaders.

Republicans: The sample included all members of the executive committees of each of the 95 counties in Tennessee, including party chairs in each county. The number of seats on these committees was much more uniform across counties than among Democrats. The state Republican Party headquarters provided names and addresses for 439 county party leaders.

TEXAS

Democrats: The sample included all 251 county chairs (three others were vacant), as well as county precinct chairs (who also serve on the county committees). Inasmuch as the state committee had not finished compiling their statewide list at the time that sampling began, lists supplied by county chairs, either by mail or reference to Web sites, were relied upon. This resulted in a precinct activist sample drawn from two large metropolitan counties (Harris and Dallas), two from suburban counties (Collin and Denton), one rural county (Grayson), and one isolated but metropolitan North Texas county (Wichita). The addition of the precinct chairs provided respondents from the most populous counties, making the proportion of respondents roughly proportional to their share of the population of the state.

Republicans: The sample included 252 people classified as county chairs by the State Republican Committee. However, this includes seven people who also served as chairs of state senatorial districts in Harris County (Houston). Hence, Republicans have a single chair in 245 of the 254 counties. Despite repeated attempts and assurances, the Texas Republican Committee would not supply a list of precinct activists, as it is not their practice to endorse such activities. Consequently, the state chair would not provide a letter of endorsement, and the Republican sample was increased slightly, (mistakenly) anticipating a lower response without the endorsement. Hence, the sample relied on lists supplied by county chairs by either mail or reference to Web sites. This resulted in a precinct activist sample drawn from two large metropolitan counties (Harris and Dallas), two from suburban counties (Collin and McClennan), one rural county (Parker), and two isolated but metropolitan North Texas counties (Lubbock and Wichita). As with the Democrats, the addition of the precinct chairs provided respondents from the most populous counties and made the proportion of respondents roughly proportional to their share of the population of the state.

VIRGINIA

Democrats: The sample included 500 randomly selected party activists, including central committee members, chairs, and county/city committee members. The sample was drawn from city or county chairs, central committee members, and county or city committee members, as Virginia's parties are not officially organized to the precinct level. The respondents were obtained from a list provided by the state Democratic Party.

Republicans: The sample included 225 committee members provided by local chairs. Despite lack of assistance from the Executive Director of the

Table A.1 Summary of Response Rates

State	*Party*	*Initial List*	*Bad Addresses*	*Valid Addresses*	*Completed Questionnaires*	*Response Rate*
AL	Dem	993	66	927	403	43.5
	Rep	989	68	921	451	49.0
AR	Dem	711	49	662	381	57.6
	Rep	291	18	273	150	54.9
FL	Dem	800	62	738	296	40.1
	Rep	800	71	729	306	42.0
GA	Dem	137	3	134	73	54.5
	Rep	346	21	325	183	56.3
LA	Dem	449	8	441	257	58.3
	Rep	384	12	372	244	65.6
MS	Dem	1,139	103	1,036	369	35.6
	Rep	1,058	80	978	462	47.2
NC	Dem	720	30	690	417	60.4
	Rep	516	21	495	306	61.8
SC	Dem	867	40	809	401	49.6
	Rep	855	34	806	404	50.1
TN	Dem	780	99	681	316	46.4
	Rep	439	14	425	247	58.1
TX	Dem	890	16	874	550	62.9
	Rep	1,100	38	1,072	686	64.0
VA	Dem	500	113	387	150	38.8
	Rep	225	41	184	118	64.1
Total	Dem			7,379	3,613	49.0
	Rep			6,580	3,557	54.0
All				13,959	7,170	51.4

Virginia Republican Party, lists were obtained of the central committee membership and local committee chairs. As with the Democrats, the sample was drawn from city or county chairs, central committee members, and county or city committee members, as Virginia's parties are not officially organized to the precinct level. Many included in the sample had given prior agreement to participate, resulting in a much higher response rate.

WEIGHTING OF THE FULL DATA SET

The full SGPA data set consists of eleven state surveys. As the description of the SGPA sample indicates, the number of cases for each state varies considerably. There are several reasons for this variation. First, the number of counties in each state varies, and since the sample in each state surveyed county chairs and other members of the county executive committees, a larger number of counties in a state tended to produce a larger number of respondents. Second, the target population of county executive committee members differed from state to state, and sometimes even within parties in a state, in large part because of differences in the availability of names. Thus, even if two states had a similar number of counties, they might have substantially different numbers of respondents, due to differences in the sampling frames for the two states. Finally, response rates vary somewhat across the states. The variations in these factors across the states are apparent from the descriptions of the state samples in the preceding document.

The variation in the sample sizes presents a problem when the eleven state files are combined into one master data set. The problem is primarily confined to the respondents who are not county chairs. Every county chair in every state was included in the sampling frame, with the exception of Arkansas Democratic chairs, where only a sample was selected. Variation in the number of chairs across the states therefore almost entirely represents variation in the number of counties and, to some extent, variation in the response rate across the states. Since the variation in the response rate for chairs across the states is not that great, we can use the unweighted chairs as a representative sample of county chairs in the South (Democratic county chairs in Arkansas are underrepresented in this sample, but this produces extremely little distortion of results in any analysis).

The problem is much greater when it comes to the county executive committee members (i.e., those who are not county chairs). Because of the variations in the sampling frame across states and parties, each member did not have the same chance of being selected. Differences in the number of members in the sample vary greatly from state to state. For example, the Mississippi sample includes 750 members (332 Democrats and 418 Republicans). Tennessee, on the other hand, has only 460 members in its sample.

However, Tennessee has both a larger population and more counties than Mississippi, so it is unlikely that Mississippi really has more grassroots party activists. To keep a state like Mississippi from contributing unduly to the total sample, it is desirable to weight the members from each state so that they contribute to the total sample in proportion to their size in the total population of grassroots party activists.

Unfortunately, we do not know the true number of grassroots party activists in each state. We are not able, for example, to determine the total number of county executive committee members for each state, as there are a significant number of vacancies in these positions in every state. Moreover, the definition of the county executive committee varies from state to state, and even between parties within a state. We have used membership in the county executive committee as a measure of significant involvement in the county party organization, but the meaning of such membership varies across the states. For example, Florida has only 67 counties, despite being the second most populous state in the region. Mississippi, on the other hand, has 82 counties, even though its population is only about one-sixth that of Florida. We would expect that being a member of the county party organization in Florida represents much more involvement on average than does being a member of the county party organization in Mississippi. Moreover, given that many of the Florida counties are large, urban ones, we would expect that there are more active members of a typical Florida county party organization than is the case in Mississippi, with many more of the active Florida members not holding a formal position on the county executive committee than would be true for Mississippi. What we ideally would like to have would be the number of individuals in each state who are significantly involved in their local party organization, but this number is very difficult to determine or even estimate accurately.

As a substitute, we have weighted the members by the population of the state. In effect, we are assuming that the number of activists in a state is proportional to its population size. This weighting procedure undoubtedly is imperfect, but it seems to us to be better than not weighting the members at all, which would have the effect of allowing the Mississippi members to count much more than the Tennessee members, for example. Furthermore, we have carried out the weighting separately by party, as the number of respondents varies by party within a state. Finally, the weights assigned to both Democratic and Republican members have been adjusted so that the overall weighted *N* is the same as the overall unweighted *N*. County chairs have been given a weight of 1.0 in each case, for the reasons already discussed.

The weight factor runs from 0.22 (Mississippi Republicans) to 5.03 (Virginia Republicans). Every county chair has a weight of 1.0. The weighted *N* is 7,171, virtually the same as the unweighted *N*, which is 7,170. The sample is divided almost equally between Democrats and Republicans (50.4 percent Dem., 49.6 percent Rep.). We have not attempted to shift the distribution by party from this 50-50 split by our weighting, as we do not know what proportion of all grassroots activists in the South are Democrats. However, given the rough parity of the parties in the region at this point in time, the 50-50 split seems reasonable to us.

In the analyses reported in this book, the weighted data set is used in most cases where all eleven states are being analyzed as a group. In cases where figures for individual states are reported, the unweighted data generally are used, as there is no reason to weight the data.

QUESTIONNAIRE

SOUTHERN GRASSROOTS PARTY ACTIVISTS PROJECT

Funded by National Science Foundation Grant SES-9986501

PLEASE NOTE: This project is being conducted by researchers at universities and colleges in the 11 southern states. Your responses to the questions below are very important to us so that we can understand how and why people choose to become involved in political party organizations. All of your answers WILL BE KEPT COMPLETELY CONFIDENTIAL and will be used only in the aggregate to describe your state or the 11 southern states together. No information will be released that will allow anyone to determine how any respondent replied.

Marking Instructions

- USE A NO. 2 PENCIL ONLY
- DARKEN THE CIRCLE COMPLETELY
- ERASE CLEANLY ANY MARKS YOU WISH TO CHANGE
- DO NOT MAKE ANY STRAY MARKS ON THIS FORM

INCORRECT MARKS ⊘ ⊗ ◒ ⊙ CORRECT MARK ●

For Office Use Only

State code:

○ AL	○ LA	○ TN
○ AR	○ MS	○ TX
○ FL	○ NC	○ VA
○ GA	○ SC	

Party position code: Ⓒ Ⓜ

Party code: Ⓓ Ⓡ

County code:

⓪ ① ② ③ ④ ⑤ ⑥ ⑦ ⑧ ⑨
⓪ ① ② ③ ④ ⑤ ⑥ ⑦ ⑧ ⑨
⓪ ① ② ③ ④ ⑤ ⑥ ⑦ ⑧ ⑨

1. First, a few questions about your party position.

1a. In what year did you occupy your **current** party position? ______

(Mark the last two digits of the year; e.g. mark 98 for 1998)

Year

19 ⓪ ① ② ③ ④ ⑤ ⑥ ⑦ ⑧ ⑨
⓪ ① ② ③ ④ ⑤ ⑥ ⑦ ⑧ ⑨

1b. When did you **first** become active in politics; that is, in doing more than merely voting? Year ______.

Year

19 ⓪ ① ② ③ ④ ⑤ ⑥ ⑦ ⑧ ⑨
⓪ ① ② ③ ④ ⑤ ⑥ ⑦ ⑧ ⑨

PLEASE DO NOT WRITE IN THIS AREA

44143

2. **Next, we would like to ask you about how you became involved in party politics.**

2a. Please indicate what role each of the following played in your decision to seek your **current party position**. Was it a major or minor consideration?

	Major Consideration	Minor Consideration	Not a Consideration
1) Urged to run by party official	①	②	③
2) Urged to run by elected official	①	②	③
3) Urged to run by candidate for elected office	①	②	③
4) Urged to run by friends or family members active in the party	①	②	③
5) Decided to run pretty much on my own	①	②	③

2b. Please indicate what role each of the following played in your decision to **first become involved** in party politics

	Major Consideration	Minor Consideration	Not a Consideration
1) Urged to participate by party official	①	②	③
2) Urged to participate by elected official	①	②	③
3) Urged to participate by candidate for elected office	①	②	③
4) Urged to participate by friends or family members active in the party	①	②	③
5) Decided to participate pretty much on my own	①	②	③

2c. Rate each of the following in terms of its importance in your *personal decision* to seek your current party position.

	Very Important	Somewhat Important	Not Very Important	Not Important At All
1) Friendship with a candidate	①	②	③	④
2) Friendship with a political party official	①	②	③	④
3) Political work is part of my way of life	①	②	③	④
4) I am strongly attached to my political party	①	②	③	④
5) I enjoy the friendship and social contact I have with other party workers	①	②	③	④
6) My family's involvement in party politics	①	②	③	④
7) I like the fun and excitement of campaigns	①	②	③	④
8) I am trying to build a personal position in politics	①	②	③	④
9) I see campaign work as a way to influence politics and government	①	②	③	④
10) I see working in the political party generally as a way to influence politics and government	①	②	③	④
11) I like the feeling of being close to people who are doing important things	①	②	③	④
12) Party work helps me make business contacts	①	②	③	④
13) Party work helps me fulfill my sense of community obligation	①	②	③	④
14) Party work gives me a feeling of recognition in the community	①	②	③	④
15) My concern with public issues	①	②	③	④
16) To support candidates whom I believe in	①	②	③	④

3. Party workers often mention the following activities as being an important part of their job. In your *current party position* which of these activities are among the important things you do?

	Very Important	Somewhat Important	Not Very Important	Not Important At All
1) Contacting voters	①	②	③	④
2) Raising money	①	②	③	④
3) Getting people to register to vote	①	②	③	④
4) Campaigning	①	②	③	④
5) Public relations	①	②	③	④
6) Contacting new voters	①	②	③	④
7) Participating in party meetings and business	①	②	③	④
8) Recruiting and organizing workers	①	②	③	④
9) County party organizational work	①	②	③	④
10) Increasing political information for others	①	②	③	④
11) Policy formulation	①	②	③	④
12) Getting candidates for local office	①	②	③	④
13) Other nominating activities	①	②	③	④
14) Helping to develop a party Web site	①	②	③	④

4. Next, we would like to ask you about your interest and affiliations in politics.

4a. Before your current party position, have you held any of the following?

1) Another party position? ① Yes ② No

2) An appointed public office? ① Yes ② No

If "yes", how many other party or appointed positions have you held? (Please mark)
○ 01 ○ 02 ○ 03 ○ 04 ○ 05+

4b. Have you ever held an elected public office?
① Yes ② No

4c. Have you ever run unsuccessfully for elected public office?
① Yes ② No

4d. Do you expect to run for public office in the future?
① Yes ② No ③ Not sure

4e. Have your parents or other relatives ever been active in politics beyond merely voting?
○ Yes ○ No

4f. How would you describe your parents' party affiliation at the time you were growing up?

Father's party:	Mother's party:
① Democrat	① Democrat
② Republican	② Republican
③ Independent	③ Independent
④ Other	④ Other
⑤ Do not know	⑤ Do not know

4g. How would you describe your own political party affiliation: In **state** politics? In **national** politics?

State politics:	National politics:
① Strong Democrat	① Strong Democrat
② Weak Democrat	② Weak Democrat
③ Ind. but lean Democratic	③ Ind. but lean Democratic
④ Independent	④ Independent
⑤ Ind. but lean Republican	⑤ Ind. but lean Republican
⑥ Weak Republican	⑥ Weak Republican
⑦ Strong Republican	⑦ Strong Republican

4h. In the 1996 election for president, how did you vote?
① Voted for Clinton
② Voted for Dole
③ Voted for Perot
④ Voted for another candidate
⑤ Did not vote

4i. In the 2000 election for president, how did you vote?
① Voted for Bush
② Voted for Gore
③ Voted for another candidate
④ Did not vote

4j. Have you ever voted for a minor party or independent candidate for any office in the past ten years?
○ Yes ○ No

PLEASE DO NOT WRITE IN THIS AREA

44143

5. **How important would you say being a member of the county party organization is to you personally?**

① Very important
② Somewhat important
③ Not very important
④ Not important at all

6. **Have you ever been affiliated with a different political party?**

① Yes → 6a.
② No
(IF "No", SKIP TO QUESTION 7.)

6a. **If "Yes", which political party?**

① Democrats
② Republicans
③ Reform
④ Other

6b. ***If you have switched political parties*, in what year did you switch? (mark the last two digits of the year; e.g., mark 95 for 1995) _______.**

Year		
19		⓪①②③④⑤⑥⑦⑧⑨
		⓪①②③④⑤⑥⑦⑧⑨

6c. **Which of the following were important or not important in your decision to switch parties?**
Please mark each question.

	Important	Not Important
1) **The party to which I switched had better, more appealing candidates**	○	○
2) **The party to which I switched was much more likely to take the right stand on issues**	○	○
3) **I switched parties because friends, relatives, or fellow workers persuaded me to do so**	○	○
4) **The party to which I switched offered greater opportunities for personal advancement (political career, business contacts, etc.)**	○	○
5) **The party to which I switched is more active and has a superior organization**	○	○

6d. **Which ONE of the above reasons (1-5 in Question 6c) was MOST IMPORTANT in your decision to switch parties?**

①②③④⑤

7. **Candidates, party workers, and party organizations emphasize different campaign activities. Which of the following activities did you do in recent election campaigns?** Please mark all activities that you did:

Ⓐ Organized door-to-door canvassing
Ⓑ Organized campaign events (rallies, forums, etc.)
Ⓒ Arranged fund-raising activities
Ⓓ Sent mailings to voters
Ⓔ Distributed campaign literature
Ⓕ Organized telephone campaigns
Ⓖ Purchased billboard space
Ⓗ Distributed posters or lawn signs
Ⓘ Contributed money to campaigns
Ⓙ Conducted voter registration drives
Ⓚ Utilized public opinion surveys
Ⓛ Dealt with campaign media (press releases, radio/TV, etc.)
Ⓜ Helped to construct or maintain a campaign Web site

8. We have found that party officials do not always work as actively during elections at one level as they do during elections at other levels. What about you?
How actively do you work:

	Very Actively	Somewhat Actively	Not Very Actively	Not Actively At All
8a. In local elections?	①	②	③	④
8b. In state elections?	①	②	③	④
8c. In national elections?	①	②	③	④

9a. Have any candidates talked with you about running for office before they announced their candidacy?

① Yes ② No

9b. Have you ever suggested to someone that they ought to run for public office?

① Yes ② No

10. Please indicate whether you agree or disagree with the following statements.

	Strongly Agree	Agree	Disagree	Strongly Disagree
10a. Good party workers support any candidate nominated by the party even if they basically disagree with the candidate	①	②	③	④
10b. Party organization and unity are more important than free and total discussion of issues which may divide the party	①	②	③	④
10c. A political party should be more concerned with issues than with winning elections	①	②	③	④
10d. Controversial positions should be avoided in party platform to insure party unity	①	②	③	④
10e. Broad electoral appeal is more important than a consistent ideology	①	②	③	④
10f. Good party workers should remain officially and unofficially neutral in primary contests even when they have a personal preference	①	②	③	④

11. Now we would like to ask you about your communication in the party organization. How often do you communicate with:

	Very Often	Often	Seldom	Never
11a. County party chair	①	②	③	④
11b. Other county party committee members	①	②	③	④
11c. State party chair	①	②	③	④
11d. State party committee members	①	②	③	④
11e. National committee members	①	②	③	④
11f. Local government officials	①	②	③	④
11g. State government officials	①	②	③	④
11h. National government officials	①	②	③	④

12. What about your political beliefs? Do you consider yourself:

① Very liberal
② Somewhat liberal
③ Middle of the road/moderate
④ Somewhat conservative
⑤ Very conservative

13. What are your views concerning the following issues?

		Strongly Agree	Agree	Disagree	Strongly Disagree
13a.	The government in Washington should provide fewer services, even in areas such as health and education, in order to reduce government spending	①	②	③	④
13b.	Women should have an equal role with men in running business, industry, and government	①	②	③	④
13c.	By law a woman should be able to obtain an abortion as a matter of personal choice	①	②	③	④
13d.	Prayer should be allowed in the public schools	①	②	③	④
13e.	The government in Washington should make every effort to improve the social and economic position of blacks and other minority groups	①	②	③	④
13f.	People convicted of murder should receive the death penalty	①	②	③	④
13g.	We need more federal government regulation of managed health care	①	②	③	④

14. Should federal spending be increased, decreased, or kept the same for the following areas?

		Increased	Kept the Same	Decreased
14a.	National defense	①	②	③
14b.	Protecting the environment	①	②	③
14c.	Public schools	①	②	③
14d.	Dealing with crime	①	②	③
14e.	Social Security	①	②	③
14f.	Health care	①	②	③
14g.	Welfare programs	①	②	③

15. What are your views concerning the following issues?

		Agree Strongly	Agree	Disagree	Strongly Disagree
15a.	The government in Washington should make every effort to improve the social and economic situation for women	①	②	③	④
15b.	The government should enact stricter legislation to control handguns	①	②	③	④
15c.	The government should provide vouchers for parents to send their children to private schools	①	②	③	④
15d.	Because of past discrimination, blacks should be given preference in hiring and promotion	①	②	③	④
15e.	The federal government should adopt a flat tax system to replace the current federal income tax	①	②	③	④
15f.	There should be laws to protect homosexuals against job discrimination	①	②	③	④
15g.	The government in Washington should see to it that every person has a job and a good standard of living	①	②	③	④

16. Would you describe your feelings toward the ***national* Democratic and Republican parties** as extremely close, extremely distant, or somewhere in between? ***State* political parties**?

		Extremely Close			Neutral			Extremely Distant
1)	National Democratic Party	①	②	③	④	⑤	⑥	⑦
2)	National Republican Party	①	②	③	④	⑤	⑥	⑦
3)	State Democratic Party	①	②	③	④	⑤	⑥	⑦
4)	State Republican Party	①	②	③	④	⑤	⑥	⑦

PLEASE DO NOT WRITE IN THIS AREA

44143

17. There is a lot of speculation these days concerning the current health and future of political parties. **In your party and in your county**, how does the strength of the party compare to 10 years ago?

	Significantly Stronger	Somewhat Stronger	Little Change	Somewhat Weaker	Significantly Weaker
17a. The over all county party organization is	①	②	③	④	⑤
17b. The party's campaign effectiveness is	①	②	③	④	⑤
17c. The party's ability to raise funds is	①	②	③	④	⑤
17d. The party's role in recruiting candidates for public office is	①	②	③	④	⑤
17e. The party's efforts to develop the organizational skills of workers is	①	②	③	④	⑤
17f. The party's use of the media is	①	②	③	④	⑤
17g. The party's use of opinion polls is	①	②	③	④	⑤
17h. The party's use of computer technology is	①	②	③	④	⑤
17i. The party's strength among county voters is	①	②	③	④	⑤

18. Political parties often represent people of differing views. How much **DISAGREEMENT** is there **WITHIN** your **STATE** party in each of the following areas?

	Great Deal	Fair Amount	Some	Very Little
18a. Between people of different ideological viewpoints	①	②	③	④
18b. Between supporters of different party leaders	①	②	③	④
18c. Between long-time residents and newcomers	①	②	③	④
18d. Between different regions of the state	①	②	③	④
18e. Between urban and rural areas of the state	①	②	③	④
18f. On the issue of taxes	①	②	③	④
18g. On the issue of abortion	①	②	③	④
18h. On racial issues	①	②	③	④
18i. On issues of government spending	①	②	③	④

19. Would you say the amount of factionalism within your **STATE** political party is:

① Very high
② Moderately high
③ Moderately low
④ Very low

20. Would you say the amount of factionalism within your **COUNTY** political party is:

① Very high
② Moderately high
③ Moderately low
④ Very low

21. How active have you been in each of the following groups:

	Very Active	Somewhat Active	Not Very Active	Not at all Active
21a. Teacher's organizations	①	②	③	④
21b. Business or professional organizations	①	②	③	④
21c. Civic organizations	①	②	③	④
21d. Labor unions	①	②	③	④
21e. Church groups	①	②	③	④
21f. Environmental groups	①	②	③	④
21g. Civil rights groups	①	②	③	④
21h. Women's rights groups	①	②	③	④
21i. Anti-abortion groups	①	②	③	④
21j. Other group (Please identify________________________)	①	②	③	④

22. Finally, we would like some information about your personal background.

22a. What is your age? _____ years.

# of Years

⓪①②③④⑤⑥⑦⑧⑨
⓪①②③④⑤⑥⑦⑧⑨

22b. How long have you lived in this state? _____years.

# of Years

⓪①②③④⑤⑥⑦⑧⑨
⓪①②③④⑤⑥⑦⑧⑨

22c. What is your gender?

○ Male ○ Female

22d. What is your racial/ethnic background?
Please mark those that apply:

① **White**
② **African American**
③ **Hispanic American**
④ **Asian American**
⑤ **Native American**
⑥ **Other**
If "Other", name______________

22e. Where did you live for most of the first 18 years of your life?

① **This state**
② **Another southern state**
③ **The eastern U.S.**
④ **The midwestern U.S.**
⑤ **The western U.S.**
⑥ **Another country**

22f. What is the highest level of formal education you have completed?

① **High school or less**
② **Some college**
③ **4 yr college degree**
④ **Graduate or professional degree**

22g. What is the approximate level of your family's yearly income?

① **Under $25,000**
② **$25,000-49,999**
③ **$50,000-74,999**
④ **$75,000-99,999**
⑤ **$100,000-150,000**
⑥ **More than $150,000**

23. What is your religious preference?

① **Protestant**
② **Roman Catholic**
③ **Jewish**
④ **Something else (name)**______________
⑤ **Nonbeliever**

23a. If Protestant, what church or denomination is that (for example, Baptist, Southern Baptist, African Methodist Episcopal, Church of God, etc.). Please write the name below,

____

DO NOT MARK HERE

⓪①②③④⑤⑥⑦⑧⑨
⓪①②③④⑤⑥⑦⑧⑨
⓪①②③④⑤⑥⑦⑧⑨

23b. How often do you attend church or synagogue services?

① **More than once a week**
② **Once a week**
③ **Almost every week**
④ **Once or twice a month**
⑤ **A few times a year**
⑥ **Never**

23c. How much guidance would you say that religion plays in your day to-day life?

① **Great deal**
② **Fair amount**
③ **Some**
④ **Very little**
⑤ **No guidance**

23d. Do you consider yourself to be a "Born-Again" Christian?

○ Yes ○ No

23e. How close do you feel toward Christian Right groups?

① **Very close**
② **Close**
③ **Neutral**
④ **Far**
⑤ **Very far**

Thank you for your cooperation in answering these questions. All of your answers are STRICTLY CONFIDENTIAL and only will be analyzed in the aggregate for each of the 11 southern states or for the southern region.

PLEASE DO NOT WRITE IN THIS AREA

44143

Mark Reflex® by NCS MM235781-1 654321 ED06 Printed in U.S.A.

References

Abramowitz, Alan I., John McGlennon, and Ronald Rapoport. 1983. "The Party Isn't Over: Incentives for Activism in the 1980 Presidential Nominating Campaign." *Journal of Politics* 45: 1006–1015.

Abramowitz, Alan I., and Kyle L. Saunders. 1998. "Ideological Realignment in the U.S. Electorate." *Journal of Politics* 60: 634–652.

Abramowitz, Alan I., and Walter J. Stone. 1984. *Nomination Politics: Party Activists and Presidential Choice.* New York: Praeger.

Abramson, Paul R., John H. Aldrich, and David A. Rohde. 2002. *Change and Continuity in the 2000 Elections.* Washington DC: CQ Press.

Agranoff, Robert. 1976. *The Management of Election Campaigns.* Boston: Holbrook Press.

Aistrup, Joseph A. 1996. *The Southern Strategy Revisited: Republican Top-Down Advancement in the South.* Lexington, KY: The University Press of Kentucky.

Aldrich, John H. 1995. *Why Parties? The Origin and Transformation of Party Politics in America.* Chicago: The University of Chicago Press.

Aldrich, John H. 2000. "Southern Parties in State and Nation." *Journal of Politics* 62: 643–670.

Appleton, Andrew, and Daniel Ward. 1994. "Party Organizational Response to Electoral Change: Texas and Arkansas." *American Review of Politics* 15: 191–212.

Backstrom, Charles. 1977. "Congress and the Public: How Representative is One of the Other?" *American Politics Quarterly* 5: 411–434.

Baer, Denise L., and David A. Bositis. 1988. *Elite Cadres and Party Coalitions.* Westport, CT: Greenwood Press.

Baer, Denise L., and David A. Bositis. 1993. *Politics and Linkage in a Democratic Society.* Englewood Cliffs, NJ: Prentice-Hall.

Baker, Tod A. 1990. "The Emergence of the Religious Right and the Development of the Two-Party System in the South." In *Political Parties in the Southern States,* ed. Tod Baker, Charles D. Hadley, Robert P. Steed, and Laurence W. Moreland. New York: Praeger.

Baker, Tod A., Robert P. Steed, and Laurence W. Moreland. 1998. "Culture Wars and Religion in the South: The Changing Character of the Party Struggle." In *Party Activists in Southern Politics: Mirrors and Makers of Change,* ed. Charles D. Hadley and Lewis Bowman. Knoxville: University of Tennessee Press.

Barth, Jay. 1992. "Dual Partisanship in the South: Anachronism, or a Real Barrier to Republican Success in the Region." *Midsouth Journal of Political Science* 13: 487–500.

Barth, Jay. 2002. "Gender and Southern Party Activists: Evidence from the 2001 Southern Grassroots Party Activists Project." Presented at the annual meeting of the Southern Political Science Association, Savannah, GA.

Bartley, Numan V., and Hugh D. Graham. 1975. *Southern Politics and the Second Reconstruction.* Baltimore: The Johns Hopkins University Press.

Beck, Paul Allen. 1974. "Environment and Party: The Impact of Political and Demographic County Characteristics on Party Behavior." *American Political Science Review* 68: 1229–1244.

Beck, Paul Allen. 1977. "Partisan Dealignment in the Postwar South." *American Political Science Review* 71: 477–496.

Beck, Paul Allen. 1997. *Party Politics in America.* 8th ed. New York: Longman.

Belloni, Frank P., and Dennis C. Beller. 1976. "The Study of Party Factions in Competitive Political Organizations." *Western Political Quarterly* 29: 532–549.

Berard, Stanley P. 2001. *Southern Democrats in the U.S. House of Representatives.* Norman: University of Oklahoma.

Bibby, John F. 1980. "Party Renewal in the National Republican Party." In *Party Renewal in America,* ed. Gerald M. Pomper. New York: Praeger.

Bibby, John F. 1998. "Party Orgnizations, 1946–1996." In *Partisan Approaches to Postwar American Politics,* ed. Byron E. Shafer. New York: Chatham House.

Bibby, John F. 1999a. "Party Networks: National-State Integration, Allied Groups, and Issue Activists." In *The State of the Parties: The Changing Role of Contemporary American Parties,* 3rd ed., ed. John C. Green and Daniel M. Shea. Lanham, MD: Rowman and Littlefield.

Bibby, John F. 1999b. "State and Local Parties in a Candidate-Centered Age." In *American State and Local Politics: Directions for the 21st Century*, ed. Ronald E. Weber and Paul Brace. New York: Chatham House.

Biggar, Jeanne C. 1984. *The Graying of the Sunbelt: A Look at the Impact of Elderly U.S. Migration*. Washington, DC: Population Reference Bureau.

Biggar, Jeanne C., and Francis C. Biasiolli. 1978. "Metropolitan Deconcentration: Subareal In-Migration and Central City to Ring Mobility Patterns Among Southern SMSAs." *Demography* 15: 589–603.

Bishop, George, Alfred Tuchfarber, and Robert Oldendick. 1978. "Change in the Structure of American Political Attitudes: The Nagging Question of Question Wording." *American Journal of Political Science* 22: 250–269.

Black, Earl. 1983. "A Theory of Southern Factionalism." *Journal of Politics* 45: 594–614.

Black, Earl, and Merle Black. 1987. *Politics and Society in the South*. Cambridge, MA: Harvard University Press.

Black, Earl, and Merle Black. 1992. *The Vital South*. Cambridge: Harvard University Press.

Black, Earl, and Merle Black. 2002. *The Rise of Southern Republicans*. Cambridge: Harvard University Press.

Blumberg, Melanie, William C. Binning, and John C. Green. 2003. "No Mo[mentum] in Ohio: Local Parties and the 2000 Presidential Campaign." In *The State of the Parties: The Changing Role of Contemporary American Parties*, 4th ed., ed. John C. Green and Rick Farmer. Lanham, MD: Rowman and Littlefield.

Blumenthal, Sidney. 1982. *The Permanent Campaign: Inside the World of Elite Political Operatives*. Boston: Beacon Press.

Bowman, Lewis, and G. R. Boynton. 1966a. "Activities and Role Definitions of Grassroots Party Officials." *Journal of Politics* 28: 121–143.

Bowman, Lewis, and G. R. Boynton. 1966b. "Recruitment Patterns Among Local Party Officials: A Model and Some Preliminary Findings in Selected Locales." *American Political Science Review* 60: 667–676.

Bowman, Lewis, William E. Hulbary, and Anne E. Kelley. 1990. "Party Sorting at the Grassroots: Stable Partisans and Party Changers Among Florida's Precinct Officials." In *The Disappearing South? Studies in Regional Change and Continuity*, ed. Robert P. Steed, Laurence W. Moreland, and Tod A. Baker. Tuscaloosa: The University of Alabama Press.

Bowman, Lewis, Dennis S. Ippolito, and William Donaldson. 1969. "Incentives for the Maintenance of Grassroots Political Activism." *Midwest Journal of Political Science* 13: 126–139.

Breaux, David, Stephen D. Shaffer, and Patrick Cotter. 1998. "Mass/Elite Linkage." In *Party Organization and Activism in the American South,* ed. Robert P. Steed, John A. Clark, Lewis Bowman, and Charles D. Hadley. Tuscaloosa: University of Alabama Press.

Broder, David. 1972. *The Party's Over*. New York: Harper & Row.

Brodsky, David, and Simeon Brodsky. 1998. "Communication Patterns." In *Party Organization and Activism in the American South,* ed. Robert P. Steed, John A. Clark, Lewis Bowman, and Charles D. Hadley. Tuscaloosa: University of Alabama Press.

Brodsky, David M., and Patrick R. Cotter. 1998. "Political Issues and Political Parties." In *Party Activists in Southern Politics: Mirrors and Makers of Change,* ed. Charles D. Hadley and Lewis Bowman. Knoxville: University of Tennessee Press.

Brown, Thad A. 1988. *Migration Politics: The Impact of Population Mobility on American Voting Behavior*. Chapel Hill: University of North Carolina Press.

Bruce, John M., and John A. Clark. 1998. "Segmented Partisanship in a Southern Political Elite." *Polity* 30: 627–644.

Bullock, Charles S. III. 1988. "Creeping Realignment in the South." In *The South's New Politics: Realignment and Dealignment,* ed. Robert H. Swansbrough and David M. Brodsky. Colombia: University of South Carolina Press.

Bullock, Charles S. III, Ronald Keith Gaddie, and Donna R. Hoffman. 2002. "The Consolidation of the White Southern Congressional Vote." Presented at the annual meeting of the American Political Science Association, Boston, MA.

Bullock, Charles S. III, and Mark J. Rozell, eds. 2003a. *The New Politics of the Old South,* 2nd ed. Lanham, MD: Rowman & Littlefield.

Bullock, Charles S. III, and Mark J. Rozell. 2003b. "Introduction: Southern Politics in the Twenty-first Century." In *The New Politics of the Old South,* 2nd ed., ed. Charles S. Bullock III and Mark J. Rozell. Lanham, MD: Rowman & Littlefield.

Burnham, Walter Dean. 1982. *The Current Crisis in American Politics*. New York: Oxford Unversity Press.

Calhoun-Brown, Allison. 1996. "African American Churches and Political Mobilization: The Psychological Impact of Organizational Resources." *Journal of Politics* 58: 935–953.

Calhoun-Brown, Allison. 1997. "Still Seeing in Black and White: Racial Challenges for the Christian Right." In *Sojourners in the Wilderness: The Christian Right in Comparative Perspective,* ed. Corwin E. Smidt and James M. Penning. Lanham, MD: Rowman & Littlefield.

Campbell, Angus, Philip E. Converse, Warren E. Miller, and Donald E. Stokes. 1960. *The American Voter*. New York: John Wiley and Sons.

Campbell, Bruce A. 1977a. "Change in the Southern Electorate." *American Journal of Political Science* 21: 37–64.

Campbell, Bruce A. 1977b. "Patterns of Change in the Partisan Loyalties of Native Southerners: 1952–1972." *Journal of Politics* 39: 730–761.

Canon, Bradley C. 1978. "Factionalism in the South: A Test of Theory and a Revisitation of V. O. Key." *American Journal of Political Science* 22: 833–848.

Carmines, Edward G., and Harold W. Stanley. 1990. "Ideological Realignment in the Contemporary South: Where Have All the Conservatives Gone?" In *The Disappearing South: Studies in Regional Change and Continuity,* ed. Robert P. Steed, Laurence W. Moreland, and Tod. A. Baker. Tuscaloosa: University of Alabama.

Carmines, Edward G., and James A. Stimson. 1989. *Issue Evolution: Race and Transformation of American Politics.* Princeton: Princeton University Press.

Clark, John A. 1997. "Georgia." In *State Party Profiles: A 50-State Guide to Development, Organization, and Resources,* ed. Andrew M. Appleton and Daniel S. Ward. Washington, DC: CQ Press.

Clark, John A., and Brad Lockerbie. 1993. "Party Integration in Southern Grassroots Parties." Presented at the annual meeting of the American Political Science Association, Washington, DC.

Clark, John A., and Brad Lockerbie. 1998. "Split-Partisan Identification." In *Party Activists in Southern Politics: Mirrors and Makers of Change,* ed. Charles D. Hadley and Lewis Bowman. Knoxville: University of Tennessee Press.

Clark, John A., Brad Lockerbie, and Peter W. Wielhouwer. 1998. "Campaign Activities." In *Party Organization and Activism in the American South,* ed. Robert P. Steed, John A. Clark, Lewis Bowman, and Charles D. Hadley. Tuscaloosa: University of Alabama Press.

Clark, John A., and Charles Prysby, eds. 2003. *American Review of Politics* 24 (Spring and Summer). Special double issue on grassroots party activists in southern politics.

Clark, Peter, and James Q. Wilson. 1961. "Incentive Systems: A Theory of Organization." *Administrative Science Quarterly* 6: 129–166.

Clarke, Harold D., Euel Elliott, and Thomas H. Roback. 1991. "Domestic Issue Ideology and Activist Style: A Note on 1980 Republican Convention Delegates." *Journal of Politics* 53: 519–534.

Clawson, Rosalee A., and John A. Clark. 1998. "Party Activists as Agents of Change: Women, Blacks, and Political Parties in the South." In *Party Organization and Activism in the American South,* ed. Robert P. Steed, John A. Clark, Lewis Bowman, and Charles D. Hadley. Tuscaloosa: University of Alabama Press.

Clawson, Rosalee A., and John A. Clark. 2003. "The Attitudinal Structure African American Women Party Activists: The Impact of Race, Gender and Religion." *Political Research Quarterly* 56: 211–221.

Cohen, Jeffrey E., Richard Fleisher, and Paul Kantor, eds. 2001. *American Political Parties: Decline or Resurgence?* Washington, DC: CQ Press.

Coleman, John J. 1996. "Party Organizational Strength and Public Support for Parties." *American Journal of Political Science* 40: 805–824.

Coleman, John J. 2003. "Responsible, Functional, or Both? American Political Parties and the ASPA Report After Fifty Years." In *The State of the Parties: The Changing Role of American Contemporary Parties,* 4th ed., ed. John C. Green and Rick Farmer. Lanham, MD: Rowman and Littlefield.

Committee on Political Parties. American Political Science Association. 1950. *Toward a More Responsible Two-Party System. A Report of the Committee on Political Parties of the American Political Science Association.* New York: Rinehart.

Conger, Kimberly H., and John C. Green. 2002. "Spreading Out and Digging In: Christian Conservatives and State Republican Parties." *Campaigns & Elections* 23 (February): 58–65.

Converse, Philip E. 1964. "The Nature of Belief Systems in Mass Publics." In *Ideology and Discontent,* ed. David E. Apter. New York: Free Press.

Converse, Philip E. 1966. "On the Possibility of a Major Realignment in the South." In *Election and the Political Order,* ed. Angus Campbell, Philip E. Converse, Warren E. Miller, and Donald E. Stokes. New York: John Wiley and Sons.

Converse, Philip E. 1972. "Change in the American Electorate." In *The Human Meaning of Social Change,* ed. Angus Campbell and Philip E. Converse. New York: Russell Sage.

Converse, Philip E., Aage R. Clausen, and Warren E. Miller. 1965. "Electoral Myth and Reality: The 1964 Election." *American Political Science Review* 59: 321–336.

Conway, M. Margaret, and Frank B. Feigert. 1968. "Motivation, Incentive Systems, and the Political Party Organization." *American Political Science Review* 62: 1159–1173.

Conway, M. Margaret, and Frank B. Feigert. 1974. "Incentives and Task Performance Among Party Precinct Workers." *Western Political Quarterly* 27: 693–709.

Cotter, Cornelius P. and John F. Bibby. 1980. "Institutional Development of Parties and the Thesis of Party Decline." *Political Science Quarterly* 95: 1–27.

Cotter, Cornelius P., James L. Gibson, John F. Bibby, and Robert J. Huckshorn. 1984. *Party Organizations in American Politics.* New York: Praeger.

Cowden, Jonathan A. 2001. "Southernization of the Nation and Nationalization of the South: Racial Conservation, Social Welfare, and White Partisans in the United States, 1956–92." *British Journal of Political Science* 31: 277–302.

Crotty, William J. 1971. "Party Effort and Its Impact on the Vote." *American Political Science Review* 65: 439–450.

Crotty, William J., and Gary C. Jacobson. 1980. *American Parties in Decline.* Boston: Little, Brown.

Cutright, Phillips, and Peter H. Rossi. 1958. "Grass Roots Politicians and the Vote." *American Sociological Review* 23: 171–179.

David, Paul T. 1992. "The APSA Committee on Political Parties." *Perspectives on Political Science* 21: 70–79.

D'Emilio, John. 2003. *Lost Prophet: The Life and Times of Bayard Rustin.* New York: Free Press.

Dodson, Debra L. 1990. "Socialization of Party Activists: National Convention Delegates, 1972–81." *American Journal of Political Science* 34: 1119–1141.

Downs, Anthony. 1957. *An Economic Theory of Democracy.* New York: Harper and Row.

Dye, Thomas R. 1966. *Politics, Economics, and the Public.* Chicago: Rand McNally.

Dyson, Michael Eric. 2000. *I May Not Get There With You: The True Martin Luther King Jr.* New York: Free Press.

Echols, Margaret Thompson, and Austin Ranney. 1976. "The Impact of Intraparty Competition Reconsidered: The Case of Florida." *Journal of Politics* 38: 142–152.

Edsall, Thomas B., and Alan Cooperman. 2002. "GOP Using Faith Initiative to Woo Voters." *Washington Post,* September 15, A5.

Eldersveld, Samuel J. 1964. *Political Parties: A Behavioral Analysis.* Chicago: Rand McNally.

Epstein, Leon. 1986. *Political Parties in the American Mold.* Madison: University of Wisconsin Press.

Erikson, Robert S., and Kent L. Tedin. 2003. *American Public Opinion: Its Origin, Content, and Impact.* 6th ed. New York: Longman.

Feigert, Frank B. 1973. "Conservatism, Populism, and Social Change." *American Behavioral Scientist* 17: 272–278.

Feigert, Frank B., and John R. Todd. 1998a. "Migration and Party Change." In *Party Activists in Southern Politics: Mirrors and Makers of Change,* ed. Charles D. Hadley and Lewis Bowman. Knoxville: University of Tennessee Press.

Feigert, Frank B., and John R. Todd. 1998b. "Party Maintenance Activities." In *Party Organization and Activism in the American South,* ed. Robert P. Steed, John A. Clark, Lewis Bowman, and Charles D. Hadley. Tuscaloosa: University of Alabama Press.

Francia, Peter L., Paul S. Herrnson, John P. Frendreis, and Alan R. Gitelson. 2003. "The Battle for the Legislature: Party Campaigning in State House and State Senate Elections." In *The State of the Parties: The Changing Role of Contemporary American Parties,* 4th ed., ed. John C. Green and Rick Farmer. Lanham, MD: Rowman and Littlefield.

Frederick, Marla F. 2003. *Between Sundays: Black Women and Everyday Struggles of Faith*. Berkeley, CA: University of California Press.

Frendreis, John P., James L. Gibson, and Laura L. Vertz. 1990. "The Electoral Relevance of Local Party Organizations." *American Political Science Review* 84: 225–235.

Frendreis, John, and Alan R. Gitelson. 1999. "Local Parties in the 1990s: Spokes in a Candidate-Centered Wheel." In *The State of the Parties: The Changing Role of Contemporary American Parties,* 2nd ed., ed. John C. Green and Daniel M. Shea. Lanham, MD: Rowman and Littlefield.

Garrow, David J. 1986. *Bearing the Cross: Martin Luther King, Jr., and the Southern Christian Leadership Conference*. New York: Vintage Books.

Geer, John, and Mark E. Shere. 1992. "Party Competition and the Prisoner's Dilemma: An Argument for the Direct Primary." *Journal of Politics* 54: 741–761.

Genovese, Eugene D. 1976. *Roll, Jordan, Roll: The World the Slaves Made*. New York: Vintage Books.

Gibson, James L., John P. Frendreis, and Laura L. Vertz. 1989. "Party Dynamics in the 1980s: Change in County Party Organizational Strength, 1980–1984." *American Journal of Political Science* 33: 67–90.

Glaser, James M. 1996. *Race, Campaign Politics, and the Realignment in the South*. New Haven, CT: Yale University Press.

Green, John C. 2002. "Believers for Bush, Godly for Gore: Religion and the 2000 Election in the South." In *The 2000 Presidential Election in the South,* ed. Robert P. Steed and Laurence W. Moreland. Westport, CT: Praeger.

Green, John C., and Rick Farmer, eds. 2003. *The State of the Parties: The Changing Role of Contemporary American Parties,* 4th ed. Lanham, MD: Rowman and Littlefield.

Green, John C., and Paul S. Herrnson, eds. 2002. *Responsible Partnership? The Evolution of American Political Parties Since 1950*. Lawrence, KS: University Press of Kansas.

Green, John C., Lyman A. Kellstedt, Corwin E. Smidt, and James L. Guth. 2002. "The Soul of the South: Religion and Southern Politics at the Millennium." In *The New Politics of the Old South: An Introduction to Southern Politics,* 2nd ed., ed. Charles S. Bullock III and Mark J. Rozell. Lanham, MD: Rowman and Littlefield.

Green, John C., Mark J. Rozell, and Clyde Wilcox, eds. 2003. *The Christian Right in American Politics: Marching to the Millennium*. Washington, DC: Georgetown University Press.

Green, John C., and Daniel M. Shea, eds. 1999. *The State of the Parties: The Changing Role of Contemporary American Parties,* 3rd ed. Lanham, MD: Rowman and Littlefield.

Gurwitt, Rob. 2003. "A Profile in Courage: Leading the Fight for Fiscal Fairness and Flexibility." *Governing* (November): 25.

Hadley, Charles D. 1985. "Dual Partisan Identification in the South." *Journal of Politics* 47: 254–268.

Hadley, Charles D., and Lewis Bowman, eds. 1995. *Southern State Party Organizations and Activists*. Westport, CT: Praeger.

Hadley, Charles D., and Susan E. Howell. 1980. "The Southern Split Ticket Voter, 1952–76: Republican Conversion or Democratic Decline?" In *Party Politics in the South,* ed. Robert P. Steed, Laurence W. Moreland, and Tod A. Baker. New York: Praeger.

Hadley, Charles D., and Harold W. Stanley. 1998. "Race and the Democratic Biracial Coalition." In *Party Activists in Southern Politics: Mirrors and Makers of Change,* ed. Charles D. Hadley and Lewis Bowman. Knoxville: University of Tennessee Press.

Harmel, Robert, and Kenneth Janda. 1982. *Parties and Their Environments: Limits to Reform?* New York: Longman.

Harris, Fredrick C. 1999. *Something Within: Religion in African-American Political Activism*. New York: Oxford University Press.

Harris, Louis. 1954. *Is There a Republican Majority?* New York: Harper and Brothers.

Hauss, Charles S., and L. Sandy Maisel. 1986. "Extremist Delegates: Myth and Reality." In *The Life of the Parties: Activists in Presidential Politics,* ed. Ronald B. Rapoport, Alan I. Abramowitz, and John McGlennon. Lexington: The University Press of Kentucky.

Hedges, Roman B. 1984. "Reasons for Political Involvement: A Study of Contributors to the 1972 Presidential Campaign." *Western Political Quarterly* 37: 257–271.

Herrnson, Paul S. 1988. *Party Campaigning in the 1980s*. Cambridge, MA: Harvard University Press.

Herrnson, Paul S. 1992. "Why the United States Does Not Have Responsible Parties." *Perspectives in Political Science* 21: 91–99.

Herrnson, Paul S. 1994. "The Revitalization of National Party Organizations." In *The Parties Respond: Changes in American Parties and Campaigns*, 2nd ed., ed. L. Sandy Maisel. Boulder, CO: Westview.

Herrnson, Paul S., and David Menefee-Libey. 1990. "The Dynamics of Party Organizational Development." *Midsouth Political Science Journal* 11: 3–30.

Hetherington, Marc J. 2001. "Resurgent Mass Partisanship: The Role of Elite Polarization." *American Political Science Review* 95: 619–632.

Hitlin, Robert A., and John S. Jackson III. 1977. "On Amateur and Professional Politicians." *Journal of Politics* 39: 786–793.

Hofstetter, C. Richard. 1971. "The Amateur Politician: A Problem in Construct Validation." *Midwest Journal of Political Science* 15: 31–56.

Hofstetter, C. Richard. 1973. "Organizational Activists: The Basis of Participation in Amateur and Professional Groups." *American Politics Quarterly* 1: 244–276.

Hogan, Robert E. 2003. "Candidate Perceptions of Political Party Campaign Activity in State Legislative Elections." *State Politics and Policy Quarterly* 2: 66–85.

Hood, M. V. III, and Mark Caleb Smith. 2002. "On the Prospect of Linking Religious-Right Identification with Political Behavior: Panacea or Snipe Hunt?" *Journal for the Scientific Study of Religion* 41: 697–710.

Huckshorn, Robert J., James L. Gibson, Cornelius P. Cotter, and John F. Bibby. 1986. "Party Integration and Party Organizational Strength." *Journal of Politics* 48: 976–991.

Hulbary, William E., and Lewis Bowman. 1998. "Recruiting Activists." In *Party Organization and Activism in the American South,* ed. Robert P. Steed, John A. Clark, Lewis Bowman, and Charles D. Hadley. Tuscaloosa: University of Alabama Press.

Ippolito, Dennis S. 1969. "Motivational Reorientation and Change Among Party Activists." *Journal of Politics* 31: 1098–1101.

Ippolito, Dennis S., and Lewis Bowman. 1969. "Goals and Activities of Party Officials in a Suburban Community." *Western Political Quarterly* 22: 572–580.

Jackson, John S. III, Barbara L. Brown, and David Bositis. 1982. "Herbert McClosky and Friends Revisited: 1980 Democratic and Republican Party Elites Compared to the Mass Public." *American Politics Quarterly* 10: 158–180.

Jelen, Ted G., Corwin E. Smidt, and Clyde Wilcox. 1993. "The Political Effects of the Born-Again Phenomenon." In *Rediscovering the Religious Factor in American Politics,* ed. David C. Leege and Lyman A. Kellstedt. Armonk, NY: M. E. Sharpe.

Jennings, M. Kent. 1992. "Ideological Thinking among Mass Publics and Political Elites." *Public Opinion Quarterly* 56: 419–441.

Jennings, M. Kent, and Richard G. Niemi. 1966. "Party Identification at Multiple Levels of Government." *American Journal of Sociology* 72: 86–101.

Kagay, Michael. 1991. "The Use of Public Opinion Polls by *The New York Times.*" In *Polling and Presidential Election Coverage,* ed. Paul J. Lavrakas and Jack Holley. Newbury Park, CA: Sage.

Katz, Daniel, and Samuel J. Eldersveld. 1961. "The Impact of Local Party Activity upon the Electorate." *Public Opinion Quarterly* 25: 1–24.

Katz, Richard S. 1979. "The Dimensionality of Party Identification: Cross-National Perspectives." *Comparative Politics* 11: 147–163.

Katzman, Martin T. 1978. *The Quality of Municipal Services, Central City Decline, and Middle Class Flight.* Cambridge, MA: Department of City and Regional Planning, Harvard University.

Kayden, Xandra, and Eddie Mahe, Jr. 1985. *The Party Goes On.* New York: Basic Books.

Key, V. O. Jr. 1949. *Southern Politics in State and Nation*. New York: Alfred A. Knopf.

Key, V. O. Jr. 1959. "Secular Realignment and the Party System." *Journal of Politics* 21: 198–210.

Key, V. O. Jr. 1966. *The Responsible Electorate: Rationality in Presidential Voting, 1936–1960*. Cambridge: The Belknap Press of Harvard University Press.

Key, V. O. Jr. 1967. *Public Opinion and American Democracy*. New York: Alfred A. Knopf.

Kirkpatrick, Evron. 1971. "Toward a More Responsible Two-Party System: Political Science, Policy Science, or Pseudo-Science?" *American Political Science Review* 65: 965–990.

Kirkpatrick, Jeane. 1975. "Representation in the American National Conventions: The Case of 1972." *British Journal of Political Science* 5: 265–322.

Kirkpatrick, Jeane. 1976. *The New Presidential Elite*. New York: Russell Sage Foundation.

Klinkner, Philip A. 1994. *The Losing Parties: Out-Party National Committees 1956–1993*. New Haven, CT: Yale University Press.

Knuckey, Jonathan. 2000. "Explaining Southern Republican Success in U.S. House Elections in the 1990s." *American Review of Politics* 21: 179–199.

Knuckey, Jonathan. 2001. "Ideological Realignment and Partisan Change in the American South, 1972–1996." *Politics and Policy* 29: 337–358.

Kramer, Gerald H. 1970. "The Effects of Precinct-Level Canvassing on Voter Behavior." *Public Opinion Quarterly* 34: 560–572.

La Raja, Raymond J. 2003. "State Parties and Soft Money: How Much Party Building?" In *The State of the Parties: The Changing Role of Contemporary American Parties*, 4th ed., ed. John C. Green and Rick Farmer. Lanham, MD: Rowman and Littlefield.

Ladd, Everett and Charles Hadley. 1975. *Political Parties and Political Institutions: Patterns and Differentiation Since the New Deal*. Beverly Hills: Sage.

Lamis, Alexander P. 1990. *The Two-Party South*. Exp. rev. ed. New York: Oxford University Press.

Lamis, Alexander P., ed. 1999. *Southern Politics in the 1990s*. Baton Rouge: Louisiana State University Press.

Layman, Geoffrey C. 1999. " 'Culture Wars' in the American Party System: Religious and Cultural Change Among Partisan Activists Since 1972." *American Politics Quarterly* 27: 89–121.

Layman, Geoffrey. 2001. *The Great Divide: Religious and Cultural Conflict in American Party Politics*. New York: Columbia University Press.

Layman, Geoffrey C., and Thomas M. Carsey. 2002. "Party Polarization and 'Conflict Extension' in the American Electorate." *American Journal of Political Science* 46: 786–802.

Lazarsfeld, Paul F., Bernard Berelson, and Hazel Gaudet. 1944. *The People's Choice*. New York: Deull, Sloan, and Pearce.

LeDuc, Lance, Harold D. Clarke, Jane Jenson, and John H. Pammett. 1984. "Partisan Instability in Canada: Evidence from a New Panel Study." *American Political Science Review* 78: 470–484.

Lewis, John. 1998. *Walking with the Wind: A Memoir of the Movement*. New York: Simon & Schuster.

Lincoln, Eric C., and Lawrence A. Mamiya. 1990. *The Black Church in the African American Experience*. Durham: Duke University Press.

Long, L. H. 1975. "How the Racial Composition of Cities Changes." *Land Economics* 60: 258–267.

Lubell, Samuel. 1952. *The Future of American Politics*. New York: Harper and Brothers.

Lyons, William, and Robert F. Durant. 1980. "Assessing the Impact of In-migration on a State Political System." *Social Science Quarterly* 61: 473–484.

MacDonald, Stuart Elaine, and George Rabinowitz. 1987. "The Dynamics of Structural Realignment." *American Political Science Review* 81: 775–796.

Maisel, L. Sandy, ed. 1998. *The Parties Respond*. 3rd ed. Boulder, CO: Westview Press.

Maggiotto, Michael A., and Ronald E. Weber. 1986. "The Impact of Organizational Incentives on County Party Chairpersons." *American Politics Quarterly* 14: 201–218.

Marchant-Shapiro, Theresa, and Kelly D. Patterson. 1995. "Partisan Change in the Mountain West." *Political Behavior* 17: 359–378.

Mayhew, David R. 1986. *Placing Parties in American Politics*. Princeton: Princeton University Press.

McAllister, Ian. 1991. "Party Adaptation and Factionalism within the Australian Party System." *American Journal of Political Science* 35: 206–227.

McClosky, Herbert, Paul J. Hoffman, and Rosemary O'Hara. 1960. "Issue Conflict and Consensus Among Party Leaders and Followers." *American Political Science Review* 54: 406–429.

McGlennon, John. 1998a. "Factions in the Politics of the New South." In *Party Organization and Activism in the American South*, ed. Robert P. Steed, John A. Clark, Lewis Bowman, and Charles D. Hadley. Tuscaloosa: University of Alabama Press.

McGlennon, John J. 1998b. "Ideology and the Southern Party Activist: Poles Apart or Reflecting the Polls?" In *Party Activists in Southern Politics: Mirrors and Makers of Change*, ed. Charles D. Hadley and Lewis Bowman. Knoxville: University of Tennessee Press.

Menefee-Libey, David. 2000. *The Triumph of Campaign-Centered Politics*. New York: Chatham House.

Miller, Gary, and Norman Schofield. 2003. "Activists And Partisan Realignment in the United States." *American Political Science Review* 97: 245–260.

Miller, Penny M., Malcolm E. Jewell, and Lee Sigelman. 1987. "Reconsidering a Typology of Incentives Among Campaign Activists: A Research Note." *Western Political Quarterly* 40: 519–526.

Miller, Warren E., and M. Kent Jennings. 1986. *Parties in Transition: A Longitudinal Study of Party Elites and Party Supporters.* New York: Russell Sage Foundation.

Miller, Warren E., and J. Merrill Shanks. 1996. *The New American Voter.* Cambridge, MA: Harvard University Press.

Montjoy, Robert S., William R. Shaffer, and Ronald E. Weber. 1980. "Policy Preferences of Party Elites and Masses: Conflict or Consensus?" *American Politics Quarterly* 8: 319–344.

Morehouse, Sarah M., and Malcolm E. Jewell. 2003. "State Parties: Independent Partners in the Money Relationship." In *The State of the Parties: The Changing Role of Contemporary American Parties,* 4th ed., ed. John C. Green and Rick Farmer. Lanham, MD: Rowman and Littlefield.

Moreland, Laurence W. 1990a. "The Ideological and Issue Bases of Southern Parties." In *Political Parties in the Southern States,* ed. Tod Baker, Charles D. Hadley, Robert P. Steed, and Laurence W. Moreland. New York: Praeger.

Moreland, Laurence W. 1990b. "The Impact of Immigration on the Composition of Party Coalitions." In *Political Parties in the Southern States,* ed. Tod Baker, Charles D. Hadley, Robert P. Steed, and Laurence W. Moreland. New York: Praeger.

Moreland, Laurence W., and Robert P. Steed. 1998a. "The Impact of In-Migration on Party Elites: The Case of South Carolina." Presented at the 1998 annual meeting of the Western Political Science Association, Los Angeles, CA.

Moreland, Laurence W., and Robert P. Steed. 1998b. "The Impact of Newcomers Among Republican Party Activists at the State and Local Levels in South Carolina." Presented at the 1998 fall meeting of the National Social Science Association, New Orleans, LA.

Moreland, Laurence W., and Robert P. Steed. 2001. "Non-Southerners in the South: Non-Natives and Party Elites in South Carolina." Presented at the 2001 spring meeting of the National Social Science Association, Las Vegas, NV.

Moreland, Laurence W., Robert P. Steed, and Tod A. Baker. 1986. "Migration and Activist Politics." In *The Life of the Parties: Activists in Presidential Politics,* ed. Ronald B. Rapoport, Alan I. Abramowitz, and John McGlennon. Lexington: The University Press of Kentucky.

Moreland, Laurence W., Robert P. Steed, and Tod A. Baker, eds. 1987. *Blacks in Southern Politics.* New York: Praeger.

Nexon, David. 1971. "Asymmetry in the Political System: Occasional Activists in the Republican and Democratic Parties, 1956–1964." *American Political Science Review* 65: 716–730.

Nie, Norman, Sidney Verba, and John Petrocik. 1976. *The Changing American Voter.* Exp. ed. Cambridge: Harvard University Press.

Niemi, Richard G., Stephen Wright, and Lynda Powell. 1987. "Multiple Party Identifiers and the Measurement of Party Identification." *Journal of Politics* 49: 1093–1103.

Norrander, Barbara. 1999. "The Evolution of the Gender Gap." *Public Opinion Quarterly* 63: 566–576.

Oldfield, Duane M. 1996a. "The Christian Right in the Presidential Nominating Process." In *In Pursuit of the White House—How We Choose Our Presidential Nominees,* ed. William G. Mayer. Chatham, NJ: Chatham House.

Oldfield, Duane. 1996b. *The Right and the Righteous: The Christian Right Confronts the Republican Party*. Lanham, MD: Rowman & Littlefield.

Persinos, John F. 1994. "Has the Christian Right Taken Over the Republican Party?" *Campaigns and Elections* (September): 21–24.

Petrocik, John R. 1974. "An Analysis of the Intransitivities in the Index of Party Identification." *Political Methodology* 1: 31–47.

Petrocik, John R. 1987. "Realignment: New Party Coalitions and the Nationalization of the South." *Journal of Politics* 49: 347–375.

Polsby, Nelson W. 1983. *Consequences of Party Reform*. New York: Oxford University Press.

Pomper, Gerald M. 1971. "Toward a More Responsible Two-Party System? What? Again?" *Journal of Politics* 33: 916–940.

Pomper, Gerald M. 2003. "Parliamentary Government in the United States: A New Regime for a New Century?" In *The State of the Parties,* 4th ed., ed. John C. Green and Rick Farmer. Lanham, MD: Rowman and Littlefield.

Price, David E. 1984. *Bringing Back the Parties.* Washington, DC: CQ Press.

Prysby, Charles L. 1989. "The Structure of Southern Electoral Behavior." *American Politics Quarterly* 17: 163–180.

Prysby, Charles. 1998a. "Party Switchers and the Party System." In *Party Activists in Southern Politics: Mirrors and Makers of Change,* ed. Charles D. Hadley and Lewis Bowman. Knoxville: University of Tennessee Press.

Prysby, Charles. 1998b. "Purist versus Pragmatic Orientations." In *Party Organization and Activism in the American South,* ed. Robert P. Steed, John A. Clark, Lewis Bowman, and Charles D. Hadley. Tuscaloosa: University of Alabama Press.

Prysby, Charles. 2000. "Southern Congressional Elections in the 1990s: The Dynamics of Change." *American Review of Politics* 21: 155–177.

Prysby, Charles. 2003. "Purist Versus Pragmatist Orientations Among Political Party Activists: Grassroots Activists in the South, 1991–2001." Presented at the annual meeting of the American Political Science Association, Philadelphia, PA.

Ranney, Austin. 1951. "Toward a More Responsible Two-Party System: A Commentary." *American Political Science Review* 45: 488–499.
Ranney, Austin. 1975. *Curing the Mischiefs of Faction: Party Reform in America*. Berkeley: University of California Press.
Ransom, John Crowe. [1930] 1977. "Reconstructed but Unregenerate." In *Twelve Southerners, I'll Take My Stand*. New York: Harper and Brothers. Reprint Baton Rouge: Louisiana University Press.
Reichley, A. James. 1992. *The Life of the Parties: A History of American Political Parties*. New York: Free Press.
Reiter, Howard L. 1981. "Intra-Party Cleavages in the United States Today." *Western Political Quarterly* 34: 287–300.
Roback, Thomas H. 1975. "Amateurs and Professionals: Delegates to the 1972 Republican National Convention." *Journal of Politics* 37: 436–468.
Roback, Thomas H. 1980. "Motivation for Activism Among Republican National Convention Delegates: Continuity and Change, 1972–1976." *Journal of Politics* 42: 181–201.
Rohde, David W. 1991. *Parties and Leaders in the Postreform House*. Chicago: University of Chicago Press.
Rosenstone, Steven J., and John Mark Hansen. 1993. *Mobilization, Participation, and Democracy in America*. New York: Macmillan.
Rozell, Mark J., and Clyde Wilcox. 1996. *Second Coming: The New Christian Right in Virginia Politics*. Baltimore: Johns Hopkins University Press.
Salmore, Stephen A., and Barbara G. Salmore. 1989. *Candidates, Parties, and Campaigns: Electoral Politics in America*. Washington, DC: CQ Press.
Scammon, Richard M., and Ben J. Wattenberg. 1970. *The Real Majority*. New York: Coward-McCann.
Schaffner, Brian F., Matthew Streb, and Gerald Wright. 2001. "Teams without Leaders: The Nonpartisan Ballot in State and Local Elections." *Political Research Quarterly* 54: 7–30.
Schattschneider, E. E. 1942. *Party Government*. New York: Rinehart.
Schattschneider, E. E. 1960. *The Semi-Sovereign People*. New York: Holt, Rinehart and Winston.
Scher, Richard K. 1997. *Politics in the New South*. 2nd ed. Armonk, NY: M. E. Sharpe.
Schlesinger, Joseph A. 1985. "The New American Political Party." *American Political Science Review* 79: 1152–1169.
Schneider, Paige L. 1998. "Factionalism in the Southern Republican Party." *American Review of Politics* 19: 129–148.
Schwartz, Mildred A. 1990. *The Party Network*. Madison: University of Wisconsin Press.
Shaffer, Stephen D. 1980. "The Policy Biases of Political Activists." *American Politics Quarterly* 8:15–33.

Shaffer, Stephen D., and David A. Breaux. 1998. "Activists' Incentives." In *Party Organization and Activism in the American South,* ed. Robert P. Steed, John A. Clark, Lewis Bowman, and Charles D. Hadley. Tuscaloosa: University of Alabama Press.

Shaffer, Stephen, and Monica Johnson. 1996. "Return of the Solid South? Exploring Partisan Realignment in Mississippi." *Southeastern Political Review* 24: 757–776.

Shaffer, Stephen D., Stacie Berry Pierce, and Steven A. Kohnke. 2000. "Party Realignment in the South: A Multi-Level Analysis." *American Review of Politics* 21: 129–153.

Shaffer, Stephen D., and Byron Price. 2001. "Electoral Politics in a Two-Party Era." In *Politics in Mississippi,* 2nd ed., ed. Joseph B. Parker. Salem, WI: Sheffield.

Sharkansky, Ira. 1969. *Regionalism in American Politics.* Indianapolis: Bobbs-Merrill.

Shin, Eui-Hang. 1978. "Effects of Migration on the Educational Levels of the Black Resident Population at the Origin and Destination, 1955–1960 and 1965–1970." *Demography* 15: 41–56.

Singer, Eleanor. 1981. "Reference Groups and Social Evaluations." In *Social Psychology: Sociological Perspectives,* ed. Morris Rosenberg and Ralph H. Turner. New York: Basic Books.

Smith, Mark Caleb. 2002. "With Friends Like These: The Religious Right, the Republican Party, and Electoral Politics." Presented at the annual meeting of the American Political Science Association, Boston, MA.

Smith, Oran P. 1997. *The Rise of Baptist Republicans.* New York: New York University Press.

Soule, John W., and James W. Clarke. 1970. "Amateurs and Professionals: A Study of Delegates to the 1968 Democratic National Convention." *American Political Science Review* 64: 888–898.

Soule, John W., and Wilma E. McGrath. 1975. "A Comparative Study of Presidential Nomination Conventions: The Democrats 1968 and 1972." *American Journal of Political Science* 19: 501–517.

Stanley, Harold W. 1988. "Southern Partisan Changes: Dealignment, Realignment or Both?" *Journal of Politics* 50: 65–88.

Stanley, Harold W. 1995. "Party Activists in the South." In *Southern State Party Organizations and Activists,* ed. Charles D. Hadley and Lewis Bowman. Westport, CT: Praeger.

Stanley, Harold W., and David S. Castle. 1988. "Partisan Changes in the South: Making Sense of Scholarly Dissonance." In *The South's New Politics: Realignment and Dealignment,* ed. Robert H. Swansbrough and David M. Brodsky. Columbia: University of South Carolina Press.

Stanley, Harold W., and Richard G. Niemi. 1999. "Party Coalitions in Transition: Partisanship and Group Support, 1952–1996." In *Reelection 1996: How Americans Voted,* ed. Herbert F. Weisberg and Janet M. Box-Steffensmeier. Chatham, NJ: Chatham House.

Steed, Robert P. 1998. "Parties, Ideology, and Issues: The Structuring of Political Conflict." In *Party Organization and Activism in the American South,* ed. Robert P. Steed, John A. Clark, Lewis Bowman, and Charles D. Hadley. Tuscaloosa: University of Alabama Press.

Steed, Robert P., and Lewis Bowman. 1998. "Strength of Party Attachment." In *Party Organization and Activism in the American South,* ed. Robert P. Steed, John A. Clark, Lewis Bowman, and Charles D. Hadley. Tuscaloosa: University of Alabama Press.

Steed, Robert P., Laurence W. Moreland, and Tod A. Baker. 1981. "In-Migration and Southern State Party Elites." Presented at the annual meeting of the Southern Political Science Association, Memphis, TN.

Steed, Robert P., Laurence W. Moreland, and Tod A. Baker. 1990. "Searching for the Mind of the South in the Second Reconstruction." In *The Disappearing South? Studies in Regional Change and Continuity,* ed. Robert P. Steed, Laurence W. Moreland, and Tod A. Baker. Tuscaloosa: University of Alabama Press.

Steed, Robert P., Laurence W. Moreland, and Tod A. Baker. 1991. "Party Change in the South: A Comparison of the Effects of In-Migration on State and Local Party Organizations in South Carolina." Presented at the annual meeting of the Southern Political Science Association, Tampa, FL.

Steed, Robert P., Laurence W. Moreland, and Tod A. Baker. 1995. "Party Sorting at the Local Level in South Carolina." *National Political Science Review* 5: 181–196.

Stimson, James A. 1975. "Belief Systems: Constraint, Complexity, and the 1972 Election." *American Journal of Political Science* 19: 393–417.

Stone, Walter J. 1982. "Party, Ideology, and the Lure of Victory: Iowa Activists in the 1980 Prenomination Campaign." *Western Political Quarterly* 35: 527–538.

Stone, Walter J., and Alan I. Abramowitz. 1983. "Winning May Not Be Everything, But It's More Than We Thought: Presidential Party Activists in 1980." *American Political Science Review* 77: 945–956.

Stone, Walter J., Lonna Rae Atkeson, and Ronald B. Rapoport. 1992. "Turning On or Turning Off? Mobilization and Demobilization Effects of Participation in Presidential Nominating Campaigns." *American Journal of Political Science* 36: 665–691.

Swansbrough, Robert H., and David M. Brodsky, eds. 1988. *The South's New Politics: Realignment and Dealignment.* Columbia: University of South Carolina Press.

Topping, John C. Jr., John R. Lazarek, and William H. Linder. 1966. *Southern Republicanism and the New South*. Cambridge, MA: n.p.

Trish, Barbara. 1994. "Party Integration in Indiana and Ohio: The 1988 and 1992 Presidential Contests." *American Review of Politics* 15: 235–256.

Valentine, David C., and John R. Van Wingen. 1980. "Partisanship, Independence and the Partisan Identification Question." *American Politics Quarterly* 8: 165–186.

Van Wingen, John, and David Valentine. 1988. "Partisan Politics: A One-and-a Half, No-Party System." In *Contemporary Southern Politics,* ed. James F. Lea. Baton Rouge: Louisiana State University Press.

Verba, Sidney, and Norman Nie. 1972. *Participation in America: Political Democracy and Social Equality*. New York: Harper and Row.

Ware, Alan. 1985. *The Breakdown of Democratic Party Organization 1940–1980.* New York: Oxford University Press.

Wattenberg, Martin P. 1991. "The Building of a Republican Regional Base in the South: The Elephant Crosses the Mason-Dixon Line." *Political Opinion Quarterly* 55: 424–432.

Wattenberg, Martin P. 1991. *The Rise of Candidate-Centered Politics: Presidential Elections of the 1980s*. Cambridge: Harvard University Press.

Wattenberg, Martin P. 1994. *The Decline of American Political Parties, 1952–1992.* Cambridge: Harvard University Press.

Weisberg, Herbet F. 1980. "A Multidimensional Conceptualization of Party Identification." *Political Behavior* 2: 33–60.

Wekkin, Gary D. 1985. "Political Parties and Intergovernmental Relations in 1984: The Consequences of Party Renewal for Territorial Constituencies." *Publius* 15: 19–37.

Wekkin, Gary D. 1991. "Why Crossover Voters are Not 'Mischievous Voters': The Segmented Partisanship Hypothesis." *American Politics Quarterly* 19: 229–247.

Welch, Susan, and Buster Brown. 1979. "Correlates of Southern Republican Success at the Congressional District Level." *Social Science Quarterly* 60: 732–742.

Whitby, Kenny J. and Franklin D. Gilliam, Jr. 1991. "A Longitudinal Analysis of Competing Explanations for the Transformation of Southern Congressional Politics." *Journal of Politics* 53: 504–518.

White, John Kenneth. 1992. "Responsible Party Government in America." *Perspectives on Political Science* 21: 80–90.

White, John Kenneth. 2001. "Reviving the Political Parties: What Must Be Done?" In *The Politics of Ideas*, ed. John Kenneth White and John C. Green. Albany, NY: SUNY Press.

White, John Kenneth. 2002. *The Values Divide: American Politics and Culture in Transition.* Chatham, NJ: Chatham House.

Wielhouwer, Peter W. 2000. "Releasing the Fetters: Parties and the Mobilization of the African-American Electorate." *Journal of Politics* 62: 206–222.

Wielhouwer, Peter W., and Brad Lockerbie. 1994. "Party Contacting and Political Participation, 1952–90." *American Journal of Political Science* 38: 211–229.

Wilcox, Clyde. 2000. *Onward Christian Soldiers? The Religious Right in American Politics.* 2nd ed. Boulder, CO: Westview Press.

Wildavsky, Aaron. 1965. "The Goldwater Phenomenon: Purists, Politicians, and the Two-Party System." *Review of Politics* 27: 386–413.

Wilson, James Q. 1962. *The Amateur Democrat: Club Politics in Three Cities—New York, Chicago, Los Angeles.* Chicago: The University of Chicago Press.

Wolfinger, Raymond, and Robert E. Arseneau. 1978. "Partisan Change in the South, 1952–1976." In *Political Parties: Development and Decay*, ed. Louis Maisel and Joseph Cooper. Beverly Hills, CA: Sage.

Wolfinger, Raymond, and Michael G. Hagen. 1985. "Republican Prospects: Southern Comfort." *Public Opinion* 49: 8–13.

Zaller, John R. 1992. *The Nature and Origins of Mass Opinion.* New York: Cambridge University Press.

List of Contributors

Jay Barth is an associate professor and the chair of the Department of Politics at Hendrix College.

David A. Breaux is a professor and head of the political science department at Mississippi State University.

John M. Bruce is an associate professor of political science at the University of Mississippi.

John A. Clark is an associate professor of political science at Western Michigan University.

Patrick R. Cotter is a professor of political science at the University of Alabama.

Samuel H. Fisher III is an associate professor of political science at the University of South Alabama.

Robert E. Hogan is an assistant professor of political science at Louisiana State University in Baton Rouge.

Jonathan Knuckey is an assistant professor of political science at the University of Central Florida.

John J. McGlennon is a professor of government at the College of William & Mary.

Laurence W. Moreland is a professor of political science at The Citadel.

James Newman is a Ph.D. student in the Public Policy and Administration program at Mississippi State University.

Barbara A. Patrick is a Ph.D. student in the Public Policy and Administration program at Mississippi State University.

Charles L. Prysby is a professor of political science at the University of North Carolina at Greensboro.

Stephen D. Shaffer is a professor of political science at Mississippi State University.

Robert P. Steed is a professor of political science at The Citadel.

Index

Note: Page numbers followed by "t" indicate tables.

R